THE FOLLY OF GENERALS

THE FOLLY OF GENERALS

How Eisenhower's Broad Front Strategy Lengthened World War II

DAVID P. COLLEY

CASEMATE

Philadelphia & Oxford

Published in the United States of America and Great Britain in 2021 by
CASEMATE PUBLISHERS
The Old Music Hall, 106–108 Cowley Road, Oxford OX4 1JE, UK
and
1950 Lawrence Road, Havertown, PA 19083, US

Hardcover Edition: ISBN 978-1-61200-974-2
Digital Edition: ISBN 978-1-61200-975-9

A CIP record for this book is available from the British Library

Printed and bound in the United States by Sheridan

For a complete list of Casemate titles, please contact:

CASEMATE PUBLISHERS (US)
Telephone (610) 853-9131
Fax (610) 853-9146
Email: casemate@casematepublishers.com
www.casematepublishers.com

CASEMATE PUBLISHERS (UK)
Telephone (01865) 241249
Email: casemate-uk@casematepublishers.co.uk
www.casematepublishers.co.uk

Front cover images:
   (top) The Allied commanders after meeting about the Ardennes strategy, December 7, 1944. (Wikimedia Commons)
   (bottom) The U.S. 39th Infantry Brigade crossing the Dragon's Teeth of the Siegfried Line. (U.S. Army)

As always, thanks to my wife, Mary Liz, my sons, Padraic and Christopher, and loyal Pips

Contents

Introduction

Many of the histories of World War II in the European Theater of Operations, the ETO, are focused on the exploits of two generals, the American, George S. Patton Jr., and British Field Marshal Bernard Law Montgomery. Patton commanded the U.S. 3rd Army; Montgomery commanded the 21st Army Group. Only they, it is often implied, could carry out swift and devastating thrusts in September 1944 to breach the German Siegfried Line defenses that protected the border, cross the fabled Rhine River, and advance deep into Germany to end the war in Europe. The Allied High Command was focused principally on the Ruhr industrial area in western Germany that was Montgomery's principal objective. Patton's primary objective was the Saar industrial zone near the French border. Both areas produced vast amounts of war materiel for the Wehrmacht, with the Ruhr producing as much as 50 percent of Germany's tanks, planes, guns and vehicles. The Allied High Command and General Dwight D. Eisenhower, the Supreme Commander in Europe, believed that if the Ruhr were lost to the German war machine, the enemy would soon collapse.

Patton's American 3rd Army, part of General Omar Bradley's 12th Army Group, romped through northern France in the late summer of 1944 before being halted in the French province of Lorraine by stiffening German defenses. Montgomery's 21st Army Group moved rapidly along the French Channel coast that same summer before advancing into Belgium and the Netherlands where German resistance stopped them. To break the German defenses Montgomery proposed and planned Operation *Market Garden*, an airborne attack on the bridge at Arnhem in the Netherlands that was designed to outflank German border defenses and open a path to the Ruhr. Patton believed he could blast his way through the German defenses and take the Saar. Both Patton and Montgomery were itching to be first.

"Monty" or Patton – which one would end the war? This has become a major theme in histories of the war in the ETO and to a large extent it is cast in stone by historians and to some extent by Eisenhower, who had to juggle the persistent demands of either one to lead the Alies into Germany.

With a bias towards Montgomery and Patton, Eisenhower and the Allied High Command (SHAEF – Supreme Headquarters Allied Expeditionary Force) neglected to exploit other opportunities where American armies and generals might have breached the German Siegfried Line defenses. There were at least four other chances for the Americans to crack the German defenses from the Netherlands to the Swiss frontier, seven or eight months before the war ended in May 1945.

Eisenhower's failure to exploit those opportunities is attributed by most histories to be largely due to a lack of supplies, mainly gasoline, and a lack of reserve forces to reinforce breakthroughs. But is this really true or is it an explanation that has been embraced and become doctrine over the decades? Little or no attention is paid to other salient reasons for a failure to breach the German border defenses, such as the U.S. Army's (or Eisenhower's) tactical ignorance of the need to concentrate its forces on a single objective, something that was

General Dwight D. Eisenhower, Supreme Commander of Allied forces in the ETO, meets with members of the 101st Airborne Division the evening of June 5, 1944 just prior to the troops embarking on aircraft for a night drop over Nazi-occupied Normandy, France. The soldier Eisenhower is speaking to is Lt. Wallace Strobel from Michigan. He survived the war unscathed.

a dominant feature in the German art of war. The Americans and Eisenhower also seemed unable to reinforce strength with the thousands of reserve forces that were actually available, many of them idle in Great Britain. The Germans always managed to reinforce critical areas under attack even as their manpower reserves were negligible after five years of war and millions of casualties.

Possibly most critical of all was the Allied strategy, imposed by Eisenhower, to adhere to what has become known as the "broad front" strategy to defeat Hitler's Germany. This meant that the Allied armies moved as one solid line from the Netherlands to Switzerland as they approached the Siegfried Line. When a possible breakthrough presented itself, the Americans didn't have the concentrated manpower, firepower, and logistical support to achieve the breakthrough. Nor did they have the military sophistication, experience, and knowledge to adapt and apply one of Napoleon's most important precepts, that an army must concentrate its forces to achieve victory. Additionally, Napoleon counseled, to concentrate his army at one point a commander must reduce his forces elsewhere and be willing to accept the risk of a flanking attack. Eisenhower and the Allied Supreme Command, SHAEF, were risk-averse and opposed to rendering their flanks vulnerable.

On June 6, 1944, D-Day, the Allies landed at Normandy and after nearly two months of bitter and costly fighting, they finally broke out of the Normandy bridgehead and began a headlong pursuit across northern France of the battered German 7th and 5th Panzer Armies. The Allies literally chased the Germans and pushed them back to the German frontier in a couple of months. One problem for the Americans and the British was Hitler's orders for the German garrisons holding the English Channel ports from Brittany to Belgium to fight to the last man, thus forcing the Allies to carry supplies hundreds of miles from the Normandy beaches to the Allied front lines. Montgomery and Patton had to be supplied over those same beaches.

Patton and Montgomery rebelled at the "broad front" strategy. Each called for a deep thrust with thousands of well-supplied troops to brush aside feeble German resistance. The problem for Eisenhower was that there were not enough supplies for an attack by two armies, only one. "My men can eat their belts but my tanks need gasoline to advance," raged Patton, who was urging Eisenhower and the Allied High Command to supply his army and unleash it for a rapid advance into the Saar. Montgomery believed that he and his 21st Army group of British and Canadian troops were in a better position to break into Germany and capture the more important Ruhr.

Montgomery won the competition with his hastily devised plan to outflank the German defenses with an end run around the northern end of the Siegfried

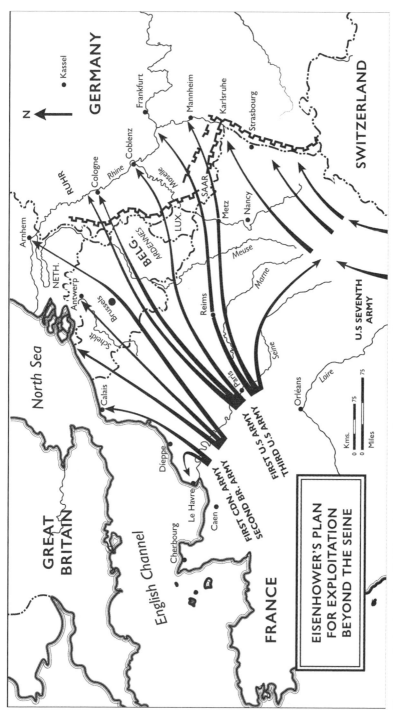

GREAT BRITAIN

North Sea

English Channel

FRANCE

Cherbourg

Le Havre

Caen

Dieppe

Calais

Scheldt

Brussels

Antwerp

NETH.

Arnhem

BELG.

ARDENNES

LUX.

RUHR

Cologne

Rhine

Coblenz

Moselle

SAAR

Metz

Nancy

Meuse

Marne

Reims

Seine

Paris

Orléans

Loire

Frankfurt

Mannheim

Karlsruhe

Strasbourg

Kassel

GERMANY

SWITZERLAND

N

FIRST CDN. ARMY

SECOND BR. ARMY

FIRST U.S ARMY

THIRD U.S ARMY

U.S SEVENTH ARMY

Kms.   0   75
Miles 0   75

**EISENHOWER'S PLAN
FOR EXPLOITATION
BEYOND THE SEINE**

The arrows depict the various British and American armies advancing on a broad front, in unison. This was termed Eisenhower's "broad front" strategy with all the armies moving like a giant bulldozer. British Field Marshall Bernard Montgomery opposed this plan and believed the Allies should form one massive force to blast its way to Berlin.

Line by capturing the Rhine river bridge at Arnhem. Once over the Rhine, Monty would plow into the Ruhr and then farther into Germany. But there was a hitch to his plan. The Arnhem bridge lay 50 miles inside German-held territory in the Netherlands and the only way to get there was to lay a carpet of paratroopers, about 50,000 in three airborne divisions, to secure a pathway for the British XXX Corps of some 60,000 men to advance with its tanks and artillery – heavy weapons the paratroopers didn't possess – all the way to Arnhem, relieve the paratroopers and advance over the bridge into Germany.

So it is the case that these two World War II generals are the focus of much of the history of the war in the west and their names are associated with fast-moving action. The irony is that neither of them succeeded in accomplishing their aim until the last weeks of the war in March 1945 when Germany was so weak that nothing could stop the Americans, the British or the Russians.

The historical focus on Patton and Montgomery overlooks the fact that several less well-known American generals had opportunities to break through the thin German Siegfried Line in the fall of 1944 and possibly accomplish what Montgomery and Patton wanted to do at much less cost in men, casualties, and materiel than were expended in Operation *Market Garden*. The commanders who might have breached the wall to exploit those opportunities have been ignored in the eight decades since the war's end – Generals Leonard Gerow, commander of the U.S. V Corps, General Lawton Collins, commander of the U.S. VII Corps, General Lucian Truscott, commander of the U.S. VI Corps, and General Jacob Devers, commander of the 6th Army Group. These opportunities came at Aachen and Wallendorf in Germany, at Belfort and at Strasbourg in Alsace, France, and might have led to a major breakthrough against the extended German front line. In all four cases, higher authority countermanded the planned attacks that might have succeeded. Farther south in Italy, higher command rejected opportunities to bag 200,000 German soldiers in the enemy's 10th Army 40 miles south of Rome in May 1944 and some 40,000 veteran German troops in Sicily in July 1943. All were allowed to escape and fight for another year or more. Had they been captured and taken out of the war, the Allies could possibly have shifted thousands of troops fighting in Italy to France and crushed the Germans there well before the war's end in May 1945. *The Folly of Generals* sheds light on the Allies' lost opportunities in the ETO in 1944 and exposes similar possibilities in the Italian campaign.

In no way does *The Folly of Generals* advocate that any one of these potential breakthroughs would have succeeded. But the potential was there for success and these opportunities should be included in any historical review of the war. All too often they are dismissed as irrelevant because of the purported lack of supplies, principally gasoline. The narrative in this book is supported by numerous comments in post-war interviews by former German generals who believed the Americans forfeited many opportunities to affect breakthroughs at several points along the Siegfried Line. They relate that had the Allies taken advantage of and reinforced one or more of these potential breakthrough possibilities, there was little the Germans could have done to stop them and the Allies could have reached the Rhine and then "leap-frogged" over it and kept going, possibly to Berlin in 1944. Or they could have driven the Germans from the Italian peninsula in early 1944. If nothing else a breakthrough in any sector of the Siegfried Line would have caused serious alarm in the German High Command and forced it to dispatch reserves to contain it when in September 1944 the Germans had virtually no reserves to plug holes in their lines.

Why did the Allies not take advantage of these opportunities to end the war in 1944? This is the substance of *The Folly of Generals*.

Note to Readers

Not all the chapters in this book are arranged in chronological order. This is done to highlight what I believe to be the command mistakes in the European Theater of WWII, from the most serious to the lesser ones, particularly those that took place over a three-month period in the fall of 1944. The man in overall command at the time was General Dwight Eisenhower, the Allied supreme commander and SHAEF.

The first chapter begins with Operation *Market Garden* on September 17, 1944, the Allied attempt to capture the bridge in the city of Arnhem, Netherlands, to breach the German border defense of the Siegfried Line. This is undoubtedly the most serious command error. Before describing the ultimate end and failure of *Market Garden*, I move in chapters 2 to 5 to relate the American V Corps' and VII Corps' attacks into the Siegfried Line at Wallendorf, Germany, and in the Solberg Corridor near the German city of Aachen. Both these operations were conducted during the same week as *Market Garden* in the Allied efforts to breach the Siegfried Line. In chapters 6 and 7 I return to the disastrous aftermath of *Market Garden* to juxtapose this failed mammoth operation with those at Wallendorf and Stollberg that could have succeeded with far fewer resources in men and materiel to achieve the same objective. But they were not reinforced and were halted after making impressive gains into Germany. In chapter 8 I shed light on another potential breakthrough in the same week as *Market Garden* that was countermanded when the American VI Corps' planned to break through the Belfort Gap and reach the Rhine in Alsace. In chapter 9 I digress to August 1944 to the bungled Battle of the Falaise Pocket to show another Allied failure to trap the remnants of two German armies, in large part because of command failures.

In chapters 11 to 18 I focus on a planned crossing of the Rhine in late November 1944, by General Jacob Devers' 6th Army Group. This operation had the support of numerous American generals and the troops were in the process of moving out to cross the Rhine when the operation was directly countermanded by Eisenhower. In chapters 19 and 20 I present two lost opportunities in the war in Italy, much of the time under Eisenhower's command, where the Allies could have destroyed two German armies but failed largely because of poor leadership. I discuss the liberation of Paris, often seen as a seminal event in WWII, as an operation that probably extended the war, possibly by several months. The book ends by describing three other situations on the battlefields where the high command might have taken advantage of German weakness and scored victories.

CHAPTER I

Why *Market Garden?*

Sunday morning, September 17, 1944 – the residents of Vlissingen and Middleburg and other hamlets in coastal Holland detected a distant drone rising over the North Sea to the west that slowly increased in volume. It was not unusual in the Netherlands at this moment in time to hear the sound of approaching aircraft after four years of war and Nazi occupation that began in 1940. The Dutch were accustomed to the pounding roar of overflying bombers, heavy British Lancasters and Stirlings at night and the deep bass hum in the early mornings from four-engine American B-24s and B-17s flying at great heights on their way to bomb targets in Germany. The nighttime British bombers always maneuvered to avoid German radar detection and antiaircraft fire and came singly or in streams, the in-line Merlin engines whining as they cut through the blackened skies. The American 8th Air Force bombers flew at 25,000 feet and were bunched in tight box-like formations to fend off German Messerschmitt and Focke Wulf fighter planes. The throb of their radial engines was muted by their extreme altitude. On this misty Sunday morning of the 17th, however, the sound was different. The drone of the oncoming planes was like low notes on an organ growing in intensity as they approached.

Soon an armada of low-flying aircraft became faintly visible on the horizon, like a far-off flock of migrating geese, hundreds of them spread in a column 10 miles wide and stretching 100 miles in length all the way back to England. The planes came in at 1,500 feet, twin-engine American C-47 Skytrains, their white star markings accentuated by their olive drab coloring, and British Dakotas, the RAF's designation for the C-47, with their red, white, and blue wing and fuselage roundels. Some of the planes trailed cables that pulled snub-nosed American Waco CG-4 gliders, and British Halifax and Stirling bombers, pressed into service, were towing even larger British Horsa and Hamilcar gliders. The aircraft were part of a huge airborne operation code-named *Market Garden,* an Allied airborne and land attack to capture a bridge over the Nederrijn River (the lower Rhine) at Arnhem in the Netherlands that the British and the Americans hoped would bring a quick end to World War II in Europe. Once the Rhine was bypassed the Allies were confident the enemy's battered armies would see the hopelessness of their cause and surrender or be destroyed with overwhelming force.

As the planes continued to their drop zones in Holland, men, women, and children poured from their homes, some climbing to the rooftops, and many coming out of church services, to witness this once-in-a-lifetime extravaganza, the sky filled with oncoming transports, fighters, and bombers winging their way into battle. Were these Allied planes and paratroopers coming to liberate the Dutch after five years of Nazi rule? The Dutch hoped and prayed that they were; the people of Holland were on the brink of starvation. Like other Nazi-occupied countries, the Germans sent many young and middle-aged men to work in German factories as slave labor and took manufactured goods and agricultural products from them for use by the German people and their armies. Little food was left in the Netherlands.

Awe-struck too were the German occupiers who saw the armada as the hand of doom for the German nation. Colonel General Kurt Student, Luftwaffe commander of the German 1st Paratroop Army stationed near Arnhem, was stunned as he gazed up at the massive fleet passing overhead. Student was no stranger to warfare and to the use of raw military power. He served as a pilot in World War I and in World War II he commanded Germany's paratrooper units. During the German invasion of Holland in 1940, Student led the first major airborne attack in history when his troops became engaged in the Battle for The Hague. He later led the airborne invasion and conquest of Crete, driving British forces out in May 1941. The German conquest of Crete motivated the British and American Allies to create and perfect their own airborne units. As he watched the hundreds of planes and gliders dropping enemy troops near his Arnhem headquarters he remarked wistfully, "Oh, if ever I'd had such means at my disposal. Just once, to have this many planes!"[1]

The night before Student had warned that an attack was imminent because of heavy Allied military ground traffic south of the Maas–Waal canal in southern Holland in a sector held by the British XXX Corps. The XXX Corps was moving up men and tanks to the jump-off line on the Dutch border in preparation for the ground attack the following day. The XXX Corps would advance overland in Holland through German-held territory to relieve the American and British paratroopers dropped along a path to Arnhem.

The townspeople in large swaths of the country also had an inkling of what might be coming that fateful next day. All during the night of September 16 they heard the crump of exploding bombs, the drone of bombers, and, during the day, the throaty roar of fighter planes swirling overhead as the Allied air forces pounded German antiaircraft positions throughout much of the country with particular attention to the Arnhem area. The Allied airmen were hoping to ensure that most of the unarmed and vulnerable air force transports arriving the next morning would have a fighting chance of getting through to prearranged drop zones.

The hundreds of C-47s and gliders that took off from bases in England in the early morning hours of September 17, were filled with paratroopers from the American 101st Airborne Division, the Screaming Eagles, the 82nd "All American" Airborne Division, and the British 1st Airborne Division, dubbed the Red Devils. The 82nd had fought in Sicily and Italy and, along with the 101st, parachuted into Normandy the night before D-Day where they were scattered all over the Cotentin Peninsula. But with so many small units spread over the countryside, the Germans were confused about the whereabouts of their enemies. The Red Devils were veterans of the campaigns in North Africa and in Italy.

If the Red Devils were successful at Arnhem they would capture the bridge in the city that arched over the Lower Rhine and open the way around the Siegfried Line defenses. They would hold the bridge and fend off German counterattacks until XXX Corps arrived three days later to reinforce them and secure the bridge. The Siegfried Line was a narrow, fortified corridor of defense points constructed in the 1930s that began at Cleve, Germany, a few miles south of Arnhem, and stretched more than 400 miles along the German border through Holland, Belgium, Luxembourg, and France to Switzerland near Basel.

The German Siegfried Line was studded with a belt of pyramid-shaped concrete tank traps known as Dragon's Teeth, four feet in height, and as many as 18,000 interconnecting bunkers and pillboxes designed to stop any invading enemy. German engineers also made use of rugged terrain in the Aachen-Hürtgen Forest region and in the Schnee Eifel farther south along the border with Luxembourg to fortify the frontier. The line was a mighty endeavor involving thousands of workers and millions of tons of concrete and steel. The Allies feared the struggle they faced trying to break through the line and devised Operation *Market Garden* as a way to bypass the border and advance to the Ruhr industrial region that supplied the Wehrmacht with 50 percent or more of their tanks, aircraft, and guns.

Market Garden was an abrupt change in Allied strategy that had been employed by American and British armies as they advanced through northern France and the Low Countries in the summer of 1944. After the D-Day landings, the German 7th and 5th Panzer Armies contained the Allies in a narrow bridgehead in Normandy for nearly two months and fought valiantly, taking heavy casualties and gaining few replacements. But the weight of the ever-increasing British and American armies in troops, tanks, and guns being shipped to Normandy was too much for the Germans. The Allies also commanded the air and attacked anything that moved on the ground. The Americans finally brought in hundreds of heavy bombers and hundreds more fighter bombers to pulverize a small section of the German front occupied by the crack panzer division, Panzer Lehr. When the smoke cleared the German front line was shattered. Both the German armies broke in late July and the Americans pushed their troops through a breach in the German lines and the enemy stranglehold on Normandy crumbled.

Hitler attempted to stem the Allied advance out of Normandy a few days later by ordering a massive counterattack designed to drive a wedge between American and British forces. Hundreds of German tanks and thousands of troops led the way and formed a narrow salient between Allied forces that was easily crushed. They were halted and there were catastrophic German losses around the Norman town of Falaise. The German High Command begged Hitler to forgo the attack but in vain, and as many as 10,000 Wehrmacht troops were killed and 50,000 more taken prisoner in the failed German counterattack. The remnants of the two once-powerful German armies barely escaped encirclement and destruction and the survivors began a disorderly retreat over the Seine River and across northern France that ended only when they reached the Siegfried Line defenses where they hoped to stop the rout. The Allies pursued their foe with a continuous, unbroken front that was a wide net, the "broad front" strategy, also referred to as the "spread formation."[2]

When planning the invasion of France prior to D-Day, Allied commanders believed the war in the ETO would be a lengthy slugging match with the German army fighting for every inch of ground across France and retreating to natural defense lines like the Seine River and then the Meuse River. It was a cautious strategy based largely on the experiences of World War I where both sides fought it out in trenches. It was also based on the Allies' experiences and knowledge of the quality of German arms in the preceding years. The D-Day plan, not only for the initial assault on the beaches, but for the invasion of northwest Europe into Germany, envisioned the Allied armies advancing like a giant plow slowly pushing the enemy back. Masterful breakouts, spearhead attacks, and end runs into the enemy's rear were not part of the plan. The Allies expected to drive the enemy to the Seine by D+90, or early September, and reach the German frontier only by May 1945. Planners thought it would take many more months after that to bring the Germans to their knees.[3]

By early September, however, the two armies of the American 12th Army Group, the 1st Army, commanded by Lieutenant General Courtney Hodges, and the 3rd Army, commanded by General George Patton, were poised on the German frontier after their lightning drives across France. Hodges' army was positioned around Aachen and Wallendorf, and Patton's was farther south and closing on Germany near Metz, France. But against the prepared defenses around Metz, the 3rd began facing stiffening enemy resistance for the first time since the breakout at Normandy.

Montgomery's 21st Army Group, with its two armies, the Canadian 1st, commanded by General Harry Crerar, and the British 2nd Army, commanded by British General Miles Dempsey, operated on the northern flank of the broad front, advancing along the French coast and into Belgium and southern Holland.

After five weeks of exhilarating advances in late July and throughout August, the troops were tired, vehicles and tanks were wearing out, and supplies of ammunition, rations, and gasoline were running low as the Allies advanced some 435 miles from the Normandy beaches to the edge of the German heartland. The German army, on Hitler's orders, continued to hold all the major French and Belgium channel ports, except Cherbourg that had been liberated by the Allies shortly after D-Day. Cherbourg's port, once restored after German demolitions, could handle only a small portion of the Allies' overall logistical needs and Hitler's strategy forced the bulk of supplies to be delivered through the Normandy beaches, several hundred miles from the German frontier, depriving the Allies of close-up logistical support. But, ironically, the order also deprived the Germans of some 250,000 troops, trapped in the ports, who might have slowed or even halted the onrushing Allies.[4]

The Normandy area was brimming with supplies of all kinds and the famed Red Ball Express swung into action to deliver supplies to the front. The Red Ball was an operation of some 6,000 trucks, mostly two-and-a-half-ton "deuce and a halfs," "Jimmies," driven mostly by African-American service troops, that transported supplies over a one-way, loop highway to delivery points near Brussels, Belgium, and to Verdun in France. Red Ball trucks raced through the French countryside, day and night, sometimes through pockets of enemy troops. They carried critical supplies, gasoline, ammunition, medical supplies, and food to the front-line troops. The 8th U.S. Air Force was called in to airlift supplies to the advancing Allied armies in England-based B-24 bombers, diverting them from their primary mission of precision bombing of German industrial targets. Hundreds of C-47s from the Allied air transports commands were also enlisted to haul supplies but there were never enough trucks, bombers, and air transports to carry all the needed supplies. The French railroads were in shambles from the pre-invasion bombing to prevent the Germans from bringing up reinforcements and concentrating their forces against the D-Day invasion beaches. By the time the Allied advance reached the Siegfried Line it was slowing to a crawl, exactly when they needed a lightning blow to end the war.

Field Marshal Montgomery had such a plan in mind as he reached Belgium after a dash across France, and so did Patton whose 3rd Army had advanced into Lorraine that bordered the German Reich. They called on Eisenhower to alter his "broad front" strategy and concentrate Allied forces for a smashing, knife-like blow into Germany. Both Montgomery and Patton argued that the German army in the west was so battered and broken it had taken 300,000 casualties in France since June 6, by some estimates more than 500,000 men, few of whom had been replaced; most replacements were men recovered from wounds. Both generals argued that a concentrated thrust employing tens of thousands of Allied troops would easily break through the thin enemy Siegfried Line defenses and smash its way to the Rhine River, Germany's last line of defense in the west. The Allies could then capture the Ruhr or the Saar industrial areas, and, if ordered, make a rapid advance to capture Berlin. The question that hung in the air was who would lead the attack, Montgomery or Patton? The Allies could not support two advances at the same time.

When the German 7th and 5th Panzer Armies gave way in late July and began their retreat in disarray across northern France, the supreme command considered using the idle Allied paratroopers in England to drop behind the retreating enemy to create a blocking force, trapping the enemy in pockets that could easily be destroyed. The call to the paratroopers went out six or seven times in late July and August only to be canceled at the last minute; the objective had already been reached by the rapidly advancing ground forces. The paratroopers returned to their barracks to fret and languish as they waited for the call to join the fight. It would come on September 17 with the Arnhem bridge as the objective, remembered today as "A Bridge Too Far."

Eisenhower chose Montgomery to deliver the fatal blow in the *Market Garden* operation using the three airborne divisions, the U.S. 82nd, the 101st and the British 1st Airborne Division, along with the 60,000 or so ground troops in the British XXX Corps which consisted of the Guards Armoured

Division and the 43rd and 50th Northumbrian Infantry Divisions. "Market" was the code name for the attack by the airborne divisions and a Polish airborne brigade, and "Garden" was the code name for the overland attack by XXX Corps, led by Lieutenant General Brian Horrocks, through an enemy-held stretch of Holland. Horrocks was a veteran of the North African campaign and the recent advance across France.

Horrocks had served during World War I and with an Allied force that landed in Russia after the 1917 revolution with the objective of helping to defeat the Bolsheviks. He was an excellent athlete as well as soldier and had competed in the pentathlon in the 1924 Olympics. At the outset of World War II he served as a battalion commander in France under Montgomery. When Monty commanded the British 8th Army in North Africa he named Horrocks as commander of XIII Corps. Horrocks was severely wounded in a German strafing attack in Tunisia in 1943 and was out of action until called back to command XXX Corps in France and on the advance to Arnhem. He was considered one of the best Allied commanders.[5]

Market Garden was to employ as many as 100,000 American and British troops, more than 5,000 Allied aircraft, thousands of vehicles, and tons of supplies including vast stores of gasoline. The American airborne troops would overfly 50 miles of enemy-held Dutch territory, drop in specific spots, and hold strategic points along a corridor for XXX Corps' advance from the Belgium border. XXX Corps had the heavy weaponry – artillery and tanks – that the airborne units lacked. The British 1st Airborne Division was designated to drop near Arnhem and move quickly to capture the bridge over the Lower Rhine.

General Horrocks was expected to push his tanks through miles of German-held territory in two to four days, to reinforce the British 1st Airborne Division and to open a supply corridor to the city. Once in Arnhem his forces were to help secure the Rhine bridge held by the British paratroopers who had been dropped on the outskirts of the city about seven miles from their objective.

The American 82nd Airborne Division was to descend on a zone stretching from Grave to Nijmegen and was to capture crossings over the Maas and Waal rivers, including the multi-span bridge at Nijmegen. The 101st was to capture canal and river crossings between Eindhoven and Veghel.[6] If the plan worked to perfection the American airborne divisions would hold open their respective territories for XXX Corps while staving off any German counterattacks along the single road to Arnhem. But even the best plans in war seldom survive once the action begins.

Market Garden had the approval of the highest-ranking officers in the Allied European command including Eisenhower. For some weeks, American army

Chief of Staff General George C. Marshall was encouraging Eisenhower to deliver a crippling blow to the enemy by employing some or all of the five airborne divisions that sat idle and restive in Britain. The airborne forces constituted a sizable reserve of about 60,000 superbly trained paratroopers, many of them combat veterans, anxious to join the fight. The men from the 101st and 82nd, and the British 6th Airborne Division, about 35,000 men, had done their job after parachuting into Normandy the night before D-Day, confusing the Germans, blowing and capturing bridges, cutting communications, and drawing enemy troops away from the landing beaches where ground troops from two American infantry divisions and British and Canadian divisions would land by sea the next morning. Their mission accomplished, the paratroopers were withdrawn to England to refit and await another call to action. American Air Force Chief of Staff, General Henry "Hap" Arnold, also lobbied to get the paratroopers into action to make use of the hundreds of transport aircraft, principally C-47s, that he believed were also under-utilized.

Other generals, British and American, thought some kind of operation that might lead to the quick, final defeat of the Germans was in order. American General Lewis Brereton, commander of the Allied Airborne Army in England, also was eager to get his divisions into action. So, when Montgomery laid out his plan for *Market Garden* there was little opposition. It was proposed during the 1st week of September and executed just over a week later on the 17th.

The Germans, including the Wehrmacht's commander in the west, Field Marshal Gerd von Rundstedt, knew of the Allied airborne reserve in England. He believed the Americans and British would soon make use of these troops, calculating that they would be dropped behind the thin German defenses along the Siegfried Line, and possibly centered on Arnhem.

While *Market Garden* had high-ranking advocates, there were those who questioned its chances for success. Colonel Oscar W. Koch, the U.S. 3rd Army's intelligence chief, warned that the Wehrmacht was still capable of putting up strong resistance and would "fight until destroyed or captured."[7]

Three months later Koch was even more prescient. In December 1944, he warned Patton that intelligence indicators pointed to an impending attack against 1st Army troops by German forces in the Ardennes. Most high-ranking officers at the time did not believe that the enemy had the capability for any kind of major attack. Patton, however, took Koch's word to heart and prepared to shift some of his 3rd Army to the Ardennes in the event of a German attack. But in the week before Operation *Market Garden* was launched, few if any were heeding Koch's warnings.

General Dempsey warned that reports from the Dutch underground should be taken very seriously, that the Germans were increasing their strength in the Arnhem area.[8] Major Brian Urquhart, intelligence chief for the British 1st Airborne Corps, who would in later years become an Undersecretary of the United Nations, also warned that aerial photographs taken by Spitfire reconnaissance aircraft showed enemy tanks in the area near the Arnhem drop zone. His findings were dismissed and he was told by higher-ups that the tanks were undoubtedly battle-damaged and would be useless in a fight. For his effort, Urquhart was declared hysterical and suffering from exhaustion and was later sent on leave.

While the shortcomings of *Market Garden* were known, its advocates believed the advantages outweighed the limitations. The Germans were reported in most intelligence reports to be on their last legs with only a thin line of troops facing the Allied armies. Beyond their front line was empty ground and the reports indicated no German reserves of any strength were available to stop the oncoming Allied juggernaut. The time to strike the mortal blow was now.

The die was cast. Nothing and no one was going to abort Operation *Market Garden*. Even Major Urquhart expressed the exhilarating tension gripping the pre-attack planning. "Everyone was so gung-ho to go that nothing could stop them... this was going to be the big show." He didn't want to miss it, but he was sidelined nevertheless and sent on sick leave.[9]

The "mightiest airborne force in history" took flight around 9:45 am on the bright Sunday morning of September 17, 1944, as people all over southern England stopped what they were doing to watch the huge airborne armada wing its way to war.[10] Once over Holland the skies filled with multi-colored chutes as the paratrooper landings went without a hitch with the exception of a few losses here and there. Some of the C-47s were shot down by antiaircraft fire but most of the paratroopers were able to exit before the planes crashed. In some cases, the gliders were wrecked on landing; killing and injuring the troops. Nevertheless, the American airborne divisions made textbook landings in their drop zones and the British airborne division came down on its objective seven miles from Arnhem. The battle for the Arnhem bridge had begun and the way into Germany and the end of the 3rd Reich was at hand. But would *Market Garden* succeed?

CHAPTER 2

Why Not Wallendorf?

On the very day, September 17, 1944, when more than 100,000 *Market Garden* airborne and ground troops began an operation that required an advance over more than 50 miles of German-held territory to outflank the Siegfried Line at Arnhem, a few thousand American troops of the U.S. V Corps had already breached Germany's border defenses nearly 200 miles to the south. The V Corps had carved out a small bridgehead on German soil and these Americans were the first Allied troops to breach the Siegfried Line and advance into the Reich. If the corps could be reinforced with a fraction of *Market Garden*'s materiel support and combat-tested troops, it might accomplish the same objective as *Market Garden*, break through the Siegfried Line and advance to the Rhine and beyond.

The V Corps' orders, from General Courtney Hodges, 1st Army commander, were to make a reconnaissance in force with its three divisions into the Nazi homeland with the prospect of capitalizing on the enemy's weakness along the German frontier. The 5th Armored Division (AD) approached the German border with Luxembourg where it was hoped that, if given logistical support and infantry reinforcements in the days ahead, the Americans might push ahead and forge a small bridgehead and expand it into an outright breakthrough. Then the troops could roll up the thin enemy front and pave the way for an uncontested advance to the Rhine.

The V Corps, one of 1st Army's three corps, which comprised the 28th and 4th Infantry Divisions (IDs) and 5th AD, arrived at the Siegfried Line after a pell-mell advance across northern France, Belgium, and Luxembourg. The corps' divisions had landed at Normandy on D-Day, June 6, and been involved in heavy fighting in the Normandy bridgehead and across northern France. Commanded by Major General Leonard T. Gerow (pronounced jeer–oh), the corps was part of Hodges' 1st Army and was positioned along the German frontier midway between Aachen and Trier. The 1st Army's right flank extended south beyond the Ardennes and was occupied by the U.S. 3rd Army advancing into Lorraine. The 1st and 3rd Armies comprised General Omar Bradley's 12th Army Group. The two V Corps infantry divisions, along with the 5th AD, were pursuing elements of the shattered German 7th and 5th Panzer Armies fleeing the Allied armies from Normandy.

The V Corps came up against the enemy's border defenses in early September along a front that stretched some 33 miles. Somewhere in the middle of this ground is Wallendorf, a small village on the banks of the Sauer River that separates Germany and Luxembourg. The bank on the German side rises sharply to a verdant plateau on the Schnee Eifel of lush fields and meandering valleys, some quite deep; copses of thick forests; and small farming villages of solid houses and farmsteads, with their ever-present manure piles.

The Schnee Eifel in Germany is a continuation of the Ardennes in Belgium, but more rugged. It was through the Wallendorf area that General Heinz Guderian launched his attacks against the Low Countries and France in 1940, driving British and French forces into Dunkirk. General Erich Brandenberger,

Schnee Eifel where U.S. troops first invaded Germany in September 1944. The terrain is rolling yet riven with gullies making difficult going for tanks. (David P. Colley)

commander of the German 7th Army, would attack the Americans through the Wallendorf area during the Battle of the Bulge in December 1944.

As V Corps approached the Siegfried Line in early September, Hodges ordered Gerow to launch reconnaissance patrols at points along his front to determine the strength of German forces in the enemy's border areas. The 1st Army's resources in gasoline and ammunition were in short supply, and tanks and equipment needed repair after the rapid, non-stop advance but Hodges was hoping to take advantage of Allied momentum and the disintegration of German forces. Intelligence estimates suggested that the enemy could muster a mere 6,000 troops along V Corps' front. Colonel Thomas J. Ford, the corps' intelligence chief, predicted that American troops advancing into the Schnee Eifel would meet only battered remnants of the three enemy divisions that the Americans had pursued across France. These included the remnants of the 5th Panzer, the Panzer Lehr, and the 2nd Panzer Divisions. If the American reconnaissance patrols met little resistance, they were to keep advancing as long as enemy resistance was not too great.

The 5th AD was moving units up to the border between Luxembourg and Germany on September 11 when it received the order from V Corps headquarters to reconnoiter across the Our River into Germany. A platoon from the 85th Cavalry Squadron, attached to 5th AD, led by Sgt. Warner W. Holzinger, crossed the Our on a semi-demolished bridge at 4:30 in the afternoon and advanced into the German town of Stolzembourg and became, officially, the first U.S. troops to enter the enemy's heartland and the first foreign soldiers to invade Germany since Napoleon 150 years before. Holzinger spoke German and interrogated local citizens and farmers who informed him and his squad that there were no enemy troops in the area. Moving a mile-and-a-half inland the men came upon the first line of Siegfried Line pillboxes, but none were manned by enemy troops. Holzinger reported his findings:

> We worked our way down to Stolzembourg, a village on the Luxembourg side of the Our River. From the citizens we learned there were no enemy soldiers in the vicinity. I have been thankful many times I could speak German.
>
> The enemy had blown to some degree the small bridge that spanned the Our River. Even at that, we were able to cross on it. We could have waded the river too. On the German side of the river there was a pillbox camouflaged as a barn. It's a good thing it wasn't manned.
>
> Lieutenant DeLille (French liaison officer) and I talked with a German farmer. He told us that the last time he had seen any German troops was the day before. He also told us that if we followed the road up the small mountain behind his farm, we would be able to see the first line of pillboxes.
>
> So, Lieutenant DeLille, Pfc [William] McColligan, the German farmer, and I went into Germany about one and a half miles, where we could get a good view. We studied the pillbox area with our field glasses. None of them seemed manned. We returned to

Stolzembourg, where we reported the information [by radio] to Lt. Loren L. Vipond [his platoon commander].

The irony for Holzinger was that he had been born in Germany in 1916 with the name Werner Willi Holzinger. He came to the U.S. with his family in 1921 and was naturalized an American citizen in 1940, changing his name to Warner William. Because of his heritage he spoke impeccable German, making him ideal on reconnaissance patrols into Germany. When the patrol returned to American lines the word was flashed to the home front that the Reich had been penetrated.

From Holzinger's report it appeared that the German border was wide open and that the Americans had arrived in this sector before the Germans had been able to establish a coherent defense. However, the situation changed the next day. Another reconnaissance platoon crossed into Germany and observed German soldiers moving into the Siegfried Line pillboxes that lined the frontier. The enemy was moving swiftly to defend the frontier but hardly in numbers that would stop a determined American advance.

The true picture of German forces opposite V Corps was described as "dismal."[1] Entire enemy divisions had been so depleted in the previous month's fighting that several were merged to form amalgamated units whose regiments were hardly more than reinforced battalions. The 2nd SS Panzer-Division "Das Reich," another division in the German mix facing V Corps, and the 2nd Panzer Division, were woefully short of equipment. Between the two of them they could muster only 17 assault guns, 26 105mm howitzers, three 150mm guns, and six tanks, three each for the two divisions. "In the feeble hands of units like these had rested German hopes of holding the Allies beyond the Siegfried Line long enough for the fortifications to be put into shape," noted military historian Charles MacDonald.[2]

A communiqué from German Army Group B, that commanded enemy forces in the Schnee Eifel opposite V Corps, stated, "Continued reduction in combat strength and lack of ammunition have the direst effects on the course of defense action."

The V Corps' attack against the Siegfried Line involved its three attached divisions that were stretched along the frontier. The 4th ID held the north end of the corps' front centered around the Luxembourg town of Wiltz, about six miles west of the German frontier. The 28th ID was positioned in the center on the plateau to the south at the eastern tip of Luxembourg that projects into Germany, and 5th AD was farther south towards the town of Echtenach, also in Luxumbourg. All three divisions attacked simultaneously into the Eifel but it was the 5th AD front, centered around Wallendorf, that "developed into a genuine opportunity for a breakthrough which showed promise of welding the three separate division actions into a cohesive corps maneuver."[3] The 5th AD's immediate task was to patrol and "secure" the southern section of the corps' front that extended to the left flank of the 3rd Army advancing in Lorraine. For this purpose, Major General Lunsford E. Oliver, the division commander, attached the 28th's 12th Infantry Regiment to 5th AD's Combat Command A (CCA). Combat Command R (CCR) he assigned to patrol the central portion of the division's front with Combat Command B (CCB) taking the northerly section. Both combat commands were ordered to be ready to conduct a "reconnaissance in force," and exploit any breakthroughs that might occur along their front. (A combat command was a regimental size unit of tanks and armored infantry.)

The V Corps and 5th AD held one great advantage over the enemy in this sector but it was unknown to the Americans at the time. The V Corps' front faced a command gap in the German line where I SS Panzer Corps abutted the German LXXX Corps. It was also the demarcation line between the German 1st and 7th Armies and German Army Groups G and B. In essence, 5th AD would advance into German territory where there was no coordinated communication between the two German corps, two armies and two army groups, and a rapid advance by the Americans might catch the enemy completely off-guard. In addition, the Germans in the sector were so insufficiently prepared for an attack that American patrols could roam at will and found many of the pillboxes in the Siegfried Line empty of defenders and weapons. On September 13, when CCR conducted a reconnaissance by fire near Wallendorf, there was no enemy response – there were few, if any, Germans in the area.

Once aware that the Wallendorf sector was lightly defended on the right flank of the German LXXX Corps, Gerow ordered Oliver to advance through Wallendorf, move up the bluff behind the village, and advance across the crevassed plateau above and behind the village, and capture the village of Mettendorf some five miles inside Germany. With the assistance of the 28th ID's 112th Infantry Regiment, the 5th AD was to advance farther still and capture the small city of Bitburg, a communication center in the area, 12 miles beyond the German border. The V Corps, with its limited resources of tens of thousands combat troops, was poised to accomplish what 100,000 men were preparing to do at Arnhem – to sweep in behind German lines and push on to the Rhine.

General Gerow chose to advance through the more rugged Wallendorf area rather than through more forgiving ground farther south near Echternach because Wallendorf put the 5th AD closer to the 28th and 4th IDs to the

The village of Niedersgegen, three miles from Wallendorf on the Schnee Eifel, where troops of the 5th AD encountered German tanks and drove them off. (David P. Colley)

north as they also began to push through the Eifel. Gerow reasoned that if the 5th AD achieved a breakthrough the three divisions would form a formidable force that could envelop the thin German front line.

The Siegfried Line around Wallendorf also was not as heavily studded with pillboxes or dragon's teeth tank obstacles; the Germans relied more on the rugged terrain to thwart any enemy incursions into this region, particularly Wallendorf's position on a steep ridge. The "bluff" was said to remind some Americans of the Palisades on the New Jersey side of the Hudson River just above New York city, although it is not as precipitous. However, once above and beyond Wallendorf, the ground levels out into an undulating plateau with sharp vales that could hamper the movement of tanks and armored vehicles. But much of the area is open farmland with patches of forest and the ground rises much more gently from village to village. The geography did not preclude maneuver by large formations.

The dearth of supplies for the rapidly moving Allied armies in the advance across France was cause for some concern at V Corps' headquarters as Gerow prepared the advance. The Red Ball Express was rushing supplies to the advancing troops but could carry only so much materiel from the Normandy area. Black marketeering and the Allied provisioning Paris after its liberation with coal and food cut into the delivery of supplies to V Corps. But 5th AD's supply situation was sufficient to begin an attack through the Siegfried Line into Germany.

> The status of supply in the 5th Armored Division was similar to that in the rest of the V Corps, although the logistical pinch might not be felt so severely since only one combat command was to see action. The three-day pause in Luxembourg had enabled the division to refill its fuel tanks and constitute a nominal gasoline reserve. Although artillery ammunition on hand was no more than adequate, a shortage of effective counter battery fires in the coming offensive was to arise more from lack of sound and flash units and from poor visibility than from any deficiency in ammunition supply.[4]

Troops in sound and flash units were positioned in the front lines to measure the distance between the flash and sound from enemy artillery fire and the time it took for a shell to strike in American lines. This enabled the artillerymen to calculate where the enemy battery was located to direct their counter fire.

General Oliver ordered Combat Command R to advance into the Siegfried Line just after noon on September 14; the bridge at Wallendorf had been blown by German engineers but the Americans were able to wade into Germany at the confluence of the Our and Sauer Rivers near the village. Enemy troops from a hastily organized Alarm battalion, thrown into the fight at the last minute, put up fierce resistance, but they possessed no antitank weapons and their artillery was desultory, directed by a Luftwaffe officer who had no experience in artillery, nor did most of his gun crews.[5] The lack of German antitank fire enabled Col. Glen H. Anderson, CCR commander, to send his tanks into Wallendorf alongside the infantry. Firefights raged through the village as the Germans were being driven out and tracer and high explosive rounds set the village ablaze.

The tanks and infantry proceeded through Wallendorf towards the plateau via a steep and narrow road that rose from the village. As the Americans advanced up the slope they knocked out the string of pillboxes that lay hidden on the ridge side. Their only opposition as they made their way to the plateau was a lone German soldier with an antitank Panzerfaust who was quickly dispatched by concentrated fire. The command dug in on the plateau as night approached and the advance resumed the following day, September 15, into the tiny crossroads village of Niedergegen along the Gay Creek. There the troops encountered an under-strength company of Mark IV enemy tanks believed to be from a remnant Kampfgruppe of General Fritz Bayerlein's crack but badly depleted Panzer Lehr Division. After a brief fight the Germans were driven out of the village and into the rolling countryside with the loss of three tanks and six half-tracks. The encounter awakened the German command to the imminent American breakthrough in the Wallendorf sector and General Schmidt von Knobelsdorff, commander of the German 1st Army, prepared to commit as many forces as possible to the Wallendorf sector. The 5th AD's CCR then pressed forward to capture a succession of farming villages situated on gentle rises in the terrain – Biesdorf, Uchten, Hommerdingen, and Nusbaum – before occupying high ground near the village of Mettendorf. The Germans at this point were virtually powerless to stop the American advance, and CCR

> moved virtually unopposed. In rapid succession, the armor seized four villages and occupied Hill 407, the crest of the high ground near Mettendorf, the initial objective. Already CCR had left all Siegfried Line fortifications in its wake. (…)
>
> By nightfall CCR had advanced through the Siegfried Line and across the western plateau almost to the banks of the Pruem (river), some six miles inside Germany. Though the combat command actually controlled little more than the roads, the fact that a force could march practically uncontested through the enemy rear augured new life to hopes of a drive to the Rhine.[6]

With his armor roaming essentially uncontested behind enemy lines, Gerow ordered Oliver to advance and capture the city of Bitburg and then swing his forces north in two columns towards the towns of Pronsfeld and Prüm, which would place elements of the 5th AD directly behind German forces opposing the 28th ID and close to the southern flank of the 4th ID, both divisions positioned just north of 5th AD in the Eifel. If this action succeeded the lightly held section of the German Siegfried Line opposing the Americans would collapse, leaving a gaping hole in the German front line.

Desperate to check the enemy, Knobelsdorff called for help from Field Marshal von Rundstedt, the overall German commander in the west, who, recognizing the gravity of the German situation, scraped together what reserves he could find, a regimental combat team from the 19th Volksgrenadier Division, which was immediately trucked to the front from some 50 miles away on the night of September 15. The rest of the division would follow in two days.

Von Rundstedt's order paid off; introduction of German reserves began to have an effect in the following days. On the night of September 16, an American engineer reconnaissance patrol ran into Germans in the village of Niedersgegen which the Americans had secured three days before. In the ensuing firefight two engineers were killed and later that day German panzers appeared near the Gay Creek in the village to block the American advances. The encounters with enemy forces on ground that V Corps had already seized

WHY NOT WALLENDORF? • 19

revealed that German forces were infiltrating American lines, sewing confusion and attacking the flanks of 5th AD penetration. Most disturbing, German artillery had been moved forward during the day of the 16th and began shelling CCR with "disturbing accuracy."[7] (German artillery spotters made use of local foresters and local citizens to pinpoint American positions.) Just to the northwest, a CCR task force tried to advance towards the village of Stockem north of Wallendorf, but stiffening enemy resistance drove the troops back.

Nevertheless, elements of the 112th Regiment, 28th ID, advanced eastward to Wettlingen on the Prüm River. Pushing across the Prüm the 112th seized high ground several hundred yards beyond Wettlingen and the infantry, supported by tank destroyers, found themselves only five miles from Bitburg and seven to eight miles beyond the Siegfried Line.

Despite evidence of stiffening enemy resistance there was a growing sense of optimism at 5th AD headquarters that a major breakthrough could be achieved. CCR may have been held up but the 112th had continued its advance and CCB was crossing into Germany at Wallendorf to take up positions to shore the left flank of the bridgehead at Niedersgegen. By the end of the day on the 16th, 5th AD's G-2 intelligence branch believed that the enemy was so weak that the most he could accomplish was to slow the American advance rather than halt it. "While the Germans had countermeasures in the making, all they actually had accomplished was to fling a papier-mache cordon about the penetration with every available man from the LXXX Corps and every man that could be spared from the adjacent I SS Panzer Corps."[8] The way was paved for a deep penetration into the enemy's heartland, to Bitburg, to roll up the enemy line facing American forces farther north in the Eifel, and maybe even an advance to the Rhine, the last line of defense for the German army.

It was now up to U.S. 1st Army, 12th Army Group, or the Supreme Command to step in and exploit the situation at Wallendorf with reinforcements. It was a potential breakthrough delivered on a platter, one that a gung-ho commander would dream about. But all the top commands were silent, possibly ignorant of the tactical situation on the V Corps' front and no reserves were forthcoming. Generals Bradley and Eisenhower may not even have been aware of what was happening in the Wallendorf bridgehead. Hodges should have been aware. The 1st Army diary makes reference to V Corps' penetration. All eyes, however, were on Arnhem and *Market Garden* where thousands of paratroopers and ground troops from XXX Corps were about to descend on Holland to open the way around the Siegfried Line to the Ruhr. The Allied High Command believed the alliance needed a spectacular show at Arnhem, and the breakthrough at Wallendorf was regarded, if it was regarded at all, as a minor skirmish. As if to acknowledge his inferior role along the Siegfried Line, on the night of the 16th just hours before *Market Garden* was launched, Gerow, somewhat inexplicably, ordered Oliver to suspend the offensive into the Wallendorf bridgehead and to consolidate his forces and "mop up" the line northeast of the village with his armor. Oliver was to make no advance towards Bitburg but would continue aggressive patrolling to reconnoiter the situation in the vicinity of the city.

Even the official army history, *The Siegfried Line Campaign*, generally conservative in its assessments of military actions and criticism of decisions by American commanders, expressed surprise at Gerow's directive for the 5th AD to assume the defensive. "It must have come as a shock to both troops and commanders. That the Germans had not stopped the V Corps armor was plain."[9] Many 5th AD troops and officers believed the division and corps was missing a great opportunity to breach the Siegfried Line and advance to the Rhine. The division's post-war history, *Paths of Armor*, asserted:

> Fifth Armored did not feel happy about withdrawing from Germany after having cut the first corridor through the Siegfried Line. Its spearhead had extended about seven miles into the Reich; two combat commands lay for two days before Bitburg; it had battered its way completely through the tough belt of pillboxes. It was fully confident then that it could have advanced the remaining 50 miles to the Rhine had it been supported by (an) additional infantry division to broaden the penetration and to keep open its supply lines. But these infantry divisions, involved in petty skirmishing to the north, were not available.[10]

CHAPTER 3

Schnee Eifel

As the 5th AD and the accompanying 28th ID's 112th Regiment were breaching the Siegfried Line around Wallendorf, the other two V Corps' divisions, the 28th – its two remaining regiments – and 4th ID, had also gone on the attack just to the north in the Schnee Eifel. The 28th was the first of the V Corps' divisions to advance along the corps' front during this operation by virtue of the fact that its troops were closest to the German frontier at a point where the German border bulges toward Luxembourg. The attack included the division's 109th and 110th Infantry Regiments, the 109th attacking on the northern flank of the advance towards commanding high ground around the village of Uettfeld. The 110th was on the southern flank moving towards the village of Grosskampenberg at the eastern edge of the Siegfried Line defenses. The 110th would sweep into Germany and link up with the 109th near Uettfeld.

The attack began on September 12, and by nightfall the Americans had made progress towards Uettfeld which lay two miles beyond the Siegfried Line defenses. The attack resumed on the 13th but both regiments were held up by withering fire from pill boxes in the belts of Siegfried Line defenses and by mortar and artillery fire. Efforts to silence the pillboxes by indirect fire and from towed 57mm antitank guns came to naught. The American attacks continued on the 14th but again failed to reach the high ground around Uettfeld, in part because tanks brought forward to support the infantry could not break through the dragon's teeth tank traps placed in rows five deep.

Interrogation of captured German POWs indicated, however, that many of the pillboxes in the Siegfried Line defenses remained unmanned and large numbers of the enemy troops in the sector were hardly battle-wise veterans, being mainly older men, young boys, and service troops thrown into the breach. One enemy defender was a 40-year-old cook who was captured only two hours after reaching the front. The fact that so few enemy troops of low quality were blocking the advance of the battle-hardened 28th angered the Americans. One American officer remarked, "It doesn't much matter what training a man may have when he is placed inside such protection as was afforded by the pillboxes. Even if he merely stuck his weapons through the aperture and fired occasionally, it kept our men from moving ahead freely."[1] The dragon's teeth tank obstacles that ran astride the border as part of the Siegfried Line prevented the Americans from calling up tanks to blast the pillboxes with their 75mm cannons. During the night, a team bringing up explosives to blow a path through the dragon's teeth was killed when the explosives detonated, killing every man.

However, there was one bright spot in the action on the 14th. A young tank commander, Second Lieutenant Joseph H. Dew, was able to maneuver his Sherman into position and methodically blasted a path through the dragon's teeth with the tank's gun. Infantry immediately followed and the Americans gained a tiny bridgehead among the pillboxes of the Siegfried Line. Dew was subsequently awarded the Distinguished Service Cross.

Although the progress was slow and costly in casualties, Gerow, "seeing the first punctures of the line as the hardest," was encouraged that a breakthrough was possible and ordered the 5th AD to send an experienced tank commander to the 28th to advise the infantry how best to use tanks and infantry in the next day's attack. The 5th AD's Combat Command B was alerted to be ready to support the 28th's infantry.[2]

September 15 brought little change on the battlefield as the advancing infantry again ran into withering fire and local enemy counterattacks drove the Americans back in some areas. For the next two days, the 109th struggled to reach the high ground around Uettfeld without success. However, late in the day on the 15th a team of engineers arrived in the 110th's sector with explosives to destroy a key roadblock that was holding up the American advance. Worming their way forward, the engineers worked under fire while placing the charges and then took off at a gallop as the explosives did the job and obliterated the concrete-encased steel I-beams. On cue, the infantry went forward at a run in a coordinated attack with supporting tanks firing point blank into the surrounding pillboxes. Within 45 minutes the 110th had gained a major objective, Hill 553 overlooking the road to Uettfeld, taking out 17 pillboxes and capturing 58 German prisoners. General Norman Cota, the 28th ID's commanding general, had high hopes for additional advances the next day.

The going would not be easy. Late that night the 110th suffered another setback. Sent ahead to position itself for an attack to take the high ground around Uettfeld, F Company was virtually wiped out in an attack by about 80 enemy troops following behind half-tracks rigged to carry flame throwers. Shortly after midnight there was an eerie silence around F Company and the men heard the approaching clatter of tracked vehicles. Then, one of the survivors recalled, "I saw the flame thrower start and heard the sounds of a helluva scrap up around Captain Schultz' position." A few minutes later a nearby company intercepted a frantic radio message from F company: "KING SUGAR to anybody. KING SUGAR to anybody. Help! We are having a counterattack – tanks, infantry, flame throwers." Before the call could be processed and action taken to relieve the beleaguered company, the sounds of the firefight diminished into silence. Most of the men in F Company were killed or taken prisoner. F Company was left with a roster of 45 men.

Despite the setback with F Company, the advance towards Uettfeld continued the next morning, September 16, when a battalion of the 110th regiment, assisted by supporting artillery fire, renewed the attack and advanced to within 1,000 yards of the objective. By day's end, the 28th ID had advanced a mile and a half beyond the dragon's teeth and taken commanding ground that overlooked the sector for miles around. "Beyond them lay only scattered Siegfried Line fortifications. Though the penetration was narrow and pencil like, the 28th Division had for all practical purposes broken through the Siegfried Line."[3]

The 109th and 110th Regiments had accomplished a breakthrough in the German Siegfried Line albeit a narrow one. Would the Allied command respond with reinforcements and supplies to exploit this additional breach? Unfortunately, as with the 5th AD just to the south, it would not. Even as the infantrymen of the two regiments gained a foothold beyond the Siegfried Line, Gerow visited the 28th ID command post, as he had visited 5th AD's headquarters around Wallendorf, and ordered Cota to suspend the attack. Presumably Gerow was following Hodges' orders to withdraw back into Luxembourg if Cota's troops ran into stiff resistance and the desperate reaction of the Germans seemed to indicate that the going beyond the Siegfried Line would become even tougher.

"Surprise" might be a judicious description of Cota's response to Gerow's order. His troops had advanced beyond the Siegfried Line to high ground around Uettfeld. When Gerow arrived at Cota's command post (CP) with orders to call off the offensive into Germany, Cota attempted to persuade Gerow to continue the fight; his infantrymen "were finally on the threshold of accomplishing their objective."[4] Gerow was concerned that he could not protect his flanks in the narrow penetration into Germany unless he was reinforced and he did not have the additional manpower. But did the Germans have the strength to seriously attack Cota's flanks and disrupt the advance? In post-war after-action reports, the Germans reported they did not. Gerow was also concerned that if he pressed farther he would not have the support of Hodges who had ordered that the troops stay "buttoned up." Gerow could have taken advice from the German general Guderian: "the Goddess of Victory will bestow her laurels only on those who are prepared to act with daring."[5]

Aides to Cota reported raised voices at the 28th's command post as Cota and Gerow discussed the withdrawal and Cota objected. But Gerow was the corps' commander and Cota had to acquiesce to his superior's order but later critiqued his own performance in the Schnee Eifel. "Most troubling to him was the plan he had developed for the attack on the Siegfried Line. He was convinced he had been overly cautious and that had he massed all six of his available battalions, the division may have broken through on the first day when the Germans were less prepared."[6] So the fight to breach the Siegfried Line in the 28th ID's sector ended. The 110th and 109th regiments consolidated their positions and fended off occasional German counterattacks. They would advance no farther.

A few miles to the north of the 28th, the 4th ID was positioned along the German border just east of the town of St. Vith, Belgium, where troops of the division's 12th and 22nd Regiments also began probing attacks into the Siegfried Line on September 12. Encountering little enemy opposition over the next two days, General Raymond O. "Tubby" Barton ordered a general attack through the enemy defenses on the 14th. The lack of German resistance and the discovery by reconnaissance patrols that many of the enemy pillboxes in the division's sector along the border were unmanned convinced Barton that the Siegfried Line was merely a thin defensive crust that, once cracked, left the entire Schnee Eifel open for exploitation. He ordered the 12th and 22nd Regiments to attack line abreast focused on the village of Bleialf and seize the crest of high ground on a central plateau east of the Prüm River. If the division succeeded in its objective, it would advance some ten miles beyond the Siegfried Line into the German heartland.

In a somewhat uncoordinated advance through thick drizzle the 12th advanced unimpeded up the western slopes of the Schnee Eifel, captured high ground on "Bogeyman Hill," and blasted their way through a few pillboxes before halting for the night on the hill. The lead battalion of the 12th had penetrated the Siegfried Line and prepared to continue the advance the next day.

As the 12th advanced, the 22nd approached Bleialf where it encountered a German panzer which knocked out one of the accompanying American

Sherman tanks. Momentarily stopped, infantrymen of the 22nd regained their footing and, after a brief skirmish, lead elements of the regiment stormed through a concentration of pillboxes and took the crest of the ridge. "Like the 28th ID's 12th Infantry farther to the south, the 22d Infantry had achieved an astonishingly quick penetration of this thin sector of the Siegfried Line."[7]

Colonel Charles T. Lanham, 22nd commander, quickly ordered the two lead battalions to continue the advance and to take control of the ridge and silence any pillboxes where the enemy was waiting. The GIs flushed out a number of enemy troops and found the defenders to be poorly trained, older men and under-age boys. The only serious enemy opposition came at a crossroads on the Bleialf–Prüm highway where the Germans put up a stiff defense that was overcome by close-in fire from several M-10 tank destroyers. As the day ended the 22nd Infantry had created a two-mile wide breach in the Siegfried Line and one battalion had reached the eastern slopes of the Schnee Eifel by the village of Hontheim a mile and a quarter beyond the forward wall of pillboxes in the Siegfried Line.

The success of the advance into Germany by the two regiments of the 4th ID encouraged General Barton to expand the division's bridgehead beyond the Siegfried Line even though the terrain in the Schnee Eifel was rugged and not overly suitable for armor. The prize was the Rhine and Barton may have taken heart from Gerow who had assigned an officer with expertise in armored warfare to assist the 28th a few miles to the south. Gerow obviously reasoned that, using armor, the 28th and the 4th might break into the open and be in a position to push to the Rhine.

General Barton thus ordered his 8th Infantry Regiment that had been held in reserve to move forward along the northern rim of the Schnee Eifel into the Losheim Gap, along the narrow corridor of the Kyll River valley. Its objective was a position along the north bank of the Kyll six miles inside Germany. The 12th Infantry was to advance northeast along the flank of the 8th and the 22nd was to move southwest to take the village of Brandscheid at the southern end of the Schnee Eifel and situated within the Siegfried Line.

"With the 8th Infantry on 15 September rode General Barton's main hope for a breakthrough. If the 8th Infantry could push on rapidly, the Schnee Eifel could be outflanked and the Siegfried Line left far behind."[8]

But, as was often the case when combating the Wehrmacht in World War II, the Germans fought back tenaciously, even these battered remnants of formations that had been mauled in France. The 8th immediately encountered blown bridges and various roadblocks and the Americans had to advance in a steady, misting drizzle without the aid of swarms of fighter bombers to ease the way. The regiment was being hit by increasing salvos of mortar and artillery fire and the enemy had mustered enough men to stage a number of counterattacks and enemy patrols began infiltrating behind American lines, forcing the Yanks to release infantrymen to guard their rear. Once-empty pillboxes in the wide belt of the Siegfried Line defenses were now occupied by infiltrating enemy troops furthering the problems for the 4th ID.

The 8th ran into heavy resistance near the village of Losheim and then, as it sidestepped to the south, more of the same near the village of Roth. The regiment saw some successes during the day as it drove the enemy back but its commanding officer, Colonel James Rodwell, with the concurrence of Barton, believed that a coordinated attack to breach the German defenses would have to be delayed until the next morning.

The Americans of the 4th ID were facing the depleted German 2nd SS Panzer Division whose ranks were stiffened by two companies of infantry and three Mark IV tanks. But much of its strength came from an assortment of fragmented units, stragglers, older men, and teenage boys who helped establish blocking positions across the Schnee Eifel. The 2nd SS Panzer launched a series of counterattacks that inflicted heavy casualties on the U.S. units. Still, the Americans held their ground; their steadfastness exemplified by First Lt. W. Wittkopf, who called for an artillery strike on his own position to halt a German counterattack.

Despite the enemy's determined counterattacks, there was hope for a breakthrough. On the afternoon of 16 September, the 1st Battalion, 8th Infantry, advanced out of the Prüm State Forest and seized a hill commanding the Bleialf–Prüm highway just west of the German-held village of Sellerich. On the 17th, Colonel Lanham ordered the attack through the Schnee Eifel to continue with two of his battalions advancing towards the high ground just beyond the village of Sellerich. But Major Robert B. Latimer, who commanded the 1st Battalion, 22nd Infantry, believed he did not have sufficient strength to take the high ground and requested artillery fire to blanket the area while he moved his troops into Sellerich. A Company proceeded down into the village and finding it empty of German troops, continued the drive to take the high ground across the Mon Creek on the road towards its objective, the town of Prüm. When B Company followed to reinforce A Company with a contingent of tanks and tank destroyers, the invisible Germans suddenly opened fire with artillery, mortar, and small arms driving A Company back into Sellerich. Trapped and unable to be reinforced when the enemy cut the road into the village, A-Company troops fought a desperate battle to avoid annihilation. Lt. Warren E. Marcum, A Company commander, requested permission to withdraw from Sellerich but his radio went silent before he could receive a reply. The company was fighting for its life and throughout the night remnants made their way back to American lines. When roll call was made the next day it was answered by two officers and 66 men.

The stiffening enemy defense and mounting U.S. casualties gave the Americans pause. The division, corps, and 1st Army did not have the immediate resources and manpower to continue the fight even though many in command believed the German defenses were little more than a thin crust that once pierced, could do little to stop a determined American attack. The divisions of V Corps had pierced the Siegfried Line, and advanced six or seven miles at its deepest penetration before its troops ran into resistance from makeshift and desperate German units. What might have been achieved if these penetrations had been exploited and reinforced?

CHAPTER 4

Miracle in the West

The Ardennes-Schnee Eifel region, as the Germans proved in 1914 and in 1940, and were to demonstrate again in December 1944 during the Battle of the Bulge, was not the treacherous ground it was thought to be by American planners. The Germans advanced through the Eifel and Ardennes to attack the British and French in World War I and later in World War II. What is more, this region in September 1944 was almost devoid of Germans, being the weakest-held enemy sector along the entire western front. The lone 5th AD proved how vulnerable the sector was at Wallendorf, but to no avail. The bulk of the U.S. 1st Army by that time was already committed in the Aachen Gap to the north and all attention was on Operation *Market Garden.*[1]

To the Allied High Command Wallendorf and the Schnee Eifel were sideshows, and SHAEF would not exploit the breakthroughs there. Certainly, Eisenhower and Montgomery were focused on Arnhem in the belief that this was the attack that would breach the German border defenses. Besides, all commands believed the Allied armies did not have the reserves in manpower and supplies to sustain V Corps' limited and potentially game-changing advances into and through the Siegfried Line defenses.

Or so it is alleged. One wonders if the same desired result of breaching the Siegfried Line and reaching the Rhine that was expected from *Market Garden* could have been achieved along the V Corps' front at a much lower cost in Allied resources and manpower. What if a few regiments or one reserve division of men and armor, along with the needed gasoline and ammunition, had been sent to reinforce General Gerow's troops instead of to the Netherlands?

Gerow's decision to suspend V Corps' attack into the Schnee Eifel begs the question, why did he order a halt to the offensive when it was showing promise of a complete breakthrough? According to the official army history, *The Siegfried Line Campaign*, Gerow was aware that the enemy forces on his front were weak and without depth. "In an optimistic farewell message to his command (a few days into V Corps' attack into the Schnee Eifel he was recalled to Washington to testify before Congress in an investigation into the Pearl Harbor disaster) he (Gerow) indicated that the opposition the Germans had mustered against his offensive had failed to impress him."[2] Why then didn't he ask for reinforcements? Yes, the Allied armies were tired and in need of rest after the race across France, vehicles and tanks were worn, and supplies were limited. There wasn't enough gasoline, ammunition, and rations to continue an advance all along the Allied front, and no commander could expect to receive additional supplies and reinforcements.

But this was only partially true. The pursuit of the enemy had slowed and 5th AD had rested and restocked for several days in Luxembourg in early September and was reasonably well supplied with gasoline and ammunition when it attacked into the Eifel at Wallendorf. Obviously there were enough supplies somewhere that the high command could provision the huge paratrooper force ready to drop into Holland and an entire British corps of three divisions advancing from Belgium to Arnhem. Eisenhower was aware that he had shifted huge resources in men and materiel to *Market Garden.* "(He) admitted he had 'sacrificed a lot to give Field Marshal Montgomery the strength he needs to reach the Rhine in the north and to threaten the Ruhr.'"[3]

Rommel or Guderian in Gerow's position would have smelled blood and driven his troops onward to force a breakthrough in the Schnee Eifel. Rommel was known to carry the attack by his Africa Corps against the British in North Africa in his command car ahead even of his most forward troops seemingly oblivious to the danger. And he was not too afraid to operate well beyond his supply lines.

Guderian would have sensed that a breakthrough was imminent if the attack were pursued. In the opening stages of the Russian campaign in 1941 his tank legions raced ahead of the main body of his troops and well behind Russian lines. The tanks encircled and bottled up the confused Russians giving the slower moving German infantry an opportunity to move in for the kill.

Another argument, sometimes cited, as to why Gerow called a halt to the advance in the Schnee Eifel was that V Corps had done its job by taking pressure off the American attack into the Siegfried Line at Aachen some 100 miles to the north where the U.S. VII Corps had also achieved a narrow breach of the Siegfried Line. The VII Corps received priority over V Corps in the overall strategic picture because the axis of its attack was through the Stolberg corridor at Aachen. This was the more direct route to the Ruhr industrial zone. Allied High Command thinking was that as long as V Corps tied up German forces around Wallendorf and in the Eifel the enemy could not reinforce his forces around Aachen, the main focus of 1st Army's attack into the Siegfried Line. However, this claim was refuted by Waffen SS Major General Fritz Kraemer, chief of staff of the 6th Panzer Army. When asked in a post-war interview whether 5th AD's attack at Wallendorf forced the Germans to shift troops away from the Aachen area he replied: "No, we did not consider it necessary to place more than our small reserve there."[4]

The Germans certainly were not immediately aware that Gerow was suspending his attacks on the V Corps' front. On the contrary, they were shifting forces and army group perimeters to contend with what appeared to them as a possible breakthrough to the Rhine.

"Unaware that the Americans had called off their attack, Rundstedt and the other German commanders saw the situation as extremely serious. Late on 17 September Rundstedt gave Army Group B a reserve panzer brigade, the 108th, for employment under the 2nd Panzer Division against the north flank of the (American) bridgehead. At the same time, General von Knobelsdorff at 1st Army laid plans to commit the 19th Volksgrenadier Division in a counterattack against the south flank on 18 September. Rundstedt also acted to remove the problem of divided responsibility occasioned by the location of the American strike along the army and army group boundaries."[5]

One explanation critical to understanding Gerow's order to stand down may lie with the psychological state of the general himself. Gerow had orders to report back to Washington to testify before a Congressional committee about his alleged failure to sufficiently warn the military commands in Hawaii and the Philippines about the Japanese attacks on December 7, 1941. Gerow had been responsible for pre-war planning at the Pentagon and in that capacity it was his responsibility to prepare American military commands in the Pacific about a possible Japanese attack. While he did issue advisories, they were not considered specific enough to motivate commanders to prepare against the destruction of aircraft and ships.

General Gerow's fault in Pearl Harbor stemmed from an ambiguously worded message. As Chief of War Plans Department, he was personally responsible for communicating with U.S. commands in Hawaii and the Philippines. On November 27, 1941, more than a week before the attack on Pearl Harbor, General Marshall instructed General Gerow to issue a warning to all American commands in the Pacific that all diplomatic means with Japan were exhausted and that Japanese military action against the United States was very likely in the immediate future. Concern that an abrupt change in U.S. military posture would raise Japanese suspicions about the security of their codes, which the Americans had cracked, led to the inclusion of a final sentence to the War Department message: "but these measures should be carried out so as not, repeat, not to alarm civil populations or disclose intent." This final sentence was not part of the Pacific original message approved by Army Chief George Marshall. Although Marshall later concurred to its addition, it was Gerow who added the sentence before sending the alert. The U.S. Army's inquiry revealed that this final phrase served to dramatically alter the tone and effect of the warning. The ensuing Army investigation of Pearl Harbor found both Marshall and Gerow at fault for their role in the pre-attack message traffic."[6] Both officers were reprimanded.

All during V Corps' attacks into the Eifel, particularly in the Wallendorf bridgehead, Gerow was aware that he would relinquish his command on September 18 to return to Washington to face a hostile reception in Congress; it weighed heavily on him. The last thing he needed before returning to Washington was a well-publicized bloody nose inflicted on V Corps by rag-tag units of a nearly defeated German army in the Eifel; better to pull back than to risk defeat and humiliation that could end his military career. In any event, he expected the war to be over in a matter of weeks and before he returned from Washington, so why go out on a limb. He was optimistic about the outcome of the war. "It is probable," he told his troops, "the war with Germany will be over before I am released to return to the V Corps."[7]

In September, many Allied generals were so confident that Germany was finished that they were taking bets among themselves as to the date they would reach the Rhine and when the German Reich would collapse. Major Chester Hansen, an aide to Bradley, noted in his diary in mid-September that "Brad and General Patton agree neither will be surprised if we are on the Rhine in a week." Hodges told his staff on September 6 that, with ten days of good weather, the war would be over. Montgomery predicted the war would end by November 1, 1944, while Bradley thought it would be a little later, but still before Christmas. Army post-exchange officials were so convinced that the war was nearly over that they planned to return to the U.S. Christmas presents from their families already in the mail to soldiers in the ETO.[8] Hansen chose November 25, 1944, as the date that he believed 1st Army would reach the Rhine. His prediction was precise by date, but he had the wrong army. It was the 7th Army that would reach the Rhine first, at Strasbourg in Alsace on November 23. (The French First Army was the first Allied force to reach the Rhine near Mulhouse, a few days before the 7th Army.) The generals' predictions were wrong, possibly because the Allies failed to take advantage of weaknesses like Wallendorf in the German Siegfried Line.

"When he (General Gerow) left for the United States he suspected that he would not return and his career was probably over. This had a profound effect on him. For an ambitious officer with over thirty years of service being summarily relieved was both professionally humiliating and personally shattering."[9] Gerow knew that he was on list for promotion to lieutenant general and would likely be given command of the new 15th Army in the ETO. But that was before he was accused of negligence in the Pearl Harbor investigation. A reprimand could derail his career and when the call came for him to testify he was devastated.

"His concern of being demoted or passed over was well founded. While he was testifying in Washington Eisenhower wrote to Bradley that Truscott had been promoted to Lieutenant General, and should be considered to command 15th Army rather than General Gerow."[10] (Major General Lucian Truscott, former VI Corps' commander in Alsace, was promoted to command 5th Army in Italy in the fall of 1944.) In fact, Eisenhower relieved Truscott of his VI Corps' command in 7th Army that landed in the south of France in August 1944 and promoted him to the command of the American 15th Army in October 1944. The 15th was being formed to operate in northern Europe in the final Allied drive into Germany. Truscott would have taken the command had not General Marshall asked him to return to Italy to take command of the American 5th Army. It was Italy where Truscott had made his mark earlier in the war commanding the 3rd U.S. ID and later the VI Corps at Anzio. He knew the difficulties of fighting in Italy better than anyone.

That the Pearl Harbor investigation interfered with Gerow's command decisions was amply demonstrated when he returned from Washington to the front a few weeks later branded with the reprimand from the Congressional committee. (General Marshall was also reprimanded for his failure to adequately warn overseas outposts. Stung by the reproof, he offered his resignation, but President Franklin Roosevelt refused to accept it. General Marshall was too valuable to lose.) Generals Eisenhower and Bradley were aloof towards Gerow when he returned to the ETO and Gerow withdrew into himself. In December 1944, Gerow took back his command of V Corps in the Battle of the Bulge and his performance was considered less than stellar and the weight of the reprimand was considered a prime reason. But he restored his reputation in the battles to subdue Germany in 1945 and later took command of the 15th Army. His lifelong friendship with Eisenhower probably helped him get back on his feet.

Whether Gerow received a direct order from General Hodges to withdraw from the Eifel and the Wallendorf bridgehead is unclear, but Hodges certainly didn't encourage Gerow to push the enemy to its limits. The meeting was contentious between the V Corps' commander and Hodges. It is not too difficult to speculate that Gerow objected to an order from Hodges to call off the attacks into the Siegfried Line.

Hodges' 1st Army war diary as V Corps' troops attacked at Wallendorf indicates that there was no unusual activity, excitement, or interest in the corps' progress in the Schnee Eifel. Entries for September 13 portray a relatively static front manned by all 1st Army's divisions from Echternach on V Corps' southern boundary to Aachen in the north. An entry for the day relating to V Corps is matter of fact: "Both the 28th and the 4th (divisions) are from six to seven miles inside the enemy's territory." The next day, the 14th, an entry reads: "4th Division made excellent progress, the 2nd Battalion, 12th Infantry reporting that it has passed through all fortifications. In the 28th Division sector the 110th Infantry is six miles inside the border while the 109th is approximately three...."[11]

Was anybody taking notice? Six miles inside Germany! Three months earlier in Normandy the 1st Army measured territory gained in yards, yet it kept pushing for nearly two months of bitter fighting until the German armies cracked. Six miles inside enemy territory would seem to be a considerable advance yet the diary notes: "because of his [General Hodges'] orders that all troops should stay tightly 'buttoned up' progress has not been so fast as before but the General believes that this is the only sound way to attack the line proper."[12] An army with orders to stay buttoned up is not one that will rampage through enemy territory nor would it encourage a commander to go on the offensive.

General Hodges initially gave Gerow permission to conduct a "reconnaissance in force," into the Eifel to determine the condition and strength of the enemy. If the German resistance proved too formidable Gerow was to retire back across the Sauer River into Luxembourg into defensive positions. That's exactly what he did after five days of fighting but surely he must have had some sense that the enemy was catastrophically weak and could be overcome with some additional hard fighting and reinforced by a regiment or two. The V Corps G-2 (intelligence) estimated that the Germans had little resources available to stop the Americans and battle-wise American commanders would have known that when the German had his back to the wall he put on a show of being much stronger than he really was by launching furious counterattacks to slow or stop an enemy. The Germans at this stage of the war were like honey badgers, relatively small, but fierce creatures that snarl, snap, and intimidate much larger predators, including lions.

It's not certain that Hodges was alert to the advances in the V Corps' sector. The diary notes: "The V Corps situation continues to worry the General as the three divisions are spread out on an exceedingly wide front…."[13] There is no mention of a possible breakthrough and a need for reinforcements. If General Hodges didn't fully appreciate V Corps' breakthrough then neither would Bradley, Hodges' superior as 12th Army Group commander, nor Eisenhower who was totally focused on *Market Garden* at the time.

The 1st Army diary during those critical five days in the Eifel devotes a great deal of space to happenings at headquarters, the general's bad cold, visiting dignitaries including Archbishop Spellman from New York, old army buddies from the pre-war period, and the war correspondent Richard Tregaskis. Hodges expressed the hope that Spellman would soon be able to deliver high mass at the Aachen cathedral. (Aachen was soon to be captured by American forces but the city was virtually destroyed.) The general's "war room trailer" was much ballyhooed: "(it) arrived today and was brought around to and parked next to his living van. It is a superb job, spacious with infinite map board, all in plexi-glass."[14] Hodges' concept of living quarters for a commanding general were a far cry from that of U.S. General John "Tiger Jack" Wood, who quartered in an army tent. Wood commanded the 4th Armored Division that smashed through German formations and believed a general should share the same hardships as his men.

The 1st Army diary doesn't reflect an aggressive headquarters searching for weakness in the enemy. A more forceful army commander might have been roaming near the front lines urging his troops on as Patton was known to do, as was General Guderian, known for his daring and lightning armored attacks. Guderian, a colonel general, the equivalent of an American four-star general, once crossed the Dnieper in Russia under fire with infantrymen in an assault boat "in order to make sure of our forces' further progress."[15] On another occasion he got so close to the Russian front line in a forward artillery observation post that he had to take cover in a mortar barrage that wounded five of his officers.[16]

One description of Hodges portrays him as "a stoic, inarticulate, and unimpressive figure…." General Hodges rarely visited his subordinate corps' and division commanders. Instead he had them return to the rear area to his headquarters and brief him there. He had earned a reputation of being intolerant of any mistake and quick to relieve subordinate commanders when he suspected they were lacking drive and initiative.

"Hodges also delegated a great deal of the command of 1st Army to his chief of staff, Major General William B. Kean, causing confusion among subordinates as to who was in command. This division of leadership and command had far reaching effects throughout the 1st Army."[17]

Another account is equally critical of Hodges: "First Army headquarters was not a happy place... General Hodges, a strictly formal, colorless man with a clipped mustache, always held himself erect and seldom smiled. He had a southern drawl, was reluctant to take quick decisions and showed lack of imagination for maneuver: he believed in simply going head-on at the enemy. More like a businessman in head office than a soldier, he hardly ever visited the front forward of a divisional command post...."[18]

One account describes Hodges as having little faith in his corps' commanders and that he "rode herd over them in such a way as to smother whatever initiative they brought to 1st Army."[19] Author Stephen Taaffe asserts that Hodges "was an old-fashioned infantryman (who) embraced straight-up fighting that sometimes led to unnecessary casualties and was reminiscent of World War I. Ernie Harmon (General Earnest Harmon) found General Hodges slow, timid and unoriginal..."[20] Taaffe states that Collins (Major General Lawton Collins) was Hodges' favorite commander and Hodges gave him a long leash and "considerable leeway" in developing and implementing plans. Brilliant as Collins was in Hodges' eyes, it was Collins who led his men into the meat grinder of the Hürtgen Forest at the same time that V Corps was breaking through the Siegfried Line around Wallendorf. In the Hürtgen several of the U.S. divisions were nearly destroyed in advances that measured a few hundred yards of ground.

Underlying the failure to exploit the breakthrough at Wallendorf was the overall broad front strategy of the Allied High Command. From the beginning, when the Allies broke out of Normandy in late July 1944, SHAEF and Eisenhower gave little thought to a concentrated drive to blast through the German defenses and roll into Germany even as Montgomery and General Patton begged for such a strategy. For the Germans this was inexplicable, especially when the Allies reached the Siegfried Line in early September. The enemy generals knew the "wall" was little more than an antiquated façade that would hardly stop a determined assault. General der Panzertruppe Erich Brandenberger, who commanded the German 7th Army during the Battle of the Bulge, dismissed the effectiveness of the wall and asserted that if the Americans had realized this and made a consolidated attack against this line of defenses, "the capture of our lines was possible." Brandenberger saw the Siegfried Line as a sham, a product of Nazi propaganda to give an enemy pause before attacking the Reich. He listed the deficiencies:

The pillboxes of the Siegfried Line were without armament. Its weapons had been removed to be used in the Atlantic Wall. No preparations for the occupation of the Siegfried Line had been made. The troops occupying the Siegfried Line had to dynamite some of the closed pillbox doors to get inside. There were no minefields in front of the emplacements. The major part of the wire obstacles had been removed. Broad paths had been blasted through the tank obstacles at many places. There were no food rations. The field of fire was not free at any place. The permanent telephone network had been put out of action... Even the permanent antitank guns had been carried off to the Atlantic Wall... Meanwhile, with the increased effectiveness of modern weapons they had become still less useful.[21]

General Brandenberger argued that the broad front strategy crippled Allied efforts to break through the German defenses. "At first we thought it was only supplies. We knew you had no great harbors. Also, spreading your forces over a great area would slow the advance." It was the dispersion of Allied effort as they reached the Siegfried Line.[22]

Other German generals in post-war interviews wondered as well why the Allies did not strike a concentrated blow. Major General Rudolf Christoph von Gersdorff, chief of staff of the German 7th Army in the Wallendorf sector, stated, "The German High Command did not think they could stop the Americans at the Siegfried Line. In addition, they did not think they could stop them before the Rhine River."[23]

When asked about a breakthrough on the V Corps' sector prior to September 20, 1944, General Gersdorff replied: "There was nothing between that point and the Rhine except for a few scattered troops." If V Corps had attacked head on in the Wallendorf bridgehead, would its flanks have been dangerously exposed to counterattacks? "If you had known about our weakness in the line, you would not have worried about your flanks," Gersdorff asserted, adding, "I told my commander that this was the time to surrender and that to continue the war any longer was a crime against the civilian population."[24]

General Kraemer, of the 6th Panzer Army, stated in a post-war interview that the American attack at Wallendorf "came as a great shock to the High Command because there were no reserves readily available. The attack was astride not only a corps' boundary (1st SS Panzer Army and Fifth Panzer Army) but also an army boundary (7th Army and Fifth Panzer Army)." When asked whether the commitment of the entire 5th AD and an infantry regiment, instead of one combat command to the Wallendorf bridgehead, would have altered the battle in the Americans' favor, Kraemer said, "No. If, however, you had even one more division to advance on Bitburg, I believe you could have made it to the Rhine. There was nothing to stop you."[25]

General Siegfried Westphal, variously chief of staff to Field Marshals Erwin Rommel, Albert Kesselring, and Gerd von Rundstedt, with whom he served in the fall of 1944, noted in his book, *The German Army in the West,* "The overall situation in the west was serious in the extreme. A heavy defeat anywhere along the front, which was so full of gaps that it did not deserve this name, might lead to catastrophe, if the enemy were to exploit his opportunity skillfully."[26]

General Westphal noted the vast resources in men and materiel the Allies possessed: British and American armored forces were four times greater than those of the Germans, the Allies controlled the air with thousands of bombers and fighters compared to a few hundred German fighter aircraft, and an equivalent number of about 41 Allied divisions were twice the size of their German counterparts and far better armed with massive stocks of ammunition and materiel. As the enemy struggled to reorganize and bring order to the rabble of forces that had been driven from France, V Corps attacked at Wallendorf.

General Westphal noted:

> Into the midst of these anxieties there burst the bombshell that an American armored division had crossed the Sauer at Wallendorf, north of Trier, and had broken through the Siegfried Line at the first assault. All the forces (German) which were available or could be spared were dispatched to drive back his incursion... After a week of fighting... the enemy retired to the western bank of the Sauer, and the mortal danger was removed. If the enemy (the Americans) had thrown in more forces he would not only have broken through the German line of defenses which were in the process of being built up in the Eifel, but in the absence of any considerable reserves on the German side he must have affected the collapse of the whole West Front within a short time.[27]

One reason the Americans failed to exploit the advances in the Schnee Eifel was their lack of adequate intelligence. The Germans knew the defenses of the Siegfried Line were more imaginary than real and that the skillful use of propaganda led the Americans to believe they were a major obstacle. While U.S. divisions, corps, and army intelligence units – G-2 – knew the Germans were in a bad way, they didn't know just how critical the enemy situation was. The Americans could not peek behind German lines to learn of the enemy's predicament. The Germans, however, had the eyes and ears of spies in many of the German-speaking border areas with Luxembourg and Belgium who were feeding them information about the strength and position of American units as they approached the Reich. Even as the Americans advanced into Germany, local citizens and foresters pinpointed American positions to German commanders thus explaining why the enemy's artillery was often deadly accurate.

General Gerow had no reinforcements to exploit the Wallendorf breakthrough, which were needed if he were to succeed in expanding the breach. "All that this bitter battle demonstrated to General Gerow was that far more strength than was presently available would be required to make a significant breakthrough in the German Siegfried Line."[28]

But there was more strength available to reinforce the fight at Wallendorf. The Allies had powerful reserves if SHAEF had chosen to use them – five airborne divisions had been stationed in Britain and even accounting for three immediately engaged in the Arnhem operation, the British 6th Airborne remained in England and was available as a reserve. Four infantry divisions and two armored divisions, along with 17 artillery battalions and an artillery brigade were engaged in Brittany, and the 83rd ID and the 6th AD were positioned along the Loire River guarding 3rd Army's southern flank. Certainly there were troops available for reinforcement. The U.S. troops in Brittany were containing the German troops left behind to deprive the Allies of the Brittany ports. The two divisions along the Loire were protecting Patton's extended right flank from the remote possibility of an attack from the bedraggled and harassed German LXIV Corps, retreating in disarray from Bordeaux and southwestern France and desperate to reach Germany.

Could not a regiment or two from the Brittany-based divisions have been trucked to the Eifel? It's not a wild idea. The Germans were able to do it with their vastly depleted reserve forces. To contain V Corps in the Eifel the Germans were calling on the few reserves they had from various parts of their front. So desperate was Rundstedt that one of the first enemy units ordered to fill gaps in the German line was the 3rd Flak Assault Regiment of the 3rd Flak Corps, hardly men trained in infantry tactics and ground warfare. The Flak regiment was 40 miles from the Wallendorf bridgehead in Traben-Trabach when it got the call to reinforce the German front line and its armament consisted of four heavy and seven light antiaircraft batteries. Two Grenadier battalions, the 291st and 294th, were thrown into the battle as was a regimental combat team from the 19th Volksgrenadier Division. It was trucked to the front the night of September 15.

The U.S. troops from Brittany could have been trucked to the Wallendorf area in five or six hours. When the Germans attacked the Bulge the 101st Airborne Division was transported by two-and-a-half-ton "Jimmies" from its base near Rheims, France, to Bastogne, Belgium, through the night of December 18, a distance of more than 100 miles. Many of the airborne troops were sent without ammunition or adequate clothing and stood packed in the truck beds the entire journey.

A regiment or two of paratroopers could have been flown into Luxembourg City or dropped in the bridgehead. Field Marshal von Rundstedt had long feared that the Americans and British would use airborne troops to drop behind the thin German defenses along the German border and bypass the Siegfried Line. His fears were not unfounded. In a spur-of-the-moment decision in late August, Montgomery had planned to use American paratroopers to drop as a blocking force at Tournai in Belgium to cut off German forces retreating to the Siegfried Line. The maneuver was called off because ground troops reached the city first.[29] *Market Garden* was somewhat spur of the moment and a much more complicated maneuver with many parts that could go wrong.

General Marshall advocated for paratrooper drops well behind German lines. Prior to the invasion of Normandy on June 6, 1944, Marshall believed Operation *Overlord* (D-Day) planners could have dropped airborne infantry and glider troops near Paris to seize a field from which to mount surprise attacks against German rear guard units. Marshall proposed that materiel, including "tractors and other things," 105mm guns, and ammunition could be airlifted in while the forces on the ground would gather in all the transport from the surrounding area, connect with local French guerrilla forces, and engage the enemy. The objective was to "to build up a force there right behind German lines before they had time to get things together and make it almost impossible for them to do anything but to fight you with small groups."[30] Forest Pogue, Marshall's biographer, noted that the chief of staff was "averse to second guessing his commanders," and may not have suggested the airborne drop to Eisenhower prior to D-Day.

The idea of trucking troops from Brittany to Wallendorf probably would have been dismissed out of hand. Every truck in the Allied armies was devoted to bringing supplies to the front – it was one reason why divisions were first stationed in Brittany; they were stripped of all but their essential vehicles and their trucks were drafted into the Red Ball Express, rendering the divisions almost immobile. Yet when General Ridgway, who commanded the two American airborne units, asked Hodges if troops of the 82nd Airborne Division could be picked up by 1st Army trucks and fed in 1st Army messes once *Market Garden* was over, Hodges agreed. "General Hodges and General (William) Kean both said that once they (the airborne troops) arrived in the Army area the food would be forthcoming and trucks could probably be gathered together in an emergency to take them where they had to go."[31]

Even if the high command had been aware of the breakthrough at Wallendorf, it is doubtful it would have been reinforced. The Allies were about to launch *Market Garden* and this was Montgomery's show and to upstage Monty with a breakthrough in the Eifel would have been unthinkable. The Anglo-American

An American MP directs traffic on the Red Ball Express in France, late summer 1944. (U.S. Army, NARA)

alliance was fragile enough with the British being overshadowed by American might at all levels. The Brits needed a victory led by one of their own.

Montgomery had been badgering Eisenhower for weeks to authorize a concentrated thrust towards the Ruhr industrial area and Ike finally acquiesced with the attack on Arnhem. One critical aspect of Eisenhower's job was keeping the peace between American generals and the British generals, Montgomery in particular. "As Supreme Allied Commander, he (General Eisenhower) had to prevent the British or the Americans alone from winning the final victory. Triumph had to be shared."[32] When the Americans seized the railroad bridge at Remagen and breached the Rhine River in early March 1945, Montgomery was still organizing his massive cross-Rhine airborne attack north of Cologne, Germany, code-named Operations *Varsity* and *Plunder*, designed to end the war in one fell swoop. The *Varsity* component called for two airborne divisions – some 16,000 men – to drop behind enemy lines around the city of Wesel and tie up German forces. The paratroopers were followed by two Allied armies, the British 2nd and the American 9th – *Plunder* – making an amphibious assault across the Rhine in the same area. The two operations involved several hundred thousand men, making it a classic, set-piece, methodical, and ponderous Montgomery undertaking.

When the Americans captured the Remagen Bridge as Montgomery was preparing for *Varsity* and *Plunder*, the GIs were first across the Rhine in a seat-of-the-pants operation that made *Varsity* somewhat redundant. The Americans took immediate advantage of the breakthrough and poured reinforcements over the span to exploit the breach. However, to preserve the Anglo-American alliance and harmony, and to salve Montgomery's and British egos, Eisenhower limited the American advances in the Remagen bridgehead to no more than 1,000 yards a day to prevent a breakthrough that would embarrass Montgomery and detract from his upcoming and massive cross-Rhine operation.[33] The war in the west was hampered by the need to foster and maintain Allied harmony, a policy that was ultimately designed to keep the peace between the Brits and the Americans, who were often feuding. Patton wanted to be the great hero of the war and so did Montgomery; their demands drew attention away from the other breakthrough possibilities along the front.

Ike also was hesitant to allow any commander to set off on a tangent that could lead to disaster similar to the defeat at Kasserine Pass in Tunisia where Rommel's troops soundly defeated green and unprepared American troops in 1943. Eisenhower could have lost his command for that debacle and he was averse to allowing another Kasserine-like disaster in Europe when he knew the war was won. With *Market Garden* he at least had encouragement from higher command in Washington.

The real issue at this juncture in the war was how long it would take to defeat the enemy. As long as the Allied juggernaut pressed on, broad front or not, the Germans would be defeated. But at what cost, possibly six more months of war and thousands more battle casualties?

When the battle for the Wallendorf bridgehead and the Schnee Eifel was over the Germans claimed it as a major victory, hailing it as "the miracle of the west." A Pyrrhic victory for the Germans, yes, but they bought themselves a respite of six months before the Allies once again began the advance into the German heartland. Lucian Heichler, in his historical account, *The Germans Facing V Corps,* notes that "it cannot be denied that the Germans accomplished an amazing feat of arms when they brought the Allied steamroller to a halt," even as they lacked men, materiel, arms, and adequate fortifications.[34] Supply difficulties may have hampered the Americans but Heichler noted: "Last, but not least, indecision at the top-level command with regard to the further strategy to be employed against Germany made itself felt down the chain of command all the way to the corps level."[35]

CHAPTER 5

The Stolberg Corridor

Aachen and the Stolberg Corridor were other battlegrounds where Americans troops breached the Siegfried Line and might have advanced deep into Germany had they been reinforced. These battles also took place at the same time as Operation *Market Garden.* It was around the ancient city of Aachen in early September 1944 that an opportunity for a breakthrough presented itself but the Allied High Command seemed indifferent. Where was SHAEF? Where was Eisenhower? Why weren't they closely watching and monitoring the situation on the ground around Aachen? Why pick the one operation – *Market Garden* – that was the most difficult to accomplish of all the possibilities to breach the Siegfried Line? *Market Garden* required precision paratroop drops, difficult supply and reinforcement operations, the necessity for clear weather for additional paratroop drops, fighter-bomber support, and an advance by XXX Corps through 50 miles of German-held territory by armored forces initially confined to single file over boggy ground on a solitary road exposed to infantry and artillery attack. In pre-war planning the Dutch saw this route as one way to halt or slow a German invasion from that region. Only when XXX Corps had run the gauntlet over this narrow highway could General Horrocks and XXX Corps reach the Arnhem bridge and relieve the British paratroopers.

The American VII Corps, commanded by General Collins, had advanced to the Aachen area by September 11. The noted World War II correspondent and later historian, Chester Wilmot, reported in his book, *The Struggle for Europe,* that General Bradley, commander of the American 12th Army Group, "missed the opportunity of outflanking the Siegfried Line north of Aachen, part of an area where German Field Marshal Walter Model had reported on September 8th, 'a very thin and totally inadequate defense line,' was held 'by only seven or eight battalions on a front of 120 kilometers'."[1] The VII Corps approached Aachen, on the border with Holland, on September 12,

1944, as preparations for *Market Garden* were underway for the attack on September 17. Because of limited supplies of ammunition and gasoline available to 1st Army, General Hodges, Collins' superior, ordered Collins to restrict his advance to a reconnaissance in force unless his divisions could force a breakthrough at the Aachen Gap and the Stolberg Corridor. While the Siegfried Line strong points were deep around Aachen, Hodges was encouraged by the rapid advance of his army through Luxembourg and Belgium and was gambling that his forces had momentum and could overrun the enemy defenses before the Germans had time to organize and man them. Collins was considering a surprise attack to catch the enemy off guard and once through the Siegfried Line he calculated that he could pause to resupply. The avenue of attack through the Aachen Gap offered a somewhat unimpeded route to the Ruhr, via the city of Düren. The route Collins selected was through the Stolberg Corridor, a 35-mile-wide section of the wider Aachen Gap.

Collins was a highly touted corps' commander who was believed capable of forcing a breakthrough. He had more combat experience than the majority of the U.S. Army's corps' commanders in the ETO, having commanded the 25th "Tropic Lightning" Division in the early Pacific battles for Guadalcanal and New Georgia in 1943 where he earned the nickname, "Lightning Joe" to suit his aggressive combat style. A favorite of the Allied High Command in Europe, including General Eisenhower, he was re-assigned to the ETO where he took command of VII Corps after being considered briefly for the command of an army in Europe. If any commander could break through the Siegfried Line, Collins was thought to be the man to do it.

As VII Corps reached the vicinity of Aachen its three divisions were advancing abreast, the 1st ID on the left flank on the southern outskirts of Aachen, the 3rd AD in the center, moving through the Stolberg Corridor, and the 9th ID on the right flank. Collins ordered elements of the 1st ID to reconnoiter towards Aachen with the possibility of seizing the city, and he ordered the 3rd AD to probe into the Stolberg Corridor, a passageway at some points less than six miles in width, that is bordered by the city of Aachen to the northeast, and the dense pine forests to the south known collectively to the U.S. Army as the Hürtgen Forest. The 3rd AD's objective was the city of Düren that lay beyond the Siegfried Line defenses deep within the Stolberg Corridor and was a gateway into Germany and the Ruhr industrial zone. The U.S. 9th ID was operating on the right wing of VII Corps' advance with orders to sweep and clear what the Germans called the "Hürtgenwald."

Aachen held great symbolism for the Germans. It was Germany proper, it was once the center of the Holy Roman Empire where Charlemagne reigned,

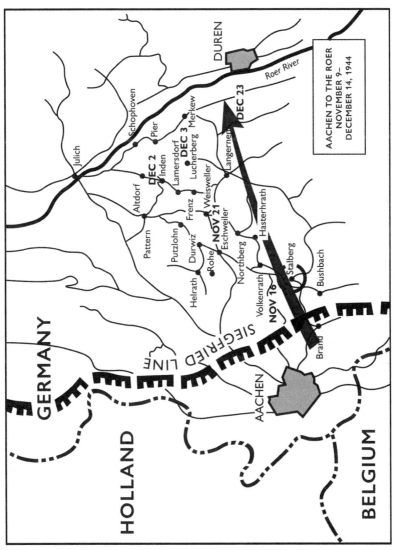

The arrow points the direction of General Lawton Collins' U.S. VII Corps as it advanced into the Stolberg Corridor south of Aachen and adjacent to the Hürgen Forest. The VII Corps skirted the city of Aachen to avoid protracted urban combat and attempted instead to break through the corridor. The attack was initially unsuccessful.

and it would be the first German city to fall to Allied forces in the war and the Wehrmacht could be expected to fight to the death to hold it. Recognizing that capturing Aachen would consume most of his forces Collins ordered the 1st ID to contain and surround the city – with the help of the U.S. XIX Corps that was advancing on Aachen to the northeast. The 3rd AD was to advance through the Stolberg Corridor towards the cities of Eschweiler and Düren. Collins' objective was to breach the two defensive lines of pillboxes and dragon's teeth in the Siegfried Line, the thinner Scharnhorst Line that paralleled the border with Holland, and the thicker Schill Line five miles deeper that defended the Stolberg Corridor. Dragon's teeth were constructed the length of the border area around Aachen.

"With the decision to bypass Aachen, the VII Corps' scheme of maneuver basically became a frontal attack by the corps' armor, protected on either flank by infantry, to penetrate the Siegfried Line," Collins later told Charles MacDonald, a World War II combat-tested company commander who fought in the battles on the German frontier, and was author of the army history about the struggles around Aachen.[2]

The main VII Corps' attack began at dawn on September 13, with the 3rd AD's Combat Command B (CCB) blasting its way through the Scharnhorst Line. To the northwest, within the corridor, Combat Command A (CCA) ran into stiff resistance in a day-long fight to penetrate the Scharnhorst Line but by nightfall had breached this first layer of the Siegfried Line.

The American advance resumed the following day, September 14, with both combat commands attacking and by nightfall CCB had breached the Schill Line. "Ahead lay open country. Task Force Lovelady (of CCB) was all the way through the Siegfried Line."[3] After fierce fighting, CCA, on September 15, had fought its way through most of the pillboxes and defenses of the Schill Line and "only a few scattered fortifications remained before CCA, like CCB, would be all the way through the Siegfried Line."[4]

On VII Corps' right flank a struggle was developing in the dense pine forests that bordered the Stolberg Corridor and this sector would become one of the most bitterly fought battles of World War II. As the combat commands continued to push deeper into the Stolberg Corridor the 9th ID's 47th Regiment advanced along the fringes of the Hürtgen Forest that straddled the corridor on 3rd AD's right flank. The 47th's objective was the road center near Düren, thus positioning the regiment just seven miles from the Roer River and an open path to the Ruhr industrial zone. While the 3rd AD began encountering stiffer enemy resistance, the 47th's advance met with "spectacular," though limited success. With the aid of a captured map that revealed German positions, the 47th advanced two and a half miles to capture the town of Schevenhütte, and "thus had advanced deeper into Germany than any other Allied unit, approximately ten miles."[5]

As in any campaign, luck played a part and smiled on the Americans. The Germans positioned the entire 116th Panzer Division in Aachen, and prepared to fight the Americans to the death if they dared enter the city. The German command, however, could not afford to release the 116th to join the fight in the Stolberg Corridor for fear that this would leave Aachen undefended and open to other advancing American forces. Had the 116th been released to counter Collins' divisions, VII Corps would likely have had to withdraw from the Stolberg Corridor. General Collins rightly elected to avoid the perils of fighting in the confines of Aachen's streets, many of them in the older sections, narrow and turning this way and that way. Thus, the Americans could advance into the Stolberg Corridor without the 116th emerging from Aachen to do battle.

While the 47th Regiment advanced in the forest in close proximity to the 3rd AD's right flank along the southern edge of the Stolberg Corridor, the 9th ID's two other regiments had much tougher going in clearing the vast tract that was the rest of the Hürtgen that stretched from the Stolberg Corridor southeast to the city of Monschau. It was a tall order; the 9th would have to clear a sector of steep ravines and ridges studded with densely planted trees and towering pines that stretched along a 17-mile-long front that has been described in myths and fairy tales as dark havens for witches and goblins. This was a gloomy region described by historian MacDonald as a place where anyone entering these mysterious woodlands must, of necessity, leave a trail of bread crumbs to find their way out. In fall and winter the Hürtgen is cold, wet, and unforgiving and even in summer it is dark and foreboding. This forest region became known in the annals of the U.S. Army as the "Bloody Hurtgen."

The enemy had no real strength in the Hürtgen that was really a number of separate forests but the Americans collectively called all of them the Hürtgen when they began their attacks. The absence of large enemy forces within the forest encouraged the American command to engage the enemy, thinking it would be something of a walk through.[6] But the Americans failed to recognize that the rugged terrain and dense woods made up for the lack of German troops and resources. It took few enemy troops, often with little combat training and manning machine guns, to slow or halt an American advance.

There were two enemy divisions opposing the American 9th ID in this 70-square-mile forested sector, the 347th and the 89th, both under-strength, fleshed out with scratch units, and few combat-tested troops. The 347th was comprised largely of troops from a fortress battalion and a battalion of men with stomach ailments. The 89th was comprised of two infantry regiments, one that had been almost completely destroyed in previous fighting and the other with only 350 men. Artillery, service troops, and engineers made up the rest of the division's combat force.

Motley crew or not, a hard core of veterans in the German 89th stiffened the resistance and these troops held fast on September 14, fighting from pillboxes and defensive terrain when the 9th ID began its attacks. The Americans were finding that the pillboxes of the Siegfried Line extended through the forest, and coupled with the terrain, made for a slow, bloody advance. The Germans had masterfully combined pillbox defenses with the terrain to create killing zones that were so well camouflaged that they often were unseen by the advancing American infantrymen until they were upon them and taking deadly fire. For the next four days, the fighting swirled through the forests with the Americans making little headway as the German fought back tenaciously. The fighting was so vicious and the American and German units so tangled that a medical aid station set up in the forest was manned by German and American doctors administering to the wounded of both armies. Adding to the 9th's difficulties, the division's three regiments were separated from each other by as many as seven miles allowing for enemy infiltration into and behind American lines. Three days of fighting in the Hürtgen had bought the Americans only a narrow opening of about a mile and a half through the Scharnhorst Line. The struggle for the forest was becoming a meat grinder for thousands of American soldiers.

Despite the 9th ID's travails, the overall situation for Collins and his VII Corps held promise. According to MacDonald, "The first five days of Siegfried Line fighting had produced encouraging, if not spectacular, results. Though success probably was not commensurate with General Collins' early hopes, the corps nevertheless had pierced the forward band of the Siegfried Line on a front of twelve miles and in the second belt had achieved a penetration almost five miles wide...." MacDonald pointed out, "VII Corps clearly had laid the groundwork for a breakthrough that needed only exploitation."[7]

Who would exploit this limited, yet promising, breach of the German border defenses, and how would they accomplish that? After nearly a week of heavy fighting Collins realized that the situation, while hopeful, was nearing stalemate. He needed reinforcements to force his way to the Ruhr, but none were forthcoming. His troops were exhausted and he recognized that as long as his adversary was throwing in reinforcements while the Americans were not, any large-scale advances were impossible. He therefore ordered the 1st ID, the 3rd AD and the 47th Regiment of the 9th ID to consolidate their positions in and on the flanks of the Stolberg Corridor. But the two other regiments of the 9th ID were to continue the fight to clear the Hürtgen Forest from Schevenhütte on the southeastern edge of the Stolberg Corridor to Monschau on the forest's southern edge. Fighting would continue in those woods until the end of November, with few results on both sides and Collins' order set the stage for one of the bitterest battles of World War II, the Battle of the Hürtgen Forest.

In the Hürtgen the 9th ID's 60th Regiment was ordered to clear the forest from the area around Monschau while the 47th Regiment operated farther to the north with the objective of seizing a critical highway that led to the town of Schevenhütte located on the edge of the Stolberg Corridor. Once positioned in Schevenhütte the American front line would be relatively straight and continuous. But in the Hürtgen that would be impossible.

The VII Corps had been stopped in its drive through the Stolberg Corridor. According to a later interview Collins stated that "a combination of things stopped us. We ran out of gas – that is to say, we weren't completely dry, but the effect was much the same; we ran out of ammunition; and we ran out of weather. The loss of our close tactical air support because of weather was a real blow…[8] The Siegfried Line had been penetrated, but the breach was not secure enough nor the VII Corps strong enough for exploitation."

The fighting in the Stolberg Corridor may have subsided but the Battle of the Hürtgen Forest raged for the next two months as the Americans continued to throw more and more men and divisions into the struggle to reach the Roer River dams and eventually the Ruhr industrial zone.

There was no front line in the Hürtgen and where it existed, it zigged and zagged through the forest. In many places it didn't exist at all, it was a series of foxholes, pillboxes, and machine-gun emplacements in the dense woods. Tanks could not negotiate in the ravines and ridges and those few that did join the fight were vulnerable to hand-held Panzerfaust antitank weapons. One American Sherman turned over and tumbled down a steep ravine as it made its way to battle.

Hampered by the terrain the Americans could not count on their overwhelming assets, artillery and airborne fire power. Their artillery was of little use; shells exploded in the tree tops and spewed deadly shrapnel downward on infantrymen, not just Germans, but Americans as well. Troops on both sides sometimes found it safer to remain standing during an artillery barrage rather than lying prone where they made a larger target. Foxholes were only considered safe if they were covered by layers of logs. American air power, vastly superior to the enemy's at this stage in the war, was useless since fighter bombers were unable to distinguish between friend and foe among the trees and to unleash ordnance in these circumstance would kill Americans as well as enemy troops.

By the end of the battle in mid-November, hardly a tree was unscathed and most were blasted into splinters. One veteran of the struggle recalled that when the fight ended, an officer offered a reward if anyone could find a tree that had not been splintered or felled by artillery fire.[9]

One advantage the Germans had that the Americans lacked in the battles fought around Aachen was their excellent intelligence about American movements. "We had many agents in your lines and both civilians and these agents kept us informed. Especially valuable were our foresters, who were very familiar with the woods and could move undetected."[10]

By late September Collins' units and those of the enemy were exhausted and the Americans in the 9th ID had little stomach to continue the fight; casualties had also depleted units to the point where few men were left to fight. "So heavy a toll did the fighting take that at the end of the month the 60th Infantry and the attached battalion from the 9th ID's 39th Infantry Regiment were in no condition to resume the attack," MacDonald wrote.[11] He added that the Germans made brilliant use of the terrain and small unit tactics to thwart the Americans. Additionally, they made excellent use of the pillboxes in the Siegfried Line that were scattered through the forest. The Americans did not have the manpower to maintain a solid front anywhere along the line.

The 9th ID was the first full infantry division to be fed into the Hürtgen meat grinder and it suffered thousands of casualties. The 9th was withdrawn and other units were later deployed in the forest, notably the 28th ID that was also badly battered in the "gloom, misery and tragedy" of the Hürtgen.[12] It was pulled from the struggle a shadow of the unit it had once been and sent to be restored to full strength in the Ardennes only to be battered again a month later in the Battle of the Bulge. The brutality of Battle of the Hürtgen will long be remembered in the American army but commanders should have learned from experiences in World War I in battle zones like the Argonne forest and Belleau Wood to stay out of heavily forested battle grounds.

The eminent World War II historian Russell Weigley weighed in on the disaster in the Hürtgen: "The most likely way to make the Hürtgen a menace to the American army was to send American troops attacking into its depths. An army (the American) that depends for superiority on its mobility, firepower, and technology should never voluntarily give battle where these assets are at a discount; the Hürtgen was surely such a place."[13] Weigley wrote that the defending German 275th Division and the other enemy units that opposed the

Americans in the Hürtgen would have been mauled by U.S. forces on an open battlefield, "but within the darks woods, battle would become a fragmented series of infantry contests, the unit cohesion lacking in the Germans' Hürtgen forces would count for little anyway."[14]

In the eyes of many, particularly the German commanders, the Hürtgen was a battle that the Americans should not have fought and did not need to fight. The advantage was with the Germans, hunkered down in foxholes, pillboxes, hidden behind trees, and awaiting their unsuspecting and vulnerable attackers. Enemy commanders were dumbstruck that the Americans persisted in efforts to clear the woods. One German general, who had served on the Russian front before being assigned to the west, reported that the bitterness of the Hürtgen fighting surpassed anything he had experienced in the east where the combat was especially brutal. In a post-war interview German General Rudolf Christoph Freiherr von Gersdorf wondered why the Americans had even bothered to attack through the forest. "Had you gone around it on both sides, you would have had almost no opposition. We did not have enough troops in the area at the time."[15]

It was more than lack of troops. "I thought you – the Americans – would concentrate on a narrow front, probably at Aachen as the terrain there was best for attack. If you had known about our weakness in the line, you would not have worried about your flanks. There was nothing between that point and the Rhine except a few scattered (German) troops."[16]

Adding to the German weakness along the Siegfried Line was the severe losses incurred during their retreat from northern France to the German frontier. Post-war German estimates pegged their losses at more than 300,000 men from the D-Day invasion to the first weeks in September 1944 when their armies were backed against the Siegfried Line. Not included in this figure were the estimated 200,000 men holed up in numerous French ports to prevent them from falling into Allied hands and easing the Allies' supply problems.

Some 300,000 men were killed, wounded or reported missing in the retreat across northern France. Of that number, an estimated 100,000 wounded might have been returned to duty. The Germans also lost two army group commanders in the retreat from France, Field Marshals von Kluge and Rommel, and three army commanders.

In the words of one German commander, "the chances for an enemy (American) to break through the Siegfried Line... were indisputably great. In the opinion of OB West – the German High Command for the western front – the Western Allies, with massed forces, could doubtless have overrun both the Siegfried Line... and have thrust to the Rhine.... However, from the subsequent, relatively hesitant, groping approach of the enemy toward the western fortifications, we could conclude that the Western Allies wanted to close up first and undertake a planned strategic concentration in front of the western fortifications."[17]

The Battle of Aachen and the Hürtgen Forest cost both sides dearly with losses neither could absorb. The Allies were running low on manpower, as were the Germans, but the Germans, by stopping the American advance through the Hürtgen and the Stolberg Corridor, had bought time to strengthen their defenses along the Siegfried Line. But it also weakened their forces that were being readied for their attack in the Ardennes, the attack the Americans call the Battle of the Bulge. Reserve forces that might have been used to bolster the Germans in the Ardennes were ground down in the Battle for Aachen and Hürtgen Forest.

The Hürtgen cost the Americans, by some estimates, 33,000 casualties – killed, wounded, and missing. The Germans are believed to have lost as many as 28,000 men in all three categories, soldiers they could never replace, but neither side could easily replace the losses.

Would a division or two of Allied troops or paratroopers, rushed to or dropped into the Stolberg Corridor have won the day and enabled the Americans to advance to the Roer and beyond? It certainly cannot be discounted. The Allied High Command was prepared to drop airborne forces on the spur of the moment as the Allies advanced across northern France in the summer of 1944 and were being dropped into the unknown at Arnhem. When Collins and VII Corps needed reinforcements in September 1944 the airborne divisions were preparing for the *Market Garden* operation. The Americans possessed other reserve forces in Britain and in Brittany – substantial forces – but they failed to use them.

Author John A. Adams in his book *The Battle For Western Europe*, suggests that "another corps attacking in team with General Collins probably would have made it over the Roer, obviating the subsequent bloodbaths in Aachen and the Hürtgen forest." Adams takes a quote from 1st Army G3 – training and operations – "You can't take chances without a reserve."[18]

Did the lack of adequate supplies imperil the possible breakthroughs? The conventional wisdom has always been that because the Germans controlled the French ports there weren't enough supplies of gasoline to keep the tanks attacking and the big guns firing in the early fall of 1944. Yet, when the Allied High Command decided to undertake Operation *Market Garden* it found plenty of gas and ammunition for the operation. Where it lacked was in enough aerial transports to ferry the paratroopers to their drop zones. The paratroopers came in relays over a three-day period allowing the Germans time to establish strong defenses. The Red Devils at Arnhem never had enough men at one time to carry out their mission as it was intended.

German General Friedrich Koechling who commanded troops in the Aachen sector of the Siegfried Line, dismissed the notion that supply difficulties disrupted the Allied advance. "At the situation at that time of the German front, being extremely weak… the alleged ammunition and gasoline shortage should have caused on no account even an only temporary halt of the U.S. armies. Under the pressure of an energetic command, every U.S. soldier should have had to 'dismount,' continuing the battle to the east as infantrymen on foot. The exceedingly insufficient combat value of the committed few German units, the absence of every reserve, the entirely not significant field fortifications built up by political ignorant to a large extent, should have guaranteed an easy fighting up to the Rhine." Koechling commented that the American command should have had greater resolve to carry the fight into Germany.[19]

As at Wallendorf, Allied strategy was also a factor. All the Allied divisions were moving in unison with no particular plan to concentrate on weak points in the enemy line. Full-blown assaults on the Siegfried Line were reduced to reconnaisances in force. The Allies operated like a football team plowing towards the goal line in bursts of "three yards and a cloud of dust," ignoring feints and flanking movements. Those were to be left to Montgomery and Patton who would smash their way into Germany, take the Ruhr and advance to Berlin before the Russians got there. The many other Allied generals in the vast tableau of war on the western front were supporting actors in this great drama.

Wilmot criticized General Eisenhower for allowing Patton's 3rd Army to advance south of the Ardennes, aimed at the German Saar industrial zone. The 3rd, Wilmot wrote, "had become a magnet drawing forces and supplies away from what General Eisenhower declared should be the main drive (north of the Ardennes). Because General Patton's right flank had been extended south to Epinal, General Hodges had been compelled to cover such a wide frontage that he could not concentrate at any one point sufficient strength to break through the Siegfried Line. Thus, far from being able to develop his own offensive 'to seize bridgeheads near Cologne and Bonn,' while Field Marshal Montgomery was advancing to Arnhem, General Hodges now could not even keep up sufficient pressure at Aachen to maintain the threat of a break-through to the Rhine."[20]

Three weeks after the fall of Paris the heady notion that the war would end within weeks gave rise to complacency and weakened Allied resolve to finish off a wounded enemy and end the war quickly. The high command took its eyes off the prize and the Germans gained time to collect themselves and establish a credible defense that they would maintain for the next six months even as Allied generals were taking bets on how many weeks the Germans would last before capitulating.

Wilmot wrote that Operation *Market Garden* was Eisenhower's last chance to retain the initiative in the west and his hopes rested on the three airborne divisions and the British XXX Corps dispatched to take Arnhem. "With them, though they could not know it, lay the last, slender chance of ending the German war in 1944."

CHAPTER 6

Disaster at Arnhem

With the opportunities for breakthroughs in the Siegfried Line in the Schnee Eifel and at Aachen being overlooked in the first weeks of September, Eisenhower and the top Allied command focused on *Market Garden*, 190 miles to the north. The generals in charge of the operation were convinced that it would succeed and force the early surrender of Nazi Germany. "Field Marshal Montgomery's ambitious plan was to sprint the troops and tanks through Holland, springboard across the Rhine and into Germany itself. Operation *Market Garden*, Field Marshal Montgomery reasoned, was the lightning stroke needed to topple the Third Reich and effect the end of the war in 1944."[1] As *Market Garden* began Monty's optimism seemed justified; the initial phases of the attack unfolded as planned. The airborne operations with the 101st, the 82nd, and the British 1st were textbook perfect with the troops coming down on their landing zones, largely without incident and with few casualties. The 101st, commanded by Major General Maxwell Taylor, dropped in a 15-mile zone with orders to capture canal and river crossings between the cities of Eindhoven and Veghel. The 82nd, commanded by Brigadier General James Gavin, was to descend on a 10-mile zone between the cities of Grave and Nijmegen. The main focus of the 82nd attack was to seize crossings over the Maas and Waal Rivers and the high rising bridge at Nijmegen. Another objective was the ridge line to the east that overlooked the bridges. Both divisions were to clear their area of enemy troops and hold them to ensure the passage of Horrocks' XXX Corps fighting its way along a narrow corridor to relieve the British 1st Airborne Division at Arnhem.

Major General Mathew B. Ridgway, commander of the American XVIII Airborne Corps that included the 101st and the 82nd, circled above the drop zone in a B-17 bomber to observe the jump that day. "The drop was beautiful, the best we've ever done.... As we circled wide, watching the skies fill with thousands of colored chutes, we could look down into the streets of the little villages. The people were all out in their Sunday best, looking up, as the great skytrain, five hundred miles long, went past... Up to this time the German occupation had brought little of war's devastation to that peaceful countryside, but I knew the German reaction would be quick and violent."[2]

Generals Taylor, Gavin, and Ridgway were pioneers in developing American airborne divisions and operations during the war. Ridgway, a 1917 graduate of West Point, was one of the great American commanders of World War II and later in Korea where he was in overall command of UN forces during that war. He took command of the 82nd Division when it was transformed from an infantry division to an airborne division in 1942. He was instrumental in the planning for the invasion of Sicily in July 1943, and deployed elements of the 82nd to the invasion of the Italian mainland near Salerno two months later. He jumped with the 82nd into France at D-Day, June 6, 1944, and two months later took command of the XVIII Airborne Corps that participated in Operation *Market Garden.*

General Gavin commanded a parachute infantry regiment of the 82nd and jumped with his troops in Sicily and later, as assistant division commander of the 82nd, parachuted into France on D-Day.

General Taylor was variously chief of staff of the 82nd and in command of the division's artillery in the early war years. He fought in Sicily and in Italy and later was named to command the 101st Airborne Division. He made the jump with the division into France on D-Day and into the Netherlands during Operation *Market Garden.* He missed the Battle of the Bulge where the paratroopers of the 101st beat off continuous German attacks at Bastogne and became known ever after as the "Battered Bastards of Bastogne."

In southern Holland Horrocks' XXX Corps was a coiled spring waiting to fight its way through the German front line and race for the Arnhem bridge. Horrocks expected to reach Arnhem in two days but allowed that it might take four; without armor and artillery 1st Airborne couldn't hold out much longer than that. The XXX Corps was a boundless army, spread out "over every field, trail and road. Massed columns of tanks, half-tracks, armored cars and personnel carriers and line after line of guns stood poised for the breakout."[3] Thousands of British troops along a demarcation line milled about awaiting the order to move out. On one side of the line was XXX Corps on the other, the enemy. Horrocks awaited the signal to advance.

It came at 2:15pm in a swirl of orange smoke after the first paratroop transports passed overhead. At that moment 350 of XXX Corps' guns opened fire on German positions in a sector one mile wide and five miles deep. Above, rocket-firing British Typhoon fighter bombers awaited the call to swoop down and blast German fortifications and artillery that survived the pounding. The long, single line of British armored vehicles rumbled forward through dust and explosions raised by the creeping artillery barrage that dropped shells no more than 100 yards ahead of them. Word came back to Horrocks, "Advance going well." The lead tanks had advanced out of the bridgehead.

But not all the German guns were silenced and a number of well-camouflaged artillery pieces survived the thunderous maelstrom. No sooner had Horrocks received encouraging news about the attack than hidden enemy guns opened fire. They had waited for the first squadron of tanks to pass before they let loose. "The Germans really began to paste us," recalled Captain "Mick" O'Cock, a tank squadron commander.[4]

Within minutes three of the lead tanks were knocked out, "brewed up," was the British term for the blazing infernos of destroyed tanks that blocked a half mile of the roadway. "The breakout had been stopped before it had really begun and nine disabled tanks now blocked the road. Squadrons coming up could not advance."[5]

The XXX Corps' advance could be likened to trying to empty a swimming pool through a kitchen funnel. Thousands of men and equipment had to advance down one narrow road that ran from southern Holland through the 82nd Airborne drop zone around Nijmegen, through the 101st Airborne sector around Eindhoven, to the British 1st Airborne at Arnhem. The ground in the initial going on either side of the highway was boggy and if the tanks and other vehicles moved off-road they would quickly find the going rough if not impossible and the advance halted.

Typhoons, fighter-bombers, were called in to ravage the hidden German positions and infantry swept forward to clean out the enemy from their trenches. Then dozer tanks were brought forward to clear the road and the advance continued but precious time had been lost and the prospects of maintaining the time schedule to reach Arnhem were dimmed. *Market Garden* was already behind schedule and the Germans were obstinate all along the way and well-placed enemy artillery shells continued to disable the lead tanks to bring the entire corps to a standstill.

By the time XXX Corps reached the zone occupied by the 101st, the division closest to the corps' jumping-off point, it was 30 hours behind schedule. The American paratroopers had captured two of the three bridges they were assigned to take; the third, the Son Bridge over the Wilhelmina Canal, was blown up by the Germans just as the paratroopers approached. The XXX Corps engineers bridged the canal when they arrived and moved on while the 101st fought to keep open the narrow highway, now dubbed "Hell's Highway," as a lifeline for supplies for the entire *Market Garden* operation.

When XXX Corps arrived in the 82nd Airborne sector around Nijmegen on September 20, its tanks assisted the paratroopers in capturing the bridge over the Waal River. The paratroopers had been in bitter combat with the enemy and were unable to shake them loose from defending the bridge without the aid of armor. The XXX Corps was losing the race against time.

As Horrocks' corps began its advance at 2:15pm the day of *Market Garden*, the British 1st Airborne hit its drop zone seven miles from Arnhem with such accuracy and with so few losses that division commander Major General Robert Urquhart, no relation to Major Urquhart, later remarked, "everything appeared to be going splendidly." His thoughts were echoed by paratroop Sergeant Major John C. Ford: "this is one of the best exercises I've ever been on. Everyone was calm and businesslike."[6] But Ford had reservations. "It's all too good to be true." Others too expressed concerns. "Everything is going too well for my liking," said one young lieutenant.[7]

It soon became apparent that taking the Arnhem bridge would not be the slam dunk some commanders, Montgomery in particular, expected. Soon after the first contingent of Red Devils landed on the north bank of the Rhine seven miles from the bridge things went awry. Squads and platoons of paratroopers were organized and set off for the objective on foot and in vehicles that had survived the landings in huge Horsa and Hamilcar gliders. The race was on – get to the bridge before the Germans had time to react. But the paras didn't get far before they were abruptly stopped by quick-acting enemy forces from makeshift German Kampfgruppen rushed into position as blocking forces. With the British landing so far from their objective, and with the capture of *Market Garden* operational plans from the body of an American officer killed in a glider crash, the Germans had time to detect their enemy's objective and threw every grenadier they could muster into the fight to stop the advancing Red Devils. Still the paratroopers approaching Arnhem were confident of success. At one point a group of paratroopers advancing towards the bridge encountered a tank that they assumed was one of their own from Horrocks' XXX Corps that had fought its way into Arnhem. They were stunned to find that it was an enemy panzer and it was firing at them. It also became apparent that the second-rate enemy troops the Brits expected to encounter were combat veterans, battle-hardened Waffen SS soldiers, and panzer units from the elite 2nd SS Panzer Corps that wasn't supposed to be in the area. Even if the Red Devils had come up against second-rate German troops, veteran Allied soldiers knew that even they could be counted on to put up a fight.

While most of the units making for the bridge were held up by enemy blocking forces, Lt. Colonel John Frost's 2nd Parachute Battalion took an undefended southerly route into Arnhem and reached the north end of the bridge by the evening of September 17 and set up defensive positions in nearby buildings. The Red Devils had arrived, some of them at least, and their objective was to capture the bridge over the Rhine. They now had to await the arrival of XXX Corps.

Frost's men made two attempts to capture the bridge but both failed. Unable to communicate with other units because of faulty radios, subject to constant artillery and mortar fire, and without equipment to fend off armor, the 2nd Battalion found itself in deep trouble. Compounding matters, the British landing zone was overrun by the enemy leaving the surviving Red Devils without renewed supplies and reinforcements.

On the fifth day of the battle, the weather cleared enough to allow the airlift of the 1st Independent Parachute Polish Brigade, commanded by General Stanislaw Sosabowski, but the unit was forced to land on the southern bank of the Rhine. This meant they had to fight their way to the Lower Rhine and cross it before they could reinforce Frost's beleaguered battalion. They made three attempts and eventually about 200 of Sosabowski's troops made it across the Rhine to reinforce Frost's men. But the battle was already lost. After days of bitter fighting the gallant troopers of the division's 2nd Battalion were forced to surrender. Only 100 men from the battalion were left to walk into captivity. The most the late-arriving Polish force could do was assist the remaining members of the 1st Airborne to escape across the Rhine to Osterbeek and the remnants made their way back to Allied lines. It was a costly fight for the Red Devils, 1,485 of them had been killed, and 6,414 were taken prisoner, of whom a third were wounded. Total strength of the division when it left Britain was 10,600. Two-thirds of the British 1st Airborne Division had been lost. As the last of the Red Devils made their way across the Rhine to the southern shore, XXX Corps was only a few miles away from its stated objective.

CHAPTER 7

The Aftermath

The fight for the Arnhem Bridge raged for nine days as the Germans methodically reduced British strong points and inflicted more and more casualties. The Red Devils had been unable to take the bridge but might have succeeded had Horrocks reached the besieged paratroopers within two to four days as planned. But XXX Corps never arrived. Was it surprising that *Market Garden* ran into trouble and ultimately failed? Some believed failure was ordained because the operation was too hastily conceived and planned and by the time it was executed it was too late, and the Germans were on the ground in force.

Planning for *Market Garden* began on September 4 and by the time it was launched on September 17 the Germans had time to bolster their defenses all along the Siegfried Line. Those in command of the operation ignored the geography of the region, the warnings of Allied and British intelligence services, the Dutch underground, the fighting potential of the enemy, and the concerns of some experienced generals. Two officers who bluntly warned of disaster for the entire operation were General Sosabowski, commander of the Polish brigade that dropped near Arnhem, and Major Brian Urquhart, intelligence chief for the British 1st Airborne Corps. Sosabowski asserted: "this mission cannot possibly succeed." Contrary to the thinking of many Allied commanders Sosabowski did not believe that the German troops around Arnhem were of poor quality, and noted that the enemy regarded Arnhem as a direct path into Germany and would fight to the death to defeat the Allied operation.[1] Urquhart believed information sent by the Dutch underground warning that elements of two German panzer divisions were positioned near the British drop zone. To ignore this information, he said, could be fatal to the entire operation. A member of the Dutch resistance had spotted German tanks in the Arnhem area bearing the insignia of the 9th SS Panzer Division,

Hohenstaufen, while another agent reported a German headquarters a few miles from Arnhem flying a red, white and black pennant, the insignia of a German army group commander. It turned out to be Field Marshal Walter Model, one of the enemy's best generals and a loyal Nazi.[2] Major Urquhart ordered a low-level flyover by a reconnaissance Spitfire that confirmed the presence of tanks hidden in woods near the British drop zone. The Red Devils would have no defense against tanks until Horrocks arrived. Urquhart's warnings, however, were ignored by his superiors and he was sent on leave, accused of suffering from battle fatigue. But he was right. The British paratroopers descended into a hornet's nest.

If *Market Garden* commanders had thoroughly studied and taken to heart pre-war Dutch military plans to counter a possible German invasion they might have been hesitant about moving ahead with the operation. The Dutch concluded that the terrain over which Horrocks' corps would pass was perceived by their Army as a likely German invasion route but any advance in this area would be confined to the single road and therefore subject to constant interdiction and interruption. That is exactly what happened to XXX Corps; it was expected to advance 13 miles in the first day but was held to only seven, even fewer miles in the days ahead.

One major problem for the operation was a shortage of transport aircraft and gliders which meant that the full force of the airborne invasion could not be delivered in one powerful blow. Men and equipment would arrive over a three-day period, weather permitting, allowing the enemy to react and concentrate his forces to defeat the invasion while the Allies could not concentrate theirs. This was particularly true in the Arnhem area where troops were lifted in piecemeal over the critical three-day period. As it turned out, the weather turned foul before all the paratroopers could be delivered to their respective landing zones, thus diluting the fighting power of their parent units.

The 1st Airborne's radios were inoperable over long distances so that the various units could not communicate. This deficiency was known to British commanders since the North African campaign but nothing had been done to correct the problem. The columns racing to the bridge from the landing zone were out of touch with each other and with division headquarters. They were blind and forced to improvise all the way to the objective.

RAF pilots returning from bombing missions over Germany prior to the launch of *Market Garden* reported about a 30 percent increase in the number of antiaircraft (Flak) batteries in and around Arnhem. Could the Germans have been prepared for the operation and increased their antiaircraft batteries in the area? They didn't have ENIGMA – the German code machine that the

Allies cracked early in the war – but they could pick up Allied radio traffic and orders from as far away as England from their stations on mainland France and Holland. They often knew when to expect an attack by simply listening to the undisciplined Allied radio operators. Just days before the D-Day invasion German radio intercepts from 100 miles away picked up American MPs chattering as they directed traffic to the invasion ships.

The information about an increase in antiaircraft batteries around Arnhem prompted the transport plane pilots, who were to carry the paratroopers and tow the gliders to a drop zone within a few hundred yards of the Arnhem bridge, to call for more distant and secure landing sites. The ideal landing site was adjacent to the structure so that the paratroopers could disembark and charge right onto the bridge. But landing so close to the span was risky; one side was crowded with buildings while the opposite side was marsh land not conducive for glider landings. The aircraft would burrow into the soft ground on landing and cartwheel, spilling their loads of men and supplies. The attack plan was altered because of the pilots' concerns and a drop zone was selected seven miles from the bridge at an ideal landing site, level and open, but this alternative site was ill-suited as well. Dropping paratroopers without heavy weapons so far from their objective would alert the Germans as to the Allies' true objective and give the enemy time to set up defensive positions around the bridge. Upon hearing in a pre-attack briefing that the British airborne division's drop zone was miles from the targeted Arnhem span, General Gavin was incredulous. "My God, he (British Lieutenant General Frederick Browning's battle plan) can't mean it," Gavin remarked. (Browning was deputy commander of the 1st Allied Airborne Army.)[3] But Gavin kept his concerns to himself reasoning that the Brits were more battle-wise than the Americans after five years of war and knew better what they were doing. Gavin may have recalled an American plan to drop the 82nd into Rome shortly after Italy surrendered in July 1943. The idea was to take control of Rome before the Germans could. Gavin's superior, General Ridgway, believed the plan unworkable because the 82nd would drop in the midst of two German infantry divisions and possibly be overwhelmed.

Lieutenant General Walter Bedell Smith, Eisenhower's chief of staff, was so concerned that the Arnhem drop zone was too far from the bridge that he approached Montgomery to suggest that Monty reinforce the British 1st Airborne Division with the British 6th Airborne Division that was sitting out the operation, or include one of the American airborne divisions at Arnhem. Montgomery dismissed Smith's fears and warnings.

Smith was in a minority of the generals who believed the operation was ill-advised, and he was up against an array of brass. The U.S. Army Chief of

Staff General Marshall had been urging Eisenhower to use the thousands of airborne troops sitting idly in Britain awaiting a call to action. Air Force Chief of Staff, General Arnold, concurred with Marshall, as did General Brereton, commander of Allied airborne forces in England.

Then there was Montgomery, the commander of the operation and the general possessed with the certainty that *Market Garden* would succeed and end the war. It was a strange position for the field marshal. Normally he took days and weeks to plan his operations down to the last detail and *Market Garden* was so hastily conceived and planned that it should have given him pause. When he outlined the operation to Lieutenant General Frederick Browning, Browning expressed reservations, "but sir, I think we might be going a bridge too far."[4] Monty, however, was confident of success.

Major Urquhart summed up the failings of *Market Garden*. The operation "depended on the notion that once the bridges were captured, XXX Corps' tanks could drive up this abominably narrow corridor – which was little more than a causeway, allowing no maneuverability – and then walk into Germany like a bride into a church. I simply did not believe that the Germans were going to roll over and surrender."[5] But opinion was against Urquhart. He noted that the prevailing judgment among the generals was that the Germans were finished and that like 1918, they were on the verge of collapse and a solid push like *Market Garden* would finish them off. It's intriguing how the chance of a big show blinded so many generals – like World War I where every big show was to end in the collapse of German forces and only resulted in hundreds of thousands of casualties.

In a postmortem of the *Market Garden* operation German officers blamed the Allied failure on the wide dispersal of the airborne troops and the slow progress of XXX Corps. The weather turned foul on the days following the first landings and prevented follow-up reinforcements. Another failing, the Germans noted, was that the 1st Airborne troops were delivered in relays over a three-day period reducing the number of troops designated to capture the bridge immediately after landing. The Germans learned this same lesson in May 1941 during the German airborne invasion of Crete where there were not enough transports to lift the German forces in one day so it was done over several days.

Additionally, a large body of British airborne troops had to take up defensive positions around the Arnhem landing zone to protect it for the arrival of their comrades in the next two days and thus these troops were not available to assault the bridge.

Montgomery termed *Market Garden* a success except for the failure to capture the bridge, eliciting a remark from Dutch Prince Bernhard: "my country cannot afford the luxury of another Field Marshal Montgomery success."[6] Thousands of Dutch civilians died as a result of *Market Garden*.

Subsequent histories and the film *A Bridge Too Far* have depicted *Market Garden* as something of a glorious operation, but in reality it proved to be a failure for the Allies, a catastrophe for the British 1st Airborne Division, and caused considerable loss of civilian life. At best, it gained some new ground in Holland, but the bridge over the lower Rhine remained in German hands. There would be no march over the river to encircle and capture the Ruhr industrial area and no dash to seize Berlin. The remaining troops in Holland, including the 82nd and 101st Airborne Divisions became engaged in a slugging match with the Germans over the next two months and little ground was taken from the enemy.

To some extent *Market Garden* reflected the thinking of the commanding generals at all levels in World War II who thought in terms of massive assaults, not unlike the World War I infantry charges, to overcome the enemy. They went for the home run rather the single to chip away at the enemy. The more powerful the attack, the more likely its chances of success, so it was believed. "My conclusion at the time, and my conclusions now, is that Field Marshal Montgomery saw a bold blow as his only chance of quick victory, and his decision to strike north (to Arnhem) ignored tactical opportunities," wrote R. W. Thompson, an intelligence officer in the British Army and a war correspondent who covered the *Market Garden* operation.[7] It would appear that the Allied High Command ignored "tactical opportunities all along the front."[8] He might be referring to Aachen and Wallendorf. The strategies of the previous war were reflected in the shameful and futile battles in the Hürtgen Forest that raged from September to November 1944 and nearly destroyed several American infantry divisions.

In the early fall of 1944 the British, in the fifth year of the war, suffering from war fatigue and with worldwide military commitments, were desperate to end the conflict by the end of 1944, thus the risky *Market Garden* plan. "He (Field Marshal Montgomery) was acutely conscious of his administrative difficulties (supply) and his lack of basic strength (in troop reserves); his blow had to succeed, it had to take advantage of the almost total disruption of the enemy and every hour was of vital importance."[9]

Thompson asserts that Monty's blow came almost two weeks too late; by the time *Market Garden* was launched on September 17 the Germans had strengthened their defenses along the Siegfried Line. At Arnhem, the two combat-tested panzer divisions that confronted the Red Devils were still in relatively good shape. General Brereton wanted *Market Garden* to begin on

September 4 but Browning, his deputy, disagreed and threatened to resign. Thompson states that Montgomery "failed to recognize the vital importance of the time factor, and his unwillingness to abandon, or modify, any plan once he had committed himself to it."[10]

The Allied High Command, including Generals Marshal and Brereton must also take great responsibility for the debacle at Arnhem for urging SHAEF and Eisenhower to make use of his strategic reserve in the five airborne divisions idling in England. By September, having been denied the opportunity to join the fight during the summer, the paratroop commanders were begging for action and Montgomery's proposed *Market Garden* offered them an opportunity.

General Ridgway weighed in on the *Market Garden* debacle. "I always felt, and still feel, that the sluggish actions of ground armies in that campaign were inexcusable. A more vigorous command supervision from the top could have driven that armored force on through. As a result of this failure, the British 1st Airborne… was almost destroyed. Its stand at Arnhem was a monument to British valor, but a monument too, to human weakness, to the failure to strike hard and boldly."[11]

In the end, *Market Garden* was a failure – a failure on a grand scale and it magnified the failure of the generals to take advantage of potential breakthrough points all along the western front with a fraction of the resources poured into *Market Garden*. This is not to say that a determined and reinforced assault on any of these points would have succeeded, but the opportunities were there and never exploited. Wallendorf was but one. Aachen was another. There were others that will be discussed later. And not all those opportunities required the detailed planning of *Market Garden* or the huge expenditure of resources just to get the fighting troops to the combat zones.

In the final analysis, neither Patton nor Montgomery accomplished a breakthrough in the early fall of 1944. Monty failed at Arnhem and Patton was stalled at Metz in Lorraine. In the years since the war, historians have offered many excuses for these failures, but the fact remains, neither of these two "greatest" generals of the war in the west succeeded in breaching the Siegfried Line in 1944.

CHAPTER 8

Lucian King Truscott, Jr.: The Man Who Would Destroy Two German Armies

In the same September period, 1944, that Gerow's V Corps and Collins' VII Corps smashed through portions of the Siegfried Line, and Allied airborne troops embarked on the ill-fated *Market Garden* operation, Major General Lucian K. Truscott, Jr. commander of the U.S. VI Corps, devised a plan to destroy an entire German army near Belfort, France, and advance to the Rhine and possibly cross into Germany.

Following the invasion of southern France on August 15, 1944, Truscott's troops, attached to 6th Army Group, raced north toward Lyon hard on the heels of the German 19th Army of seven infantry divisions, most understrength, and the crack 11th Panzer Division. The 19th was scurrying up the Rhone River valley in a retreat that ran through Montelimar, Lyon, Dijon, and Besancon and into Alsace.

The 19th Army's objective was to reach the Belfort Gap, a narrow defile in the mountain chain between the French Vosges and Swiss Jura Mountains that led to the safety of the Alsace Plain and the adjacent German heartland across the Rhine. General Friedrich Wiese, 19th Army commander, could fortify the Gap and hold off Truscott and possibly the entire U.S. 7th Army to which VI Corps was attached, The Belfort Gap, also known as the Burgundy Gate, had been a gateway for centuries to and from Germany and France and had seen armies from the time of Caesar and before advance and retreat through this narrow plateau that ran between the two mountain ranges.

The enemy's LXIV Corps, garrisoned along the French Atlantic coast to protect against a possible Allied invasion from the sea, was also in headlong retreat across central France as it too struggled to reach safety in Alsace and the protection of the 19th Army and the Belfort Gap. Without transportation some 30,000 enemy personnel, clerks, medics, nurses, and a smattering of combat troops, literally walked across France. The rabble was under constant

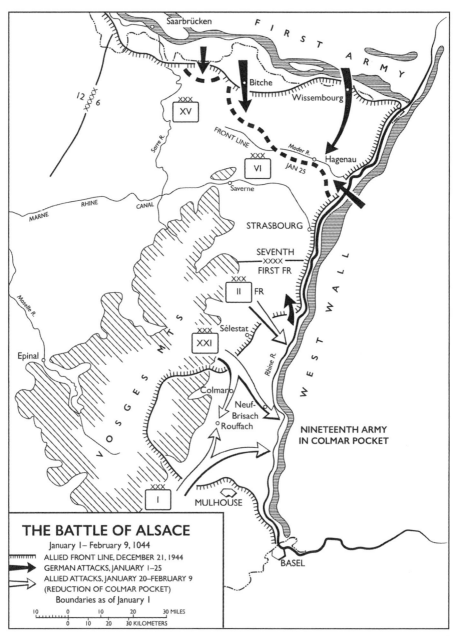

THE BATTLE OF ALSACE

January 1– February 9, 1044

ALLIED FRONT LINE, DECEMBER 21, 1944
GERMAN ATTACKS, JANUARY 1–25
ALLIED ATTACKS, JANUARY 20–FEBRUARY 9
(REDUCTION OF COLMAR POCKET)
Boundaries as of January 1

The lines from the south of France depict the path of the 6th Army Group, commanded by General Jacob Devers, from the Marseilles area to Alsace. The American 7th and the First French Armies advanced up the Rhone valley into Alsace which is separated from Germany by the Rhine river.

attack by Resistance fighters and by American fighter bombers patrolling the skies above monitoring the corps progress. Had it remained in the Bordeaux region it would have been cut off from the rest of German forces in eastern France.

Truscott saw the possibility of cutting off the 19th's and LXIV Corps' retreat by reaching the Gap before the enemy and blocking his escape onto the Alsace Plain and the Rhine. The enemy's only avenue of retreat would then be over the rugged slopes of the Vosges Mountains, or if desperate enough, to bypass the Gap and conduct an end run through Switzerland. But the well-trained Swiss army was determined to maintain the country's sovereignty and independence and was prepared for any intruder, Allied or German.

General Friedrich Wiese, commander of the German 19th Army. (unknown)

If trapped on the western slopes of the Vosges Mountains the 19th and the LXIV would be caught between two hard-charging American armies, Patton's 3rd, bearing down from the northwest as it advanced across northern France, and General Alexander Patch's 7th Army and Truscott's VI Corps, advancing from the south. With General Friedrich Wiese's 19th Army destroyed, Truscott could lead the 7th Army onto the Alsace Plain on the east side of the Vosges, capture Mulhouse, Colmar, and Strasbourg on the Rhine, and be in position to invade the German heartland just across the river. Truscott's corps and the 7th Army fell under the command of 6th Army Group, commanded by General Jacob Devers. The 6th Army Group also included the French 1st Army advancing from southern France alongside the U.S. 7th.

The 19th suffered thousands of casualties and the loss of hundreds of vehicles and tanks in its flight north from southern France and thousands more of its troops were lost as prisoners of war. If Truscott's Belfort Gap plan worked, he could not only destroy what was left of the 19th but possibly unhinge the enemy's southern front from Lorraine to the Swiss frontier. The entire German line stretching north to the Netherlands might then also be in danger of disintegration as the enemy retreated behind the Rhine. Would

General Eisenhower and the high Allied command grab at the opportunity offered by General Truscott and his hard-charging VI Corps?

This was not the first time that Truscott saw an opportunity to trap and destroy an entire German army. Four months earlier in Italy, where the VI Corps had fought for ten months before being transferred to France for Operation *Dragoon*, the invasion of southern France, Truscott was deprived by misguided leadership of the chance to trap and possibly destroy the German 10th Army south of Rome. This will be the subject of chapter 19.

As VI Corps approached the Belfort Gap, after a rapid advance from the Riviera coast of southern France, Truscott had already made a name for himself as one of the ablest commanders in the American army, and he would soon be the subject of a *Life* magazine cover story; Eisenhower rated him second only to Patton. To some, Truscott was superior to Patton, having fought against greater odds than Patton, against the likes of Field Marshal Rommel in North Africa and in Italy against "Smiling Albert," Field Marshal Albert Kesselring, considered a master at blunting his opponents' attacks. While Patton talked of defeating Rommel in Tunisia, he faced the German field marshal for only about three weeks and Rommel was not in command of the Army Group Africa at the Battle of El Guettar in March 1943, where Patton turned back a determined German attack. The German assault was led by General Jurgen von Arnim while Rommel was back in Germany on medical leave.

Truscott began his professional career as a provisional second lieutenant in the cavalry when the U.S. entered World War I in 1917. He was not a West Pointer but graduated from the Oklahoma Normal School at Norman and spent six years teaching in rural Oklahoma.

In World War II, Truscott got his first taste of combat as an observer during the British–Canadian commando attack on Dieppe in August 1942. The attack was a terrible defeat, some believing that it was a planned disaster, orchestrated by British Prime Minister Winston Churchill, to demonstrate to the Americans that the Allies were not ready and capable of invading France in 1943, as General George Marshall hoped. Truscott, however, came away believing that Dieppe was a success for the Americans; it was a hard lesson in warfare that the Americans had yet to experience. Truscott learned from British commando training that he could instill higher standards on his own American troops. He was charged with developing a commando unit in the American army and oversaw creation of the 1st Ranger Battalion, fashioned after similar units in the British army. Some 50 American Rangers participated in the Dieppe attack, believed to be the first American ground troops to do battle against the Germans in World War II.

Shortly after Dieppe, Truscott, now a brigadier general, commanded infantry and armored units in the invasion of North Africa in November 1942. Truscott solidified his image as a fighting general during this invasion:

> Known to his men as "old stone face," and "Injun Joe," because of his hawk nose, square face, and roots in Oklahoma Indian territory, "the ... rough-hewn Truscott possessed all the qualities needed for success on Earth's deadliest place: the modern battlefield. He had toughness, courage, tactical ability, and professional competence. He also had an intangible only the best possessed: great leadership under fire – the genius for doing what must be done in the heat and chaos of battle that separates the adequate from the exceptional. Supreme Commander General Dwight D. Eisenhower knew what he had in Truscott; in 1945, Eisenhower rated Truscott as his most able army commander, second only to General George S. Patton.[1]

In March 1943 he took command of the 3rd ID as it prepared for the invasion of Sicily. Truscott's motto learned from the Dieppe raid might have been "train hard, fight easy." The 3rd was in the vanguard of the American forces that invaded Sicily in July 1943 and his troops became known for the "Truscott trot," in which his infantry was trained to cover ground at four miles per hour instead of the usual three. Roman legions moved at that pace, he noted, as did Stonewall Jackson's Confederate troops during the Civil War, and Truscott's troops were expected to move just as fast. The training paid off. When the 3rd covered 100 miles in three days in Sicily in July 1943, from the south coast around Gela to Palermo on the north coast, one general remarked in surprise that Truscott had turned his infantry into cavalry. The division then made a dash along the north coast of Sicily from Palermo to capture the city of Messina as the Germans retreated to the Italian mainland.

Truscott took the 3rd ID to the Italian mainland where it landed at Salerno in mid-September 1943. What was expected to be a "walkover" turned into a bloody fight on the beaches at Paestum. The Germans were not surprised; they had seen the massive Allied fleet approaching the day before and were prepared. The Americans landed in a zone protected by a German armored division with over 100 tanks and 17,000 troops. For several days the fighting seesawed back and forth and at one point German tanks penetrated almost to the sea. General Mark Clark who commanded the American 5th Army landings at Salerno considered withdrawing the troops to prevent a disaster. Instead he called on paratroopers from North Africa and fierce naval gunfire to stabilize the situation. The Americans prevailed and from Salerno Truscott and the 3rd advanced up the Italian boot with the U.S. 5th Army through Naples to Cassino, 63 miles above Naples on the road to Rome. Promoted to VI Corps' commander, Truscott was later placed in command of Allied troops at Anzio in February 1944. His time at Anzio was cut short when VI Corps,

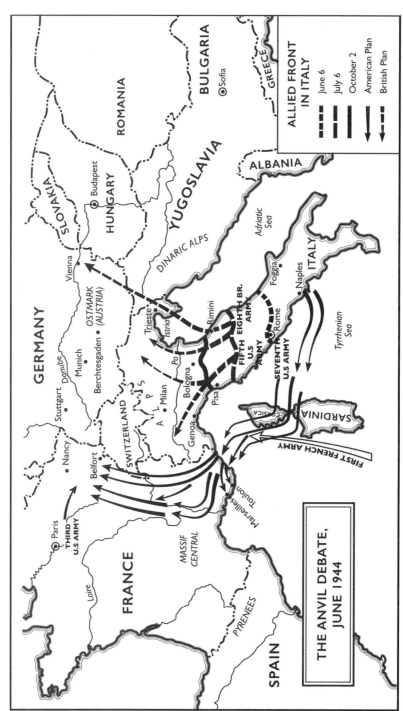

The lines show the Allied commanders' planning for the invasion of southern France. The units, French and American, came from Italy, the U.S. VI Corps and elements of the French 1st Army, and landed near Marseilles. Other units for the invasion came from North Africa. The landings, at various locations in southern France, were the largest naval invasion force, second only to Normandy.

comprising the 3rd, 36th, and 45th Divisions, the most combat-tested and experienced divisions in the American army, was pulled out of the line in late May 1944 to prepare for Operation *Dragoon*.

The *Dragoon* landings east of Marseilles on August 15 were supported by a vast armada of 553 vessels, including five battleships, four heavy cruisers, 18 light cruisers, nine aircraft carriers, 85 destroyers, and 20 large transports. Complementing this fleet was a massive force of 1,300 B-17s and B-24s, flying from Italian bases, that unleashed their sticks of bombs on the landscape once depicted in bright hues by Van Gogh and Cezanne. The fabled beaches around the seaside village of St. Tropez, a pre-war playground for royalty and the rich, were now part of the tableau of war.

Sergeant Audie Murphy, the most decorated World War II soldier, recalled the landings that day on the southern coast of France:

> About us in the bay lying between St. Tropez and Cavalaire is the now-familiar design of an amphibious invasion.
>
> We jump from the landing craft and wade ashore through the swirling water. From the hills, the German guns begin to crack. An occasional shell lands in our midst. The medics roll up their sleeves and get busy. An explosion sounds on my left; and when the smoke lifts I see a torn body of a man who stepped on a mine. A medic bends over him, rises, and signals four litter bearers that their services will not be needed.[2]

The German 19th Army occupied all of southern France from the Italian border to Spain. (The Italian army had occupied southern France from Menton to Marseilles until the Italians surrendered to the Allies in the summer of 1943.) The Germans in the south of France were spread so thin along the Mediterranean coast that it would have been impossible for their troops to drive a large invasion force back into the sea. The Wehrmacht troops, many youthful and without combat experience, were suddenly roused from their torpor after months of waiting for the enemy to appear, but they were no match for the combat-tested American and French troops who arrived in greater numbers and with vast amounts of equipment and materiel. The French troops had also fought in Italy and had recently invaded and liberated the island of Elba off the Italian coast from the Germans. Truscott remembered the Allied debacle at Anzio where U.S. General John Lucas, VI Corps' commander before Truscott, failed to immediately exploit the undefended landings and the Germans quickly moved in troops to surround the beachhead and contain Lucas' forces, thus defeating the whole purpose of the Anzio plan. The Anzio forces were expected to break out and cut off the German 10th Army fighting to the south. Now they were locked into a small perimeter with enemy on all sides. The sea was the only escape. Truscott knew from experience at Anzio that he had to press inland immediately from the southern French coast if he was to overtake Wiese and his 19th Army as it retreated north up the Rhone River. "We were attempting to set the stage for a classic – a 'Cannae' – in which we would encircle the enemy against an impassable barrier or obstacle and destroy him. There was some question as to how many of the enemy we would trap, and more debate about whether or not we could build up sufficient strength in the enemy's rear to prevent his escape." Truscott wrote.[3] The Rhone valley for centuries was the natural link between the north and south of France and is confined on either side by high ground, the Massif Central to the west and the Jura-Alps to the east. Within the first 24 hours of the invasion, VI Corps advanced inland farther and faster than *Dragoon* planners had anticipated. The Germans had no time to react to and confine the Allied forces by bringing up additional forces. As a result, casualties had been light, 95 U.S. troops killed and 385 wounded, and 94,000 Allied troops were landed along with 11,000 vehicles. Some 2,300 enemy troops had been taken prisoners, many of them of questionable value as combat soldiers, "Ost" (east) troops from Russia, Poland, and other Eastern European countries, reluctant soldiers at best.

Truscott faced a formidable opponent in General Wiese, a master of defensive warfare, who had served in Russia where, of necessity, he was involved in defensive retreats to stave off disaster by the advancing Soviet armies. A combat veteran of World War I he had survived four years in the trenches. He looked like a farmer with a slender, weather-beaten face, but his eyes showed intelligence. He had been a battalion commander in the 1939 Polish campaign and took command of a division in 1942. In 1943, he took command of the German 19th Army in France. Wiese realized quickly that the only available option to save his army was to retreat northward through the Rhone River valley. The German High Command came to the same conclusion. With the German armies in Normandy in headlong retreat across northern France and making for the safety of the Siegfried Line along the German frontier, and 19th Army threatened with annihilation, the high command ordered a complete withdrawal of all German forces in the south of France.

Within hours of the Allied landings the Americans began advancing rapidly northward to cut off the enemy's retreat. The 36th ID advanced on the right wing towards Grenoble while the 3rd ID pursued Wiese's army up the Rhone. After the French Army secured the ports of Toulon and Marseille from German garrisons, they began an advance on the west side of the Rhone. The German 19th was effectively boxed in and fleeing for its life. As the 36th ID moved north it wheeled west to trap the 19th in the Rhone gorges around the city of Montelimar as the 3rd ID advanced on the heels of the enemy army.

If Truscott could catch the Germans as they passed through the narrow gorges around the city of Montelimar, he could cut off their retreat and smash their army. He issued his orders: "Keep in mind that your primary mission is to block the Rhone Valley... every road between Montelimar and Highway 19 must be blocked and roads south thereof covered by reconnaissance... If humanly possible, create roadblocks... You must intercept all enemy traffic on the main north–south roads in the Rhone Valley."[4]

General Patch was also direct. "Your primary mission is to block the Rhone Valley and I expect you to do it... And when you run out of gas you park your trucks and move on foot." In a follow-up call he ordered, "interrupts by demolitions that main road... on the Rhone valley. I don't want a single vehicle to go up that road."[5]

Patch was a combat-tested commander who had served on Guadalcanal in the Pacific before being selected to command 7th Army. A 1913 graduate of West Point, General Patch served with General John Pershing during the 1916 Mexican incursions and saw combat in World War I in command of a machine-gun detachment. He fought in the Second Battle of the Marne, the Battle of Saint-Mihiel and the Meuse–Argonne Offensive. In the Pacific in World War II he took command of the Americal Division on Guadalcanal and later the XIV Corps in the final stages of the struggle for Guadalcanal.

Lead elements of VI Corps reached the Montilemar area as did elements of the enemy's 11th Panzer Division and the two forces slugged it out for several days in mid-August. The Germans controlled the heights north of Montilemar and were able to break up repeated American attempts to drive the enemy from their positions thus preventing the Americans from closing the Gate of Montilemar. The battered 19th slipped through the defile, but the Germans paid a terrible price. They left behind in Montilemar vast quantities of smashed equipment.

While the combat troops hammered the retreating 19th Army, so too did American air forces. They dubbed their attacks a "Roman Holiday," in which attacking Allied aircraft, including U.S. Navy Hellcats from several of the escort carriers that accompanied the invasion fleet, destroyed more than 1,500 enemy vehicles and killed 1,500 horses, the mainstays of the German army's transport corps. Rail cars were blasted and 3,000 German troops were taken prisoner and more than 1,000 enemy dead littered the battlefields.

Sergeant Murphy recalled the carnage he and his comrades came across in his wartime memoir, *To Hell and Back*:

> The destruction surpasses belief. As far as the eye can see, the road is cluttered with shattered, twisted cars, trucks and wagons. Many are still burning. Often the bodies of men lie in the flames; and the smell of singed hair and burnt flesh is strong and horrible.

> Hundreds of horses, evidently stolen from French farmers, have been caught in the (artillery) barrage. They look at us with puzzled, unblaming eyes, whinnying softly as their torn flesh waits for life to drain from it. We are used to the sight of dead and wounded men, but these shuddering animals affect us strangely. Perhaps we have been in the field too long to remember that innocence is also caught in the carnage of war.[6]

While the Germans lost heavily, the bulk of the 19th Army, including the 189th, 198th, 338th, and the 716th Infantry Divisions, and the 11th Panzer Division, escaped and continued its retreat north toward the city of Lyon. Beyond Lyon, just under 100 miles to the north, was the city of Belfort at the opening of the Belfort Gap. The 19th may have escaped Truscott's clutches, but he was off and running, planning another trap before Wiese reached the Gap where the Germans could set up defensive positions to hold off the hard-charging Americans and French. The Americans continued at attempts to block the 19th as it made its way northeast but the Germans were always able to break through roadblocks along the way.

The Allied battering of the German 19th Army as it approached the Franco-Swiss border raised fears among the Swiss that if the 19th Army's retreat to the Belfort Gap were blocked, Wiese and his superior, Field Marshal Johannes Blaskowitz, commander of Army Group G, might opt to counterattack VI Corps' flanks by passing through portions of Switzerland. Or the 19th might choose to fight its way through Switzerland to escape into Italy where it would link up with Kesselring's armies and be welcomed by Mussolini's fascist forces.

Brigadier General Kenneth McLean, chief planner for SHAEF, laid out possible scenarios for such possibilities: "Just possible the Germans might wish to widen Belfort Gap slightly by trespassing on small outlying piece of Switzerland," McLean opined. "Most unlikely they would attempt a wide turning movement through the Jura (mountain chain). Object presumably to turn the Belfort position from the south and advance on Besancon (France)."

McLean's report also speculated that the Germans might invade Switzerland to:

> Assist in the evacuation of their troops in Italy by providing more routes. Politically, more unlikely. Germans in the past have never violated Switzerland. The Swiss would fight and have a good army which knows own ground. Swiss presumably have taken full precautions and concentrated in area bordering on battle zones… all railroad lines from Italy run through tunnels prepared for demolition. Consider German violation move unlikely as disadvantages would outweigh advantages.[7]

The 19th Army retreated by whatever means the troops could find: "trucks, cars, buses, horse-drawn carts, bicycles, pushcarts, on foot. Columns lived off the land, usually marching only at night, hiding by day. Fearful of being cut off by the converging American armies, they lost men and equipment daily to air attack and ambush by the Maquis."[8] Field Marshal Blaskowitz later wrote that 19th Army was "barely able to pull its head out of the noose which is already tied."

By the first days of September, Truscott was convinced that the 19th was doomed and the possibility of trapping it between the French and Americans of 6th Army Group and Patton's oncoming 3rd Army divisions from Normandy grew with each passing day. The 19th had little left to defend itself and Wiese and Blaskowitz saw the imminent danger.

Original *Dragoon* battle plans called for 7th Army to pause after the capture of Lyon to regroup and resupply. Truscott realized however, that a pause at this juncture would give Wiese the break he needed to reach and prepare the Belfort Gap defenses. It would also give the German LXIV Corps more time to link up with the 19th and give it added strength. The LXIV Corps' exodus across central France was largely made on foot and the troops making the trek were constantly subject to air attacks by American fighter planes and ambushes by French resistance fighters. Of the 82,000 military personnel in retreat about 32,000 were combat troops.

Truscott queried Patch seeking permission to continue the advance without pausing to regroup and resupply around Lyon. Generals Patch and Henry Maitland Wilson, the British commander of Allied forces in the Mediterranean, which included 6th Army Group, agreed, noting, as Truscott did, that the 19th Army was now little more than a rabble of panic-driven troops incapable of mounting a concerted defense. Destroy it now, before it had time to regroup and become a threat. ULTRA intercepts revealed just how desperate Wiese was. In one effort to reinforce the 19th he received nine German and half a dozen old French tanks and five 88mm guns with 400 rounds between them to bolster the enemy defenses.

Wiese's troops took a stand at the ancient citadel of Besancon but Truscott ordered the 45th Division to go around the city with its ancient citadel. The 3rd Division would attack and neutralize the enemy garrison there, the site of a Roman bastion two millennia before, while the 45th continued its advance toward the gap, hoping to arrive there before the 19th.

On September 12, Truscott briefed Patch on VI Corps' plan to attack and control the Belfort Gap with Truscott confident that his troops could reach the objective and deny it to Wiese despite the "precarious" supply situation. The 7th Army troops had been moving so fast that it was difficult to provide all their needs, gasoline for the tanks and vehicles, and small arms and artillery ammunition in particular. Truscott noted, "Our supply problem has been difficult and, of course, will become more so when heavy fighting incident to the reduction of the Belfort Gap requires enormous ammunition expenditures. However, I have no doubt that, by strenuous effort, solutions can be found and adequate supplies for the operation can be provided."[9]

For Truscott the value of the Belfort Gap – the "Gateway to Germany," as Patch described it – was worth the risk and the effort. Patch agreed with Truscott's plan and gave him the go-ahead to charge headlong for the objective. Truscott was about to unhinge the enemy's southern front line.

But the date and Eisenhower, rather than supplies, were Truscott's biggest roadblock. On September 15, as he readied his plan to take the Belfort Gap, 6th Army Group fell under the command of Eisenhower and SHAEF. Generals Devers, Patch, and Truscott would no longer be a separate command under the loose control of the Allied Mediterranean Command under British General Wilson, with Devers as his deputy as well as commander of 6th Army Group. SHAEF was now in command of 6th Army Group and the high command had different plans on how to defeat the Germans and its focus was on breaching the German front line to the north at Arnhem and at Aachen. With SHAEF's ultimate objective the German Ruhr industrial area to the north where the Allied command believed the final battle of the war would be fought and won, 6th Army Group would now play only a supporting role in the defeat of the German Army on the west front. Its new assignment was to guard the flank of Patton's 3rd Army as the 3rd advanced into the Saar industrial area. To SHAEF and Eisenhower, southern France and the 6th Army Group were sideshows.

Immediately on the transfer to SHAEF, Truscott's plan to take the Belfort Gap and destroy the enemy 19th Army was scuttled. The order to shelve the plan came from Devers' 6th Army Group but undoubtedly was ordered by SHAEF and reflected the high command's bias for an advance into Germany in the north as well as a conservative approach to combat tactics and strategy.

Devers would not have made that decision. The new order allowed Wiese's 19th Army to elude defeat and capture and resulted in the creation of the Colmar Pocket, a bulge of German troops in the Allied line around Belfort and the nearby city of Colmar. The pocket unnerved Eisenhower and SHAEF for the next six months and strained relations between Devers and the Supreme Commander. The high command feared that the 50,000-plus German troops remaining in the pocket constituted a threat that could unhinge the Allied front.

SHAEF's new orders were for 6th Army Group to shore up the Allied front south of 3rd Army and tie in with Patton's 3rd Army to form a continuous front from the Netherlands to Switzerland. Truscott's VI Corps would also swing east to attack through the Vosges to reach the Alsace Plain and the Rhine. No army in military history had even broken through the Vosges, especially in winter.

Truscott exploded at the new orders. As in Italy in May 1944, when he had an opportunity to surround and destroy the German 10th Army, a myopic higher commander drew back and allowed the enemy to escape destruction. The orders were also in direct contradiction to Devers' dictum that the objective of any commander is to destroy an opponent's army and not to capture terrain. It was also in direct contradiction to Eisenhower's and SHAEF's directive for the Allied armies wherever possible to advance to the Rhine and establish bridgeheads on the east bank. Allied commanders were living up to their reputation, as universally noted by the Germans, of being risk averse and timid in the face of opportunities to defeat the enemy. Patton would have agreed with the German assessment. He noted in his diary as his troops were attempting to encircle huge German forces at Falaise in Normandy but were constrained by Bradley: "If I were on my own, I would take bigger chances than I am now permitted to take. Three times I have suggested and been turned down and each time the risk was warranted."[10]

General Devers weighed in about the importance of smashing ahead to the Belfort Gap regardless of perceived hurdles. He noted in his diary of September 3, 1944, before the order to cancel the attack on Belfort:

> I urged on (General) Patch and (General) Saville, (commander of the 12th Tactical Air Command) and all the supply people that they must keep up this drive until they have crossed the Rhine River and established bridgeheads, at which time we would undoubtedly have to pick up the pieces before we could go on unless SHAEF could supply us with fresh troops. I have hopes that this may be accomplished as SHAEF has the 35th Division and the 6th Armored Division who have been resting north of us. I was confident that we would be able to block the Belfort Gap, cutting off many of this large group of unorganized German specialists, civilian and otherwise retreating toward Germany....[11]

Adopting the universal military axiom to reinforce strength with strength, Devers had counseled that the U.S. High Command should assemble greater forces in the campaigns in France to end the war quickly. In particular, he recommended that the U.S. remove the five American divisions from Italy and transfer them to southern France where they could be used in the drive through places like the Belfort Gap and across the Rhine into Germany, or aid in the advance across northern Europe. The war in the west would be won, Devers knew, in France, not in Italy. He believed that American divisions were being wasted in Italy in a fight designed by the Germans to contain as many American and British divisions as possible so they would not be transferred to

France. The Italian campaign tied up as many as 15 Allied combat divisions. Even if the Allied armies in Italy drove the Germans out, the Allies would be up against the Italian, Austrian, and German Alps, hardly terrain for a rapid advance and the Germans would require few men to stave off any Allied attempt to break through this mountainous region.

On September 15, Devers conferred with French General de Lattre (Jean de Lattre de Tasigney, French 1st Army commander) who was preparing not only to take his 1st Army troops across the Rhine, but to advance deep into the Reich. Devers' diary notes on the same day, "General de Lattre thought that by the 25th (September) he would have enough ammunition behind him to carry out his attack and bypass Belfort and drive on to Mulhouse; that then he could get his army together and force a crossing of the Rhine and drive north through the Black Forest toward Stuttgart."[12]

Truscott was of the same mind as Devers, Patch, and de Lattre. Furious and fuming that 6th Army Group, and specifically his VI Corps, were prevented from taking advantage of such a promising opportunity at Belfort, Truscott penned a sharply worded letter to Patch reminding him that they both had agreed to an advance to close the Belfort Gap:

> As you stated the other day, the Belfort Gap is the Gateway to Germany. It is obvious that the Boche (Germans) is making strenuous effort to strengthen the defense of this area (the Vosges) and that he expects to hold the area as long as possible. While the permanent fortifications face generally eastward, the natural defense strength of the area needs little comment. Given sufficient time, the Boche can increase the defenses and make reduction of this area a slow and costly process, even against our superior power. Every consideration points to the fact that time available to him should be reduced to a minimum. Consequently, the assault on the Belfort Gap should begin at the earliest moment that sufficient troops can be made available and sufficient supplies can be built up.[13]

Truscott asserted in the letter that three American and "one-plus" French divisions were in position to advance toward Belfort and that a French armored division would also be available for the attack within three days. He continued:

> The axis prescribed in FO 5 (the new order to avoid Belfort) leads through the Vosges Mountains, where roads are limited, terrain rugged and easily defended. With the approach of weather in which rain and snow are to be expected, operations will be most difficult. As demonstrated in Italy during the last winter, the Boche can limit progress to a snail's pace and even stop it entirely, even against superior strength. With the SHAEF main effort in the direction of Aachen-Bonn-Berlin, this mountainous area (the Vosges) has little value if the Belfort Gap is breached and operations therein can contribute little to the success of SHAEF's main effort. It would be wasteful to employ the three most veteran divisions in the American Army in an operation where they can be contained by a fraction of their strength and where their demonstrated ability to maneuver is so strictly limited.[14]

Generals Truscott, left, helmeted, Patch, center, and Devers confer during 6th Army Group's advance through southern France. (U.S. Army)

Truscott was confident that his VI Corps could muster the strength and the supplies to carry out the advance and the taking of the Belfort Gap. He wasn't through with his letter to Patch. In what would appear to be a case of extreme pique, but wasn't (it had considerable merit), the VI Corps' commander seemingly threatened to take his ball and go home – he suggested to Patch that if the VI Corps weren't going to be used to breach the Belfort Gap it should be sent back to Italy to engage the enemy there.

> The Italian front seems to have bogged down in the face of determined opposition on the Gothic Line (a defensive line across the width of the Italian boot). An approach from the Nice area toward Genoa is a feasible operation, especially if supported by sufficient landing craft to permit "end runs" such as contributed to the success on the north coast of Sicily. The appearance of this veteran corps in the Genoa area would almost certainly break the stalemate in Italy and might bring results as decisive as those which have characterized the operation through the Belfort Gap. I believe that this operation for the VI Corps might contribute more to the German defeat than the operation ordered through the Vosges Mountains. It could be supplied from bases in the Marseilles area and would considerably alleviate the supply situation for troops in this area.
>
> It seems to me that the following conclusions are justified:
>
> The greater assistance to the SHAEF main effort by troops in this area is through the Belfort Gap.

If the gap is to be breached, the operation should begin at the earliest practicable time permitted by available troops and logistical considerations.

The French Army B (soon to be designated the French 1st Army) will not dispose more resources than are available now or will be within the next few days.

VI Corps is already engaged in the operation of driving the German covering forces and is well disposed to assist the assault on Belfort.

The operation prescribed in FO 5 for VI Corps can have little effect on the Belfort operation or on the SHAEF main effort and may bog down in winter warfare in the mountains.

An operation towards Genoa and the PO Valley would break the Gothic Line and might insure the destruction of German forces in Italy. This would probably be the most valuable use that could be made of these three veteran divisions.

Therefore, I recommend that the VI Corps: (1) Be employed in opening the Belfort Gap; or (2) That it be employed to capture Genoa and assist in the destruction of the German forces in Italy. It is requested that this letter proposal be submitted to the Army Group Commander for consideration.[15]

Whether Patch ever submitted Truscott's letter to Devers is not known, but Patch declined to follow Truscott's advice since the order not to breach the Belfort Gap undoubtedly came from SHAEF. If the decision to storm the Gap and advance to the Rhine and beyond had been left to Devers he would have allowed Truscott to keep advancing to block the Gap and cut off the escape route for the German 19th Army. In an entry to his diary on September 9, Devers stated his aggressive military philosophy as it related to the fighting in Italy in contrast to that in southern France: "Great leaders in war take calculated risks and they always pay dividends."[16]

The VI Corps would now be committed to the same kind of fighting its troops had experienced in the mountains of Italy. The divisions would have to fight their way uphill against German defenses in wooded and rugged terrain. Truscott knew the hurdles and struggles of infantry on this sort of ground. He "had had his fill of winter fighting in the mountains of Italy, and neither he nor any of his troops desired to repeat the experience in the Vosges. The terrain and weather, he pointed out, would allow the Germans to control the pace of any Allied offensive and, in his opinion, would waste three fine American divisions with little benefit to either SHAEF's efforts in the north or to the French 1st Army's drive against Belfort."[17]

The campaign in the Vosges, however, ultimately proved successful when VI Corps broke through the German defenses and reached the Alsace Plain and the Rhine River, but it took an additional two months of combat in the cold, mud, and drizzle of the European winter. In late November the 7th Army troops broke out onto the Alsace Plain when Devers planned a cross-Rhine attack north of Strasbourg at Rastatt. But by that time Truscott, promoted to three-star general, was long gone to Italy to command 5th Army before his VI

An American machine-gun crew in Alsace, winter 1945. (U.S. Army, NARA)

Corps' troops breached the Vosges Mountains and reached the Alsace Plain. But he felt the sting, knowing that the Belfort Gap was one of the primary gateways to the German heartland. By the time the Allies (VI Corps and the French 1st Army) regrouped their forces in mid-September in preparation for the attack through the Vosges, the Germans had slammed the gate shut.

In the view of Generalleutnant Walter Botsch, who succeeded Wiese as 19th Army commander, "it would have been the most unpleasant thing for the German 19th Army if a strong force of troops (either the entire French Army B of the U.S. VI A.C (army corps), with the French 1st Armored Division in any case) had immediately been used for an encircling maneuver northwest toward the Belfort Gap between Saone and the Swiss frontier. The 19th Army probably would have been cut off from its communicating with the Rhine."[18]

The French 1st Army command serving with 6th Army Group certainly understood the significance of taking the Belfort Gap. "Bethouart's (Major General Antoine Bethouart, commander of the French 1st Corps) troops were well positioned now to drive to the Belfort Gap. Generals Bethouart and de Lattre could practically taste it."[19] But with new 7th Army orders and before SHAEF signaled on September 15 that the Belfort Gap was not the main objective, the French would have to wait to take the prize.

"De Lattre was furious; (at the order to call off the attack to the Gap) he and Bethouart were both convinced that they could have gotten to Belfort and plugged the gap."[20] The French combat striking power had nearly doubled as new units were added and existing units fleshed out. The Americans also didn't know or they disregarded de Lattre's plan to drop airborne forces into the gap to seal the conquest. "Bethouart was convinced that until September 10, when German reinforcements started coming from the east, his forces could have gotten to the gap. A post-war discussion with Generalmajor von Wietersheim, former commander of the 11th Panzer Division, only reinforced Bethouart's view."[21]

It is worthy speculation to wonder what effect it would have had on the war in Europe had Truscott had been authorized to plug the Belfort Gap before Wiese and his 19th Army reached it. In post-war interviews, several German generals wondered why the Americans and French did not carry out a full-blooded thrust to advance and capture the gap before the Germans could get there. "It was an enigma to the army," wrote Wiese in a post-war debriefing, "why the enemy did not execute the decisive assault on Belfort between 8 and 15 September 1944 through a large-scale attack. The re-grouping of the American and French forces of which I learned now, came just in time for the (German) Army and gave it the necessary breathing spell to block and to hold the Belfort Gap." Wiese stated that had Truscott's troops moved to take the Belfort Gap his army would not have been able to counter a large-scale attack.[22]

The 6th Army Group's failure to exploit the German weakness at the Belfort Gap did not surprise several German generals who noticed this trend in the American Army's method of warfare. In a post-war interview General Alfred Schlemm, whose last command in World War II was the 1st Parachute Army on the western front, spoke out: "we seldom noticed exploitation of favorable opportunities, swift pursuit of the retreating enemy, surprise attacks by infantry at dusk or at night without the support of artillery or tanks…. The disadvantage for the enemy was that he never surprised us."[23] Wehrmacht General Walter Botsch noted, "It strikes a German military observer very forcibly that the American Army does not greatly believe in the formation of centers of gravity to the extent that the German Army has practiced in the past. It was as if the Americans still saw themselves fighting widely separated bands of Indians."[24]

Had Truscott reached and blocked the gap the 19th Army might have escaped over the Vosges to the Alsace Plain but it would have been met on the eastern flanks of the Vosges by Truscott's corps that had broken through the Belfort Gap and controlled the Alsace Plain from the Vosges foothills to the Rhine.

Another route of escape apparently contemplated by Wiese was through the mountain passes from France into Italy where the 19th would have linked up with German forces occupying northern Italy and with Field Marshal Kesselring's 10th and 14th Armies. According to Generalleutnant Walter

Botsch, then chief of staff of the 19th Army, "the 19th Army planned to fight its way to Italy through the passes, in case its northern route of retreat into the Belfort Gap was blocked by the American forces."[25]

Capture of the Belfort Gap would have provided an avenue east to the Rhine and the Alsace Plain and the city of Strasbourg that wasn't reached by Allied forces until late November. The Alsace Plain would also have provided a springboard to cross the Rhine as Devers proposed two-and-a-half months later in November. At that time Devers found the area immediately across the Rhine undefended and Truscott and Patch undoubtedly would have found the same in September. The Germans left the area virtually undefended because they had few reserves and they calculated that the principal objective of the Allied drive was to the north and the Ruhr industrial area, with the Saar industrial area as a secondary target. Their calculations were correct. But a force of Allied troops across the Rhine on the German southern front would have been a major psychological blow to the Germans, if not a major military threat. They regarded the river as a last line of defense of the German heartland. It would also have constituted a worrisome invasion with troops ready to break out behind the enemy front, just as the Colmar Pocket unnerved Eisenhower and the Allied High Command. Ironically, SHAEF planning, developed earlier in the campaign in France, called for each Allied army, including 6th Army Group, closing on Germany, to take advantage of opportunities to "jump" the Rhine to establish bridgeheads from which Allied forces could prepare to advance deep into the German heartland. But as Devers discovered in September and later in November with his proposed attack across the Rhine at Rastatt, SHAEF did not intend the cross-Rhine order to extend to 6th Army Group.

General Siegfried Westfall, who served under a number of German generals including Field Marshals von Rundstedt, Rommel, and Kesselring, noted that at the time Truscott planned to breach the Belfort Gap the German army was in such disarray that it would have been unable to stop any concerted and concentrated Allied advance through the Siegfried Line defenses. "The overall situation in the West was serious in the extreme. A heavy defeat anywhere along the front, which was so full of gaps that it did not deserve this name, might lead to catastrophe, if the enemy were to exploit his opportunity skillfully."[26]

When VI Corps advanced north along the eastern face of the Vosges and then wheeled east and attacked through the Vosges, Truscott's predictions of a slugfest resembling the fighting in the Italian campaign were realized. Truscott wrote while still in command of VI Corps in France: "Operations made slow progress during the first two weeks of October. Rain was almost incessant and vastly increased the hardships of moving and fighting. Cold caused acute discomfort, and the losses and exertions of preceding weeks were having their effect…. North of the Moselle, rugged foothills covered with dense forests made operations almost arduous. Thick woods required greater concentrations of troops to wipe out the enemy, while the corps was extended on such a wide front that any concentration was difficult."[27]

Truscott's suggestion that VI Corps be sent back to Italy wasn't as far-fetched as it might appear; it wasn't a harebrained suggestion made out of pique. Truscott believed that the rapidly expanding French 1st Army, beefed up by recruitment of thousands of resistance fighters, could hold the line in lightly defended Alsace while VI Corps disengaged from the Alsace area, moved south and advanced into Italy via Nice and Menton or by an amphibious assault on the Ligurian coast near Genoa. This would have placed it in a position to threaten German forces in Italy farther to the south under Field Marshal Kesselring and might have forced German forces in Italy to retreat into the Italian and the Austrian Alps. The VI Corps could then have formed a blocking force against any enemy forces to the south in Italy. General Botsch added: "The menace of an Allied advance into Italy not only caused certain misgivings in the German command but downright worry."[28]

Kesselring was well aware of the threat to his western flank from the Cote d'Azur east of Nice:

> Throughout the spring and summer of 1944, Hitler and OKW (the German High Command) were more concerned with an amphibious assault against northern Italy along either the Ligurian or Adriatic coasts, behind German lines. Such a landing could cause a complete collapse of the theater and project Allied land and air power dangerously close to the German heartland. Their fears were undoubtedly strengthened by Kesselring's estimates that the next major Allied offensive in the Mediterranean would be an assault in the Genoa area, outflanking German defenses north of Rome and forcing him to evacuate the Italian peninsula.[29]

Two weeks before the Allied invasion of southern France on August 15, 1944, when the Germans wondered where a new Allied amphibious landing in the Mediterranean would take place, Kesselring's fear of an attack on the Ligurian coast near Genoa caused him to reinforce the area with two under-strength German divisions and two pro-German Italian divisions of doubtful reliability and quality. He also began assembling several German divisions in northern Italy to form a central reserve to counter a threatened Allied landing around Genoa and "to hold the Alpine mountain passes from France into Italy and block any possible Allied incursion from the French Alps Maritime into northern Italy."[30] Truscott might have found it difficult going, had Generals Patch and Devers acceded to his plan to lead his VI Corps in an invasion of

Italy via the Ligurian coast, but any Allied incursion into Italy would have been a serious threat to German forces there.

The successful landing in southern France was of special concern for German forces in Italy. Several weeks after the landings in mid-August a force of American paratroopers advanced along the southern French coast, liberated Nice and reached the Italian frontier. An advance by American troops over the passes into Italy or along the coast into the rear of the German front could mean the enemy's destruction. The Allies in southern France likewise took steps to guard against a German attack through the Nice area against the eastern flank of 6th Army Group.

Nice and the surrounding Alps Maritime border area with Italy were then sealed by French Moroccan troops to prevent infiltration by German forces from Italy into France. The 6th Army Group was taking no chances of a German attack from Italy, even though ULTRA intercepts indicated the enemy had no intention of invading southern France to relieve the pressure on Wiese and the 19th Army. The Nice region was held by a second-rate German division comprised of wounded veterans and new conscripts who were being introduced to army life before being sent to veteran units at the fronts. By late August 1944 the Germans were driven out of southern France and into Italy by Allied forces and French resistance groups eager to emerge after years in the shadows to drive the Germans from French soil.

In November 1944 Truscott was again back in Italy, and placed in command of the U.S. 5th Army when General Clark was promoted to lead 15th Army Group, replacing British General Sir Harold Alexander. Truscott would have preferred to remain in France but with the offer of a third star and command of an army, he returned to the sideshow of the Italian campaign, no doubt painfully aware of the lost opportunities at the Belfort Gap. In Italy, he also remembered another lost opportunity the previous May when his VI Corps advanced out of the Anzio beachhead during a general Allied spring offensive.

CHAPTER 9

Fateful Decision at Falaise

While the focus of this book has been on the fall of 1944, I digress to the middle of July 1944, before Arnhem, before Wallendorf, Stolberg, and Belfort, to when the high command and Eisenhower failed to trap two battered German armies in Normandy and possibly shorten the war in Europe. The growing British and American armies in Normandy had been boxed in to a narrow sliver of land along the Norman coast for six weeks by the German 7th and 5th Panzer Armies and the leaders of the Anglo-American alliance feared that the Allies would never break out of the Normandy bridgehead where they had landed on D-Day, June 6. By some estimates the American 1st Army had suffered 125,000 casualties during the Battle of Normandy; the British and Canadians in Montgomery's 21st Army group suffered another 83,000 dead, wounded and missing. The Allies had little to show for the cost in lives and blood and the Normandy bridgehead was not considerably larger in mid-July than it was in the first weeks after D-Day.

The Germans also had suffered huge casualties. Army Group B, which controlled the German 7th and 5th Panzer Armies, suffered some 160,000 casualties from D-Day to August while receiving only about 10,000 replacements. It was the skill of the German army and its leadership, however, that kept the enemy fighting with such determination.

As the battle extended from June into July the Allies were desperate to find a way to break the stalemate and drive the Germans back. At the northeastern end of the bridgehead Montgomery's troops failed to break out in the vicinity of Caen and were repulsed with heavy losses. On the western end, in the direction of St. Lo, the Americans were stymied by the difficulties of the *bocage,* a landscape of towering and centuries-thick hedgerows where the enemy set up defensive positions to thwart an American advance. Neither man nor tank could get through the hedgerows and the fighting turned into isolated and bloody struggles between squads of Germans and Americans battling for small plots of ground. (Later in the battle the Americans devised a steel-pronged device with sharp blades attached to the front of Sherman tanks that could plow through the thickest of hedgerows.) The American VII Corps, commanded by General Collins, captured the port of Cherbourg but that did little to expand the bridgehead to the west and east. Frustrated, the Allied command needed an extraordinary measure to break the German hold on Normandy.

That measure came in the form of a massive aerial bombardment, Operation *Cobra*, on July 25, when American Air Force bombers and fighters based in England unleashed 4,000 tons of bombs on a mile-wide section of the German front line in the St. Lo–Periers sector. The bombs from 1,500 B-17s and B-24s, 380 medium B-26 and B-25 bombers, and 550 fighter planes P-47s and P-51s, landed squarely on the section of German front held by the Panzer Lehr Division, arguably the finest armored division in the German Army. Panzer Lehr was virtually wiped out and its commander, General Fritz Bayerlein, found himself without a division to command: "After an hour I had no communication with anybody, even by radio. By noon nothing was visible but dust and smoke. My front line looked like the face of the moon and at least 70 percent of my troops were knocked out – dead, wounded, crazed or numbed."[1] The next day the Americans followed through with a second bombardment and when the dust cleared the U.S. VII Corps advanced over once-peaceful farmland pitted by huge craters and piles of debris along with the bodies of hundreds of German soldiers. The ruptured landscape at first hindered the American attacks, particularly armored formations that had to navigate the cratered landscape, but the momentum increased and the advance continued.

Operation *Cobra* broke the German stranglehold on Normandy and American divisions poured through a narrow opening at the edge of the German lines near the town of Avranches on the Channel coast in sight of Mont St. Michel. Patton took command of the newly activated 3rd Army on August 1 and began funneling divisions through the breach and swinging his forces west into Brittany with the objective of securing the ports, and to the east towards Le Mans.

The German generals, especially Field Marshal Gunther von Kluge, overall German commander in the west after the departure of Field Marshal Erwin Rommel, saw the writing on the wall. By moving west, the Americans were cutting off the German troops in Brittany and by advancing east at the same time the Americans were maneuvering behind the bulk of German forces in

Normandy. Unless the depleted Germany army began extricating itself it faced encirclement and annihilation. Von Kluge ordered a series of counterattacks to delay the American advance, hoping to gain time for a retreat, but all were beaten off. Then came the order from Hitler that the German 7th and the 5th Panzer Armies were to attack west toward Avranches to cut off Patton's 3rd Army from the American 1st Army still in Normandy. "We must strike like lightning," Hitler announced to his high command. "When we reach the sea, the American spearhead will be cut off.... We might be able to cut off their entire beachhead."[2] Von Kluge considered the order madness, knowing that his forces, particularly his panzer divisions, were badly depleted and did not have the strength of launch a successful attack to reach the sea and isolate Patton's 3rd Army.

The attack kicked off nevertheless on the night of August 6 with four German panzer divisions advancing abreast toward the towns of Mortain and Avranches. Unfortunately for von Kluge, the Americans knew from ULTRA intercepts the attack was coming and were prepared. Thus, the stage was set for a huge Allied victory and a devastating German defeat, one that could possibly determine the outcome of the war in western Europe. If the Allies could capture or kill over 300,000 German troops around Mortain and in Normandy, the enemy's homeland would be wide open to invasion. There would be little to stop the Allies from reaching the German border without opposition.

Von Kluge's panzers came on relentlessly in the attack on Mortain overpowering everything in their paths until they confronted the U.S. 30th ID astride the road with the GIs of the 2nd Battalion, 120th Infantry Regiment dug in atop Hill 314 that rises 600 feet above the nearby valley floor. The town of Mortain is located halfway up the western slope of a steep hill and from the top Americans had a clear view of the Mortain–Saint-Hilaire-du-Harcouët road that leads to Avranches and the sea. This was the road on which the panzers were mounting their attacks.

The enemy surrounded 700 Americans from the 2nd battalion atop the hill who faced a division-size force of the 17th SS Panzergrenadier Division. Despite running low on food and ammunition and suffering serious casualties, the battalion held out, fending off attack after attack by the German grenadiers. The American enclave was difficult to supply by air drop so the 230th Field Artillery Battalion took to firing shell canisters with needed supplies.

The Americans had the advantage of height and from their vantage point were able to direct artillery fire on enemy troops and tanks alike. The German assaults were stopped by these concentrated artillery barrages from tanks and tank destroyers directed from the hilltop observation point and from the determined and dug in American infantrymen who refused to retreat. The next day droves of Allied fighter bombers came swooping down on the hapless enemy tanks and forcing their retreat. The battalion was relieved on August 12 but the force had been whittled down to 400 effectives. Four hundred men had either been killed or wounded.

The Germans faced additional devastation as they retreated, when they faced simultaneous attacks by Montgomery's 21st Army Group attacking out of the eastern end of the Normandy bridgehead. The Canadian Army was leading the way as it advanced south out of the bridgehead toward the town of Falaise. As the battle raged both in the west of the bridgehead where the Germans faced the Americans, and the east with Monty's troops, the Germans, on Hitler's orders, made one more attempt to break through the American defenses and reach Avranches. It failed.

As von Kluge predicted, the Germans of 7th and 5th Panzer Armies suffered huge losses and were now fighting for their very existence. Their attack toward the sea had carried them forward into a narrow tubular pocket about 12 miles wide between the Americans to their south and the British and Canadians to the north. Hitler had created a trap for his own soldiers just as his armies had trapped pockets of French soldiers in the defeat of France in 1940 and Russians in early stages of *Barbarossa*, the invasion of Russia in 1941. This was *Blitzkrieg* as the German panzers swept around entire French and Russian armies, entrapping them into huge pockets and then closing off their means of escape. German infantry then moved to seal the pocket and that way the Wehrmacht captured hundreds of thousands of French and Russian troops. Now at Falaise it was the Allies practicing *Blitzkrieg* and preparing to encircle the enemy and close off his means of escape. More than 300,000 Germans in two veteran armies would be trapped and at the mercy of Allied assaults on the ground and from the air.

But did the Allies have the command experience and the will to bag two German armies? They needed perfect timing and the ability to take risks, and risk taking wasn't always their forte. For nearly a week, between August 15 and 21, the trapped Germans fought desperate actions to escape from what became known as the Falaise Pocket. As they struggled they were bombarded and strafed from the air, blasted by ranged artillery fire on all sides, and shot at by closing infantry. Allied fighters and rocket-firing British Typhoon fighter bombers circled above the melee in the lush green Normandy hills waiting to pounce like circling vultures on anything that moved. The scenes in the pocket began to resemble scenes imagined from Dante's Inferno, blood, ravaged bodies of men and beasts – the German army was largely horse-drawn – smashed trucks and horse carts, artillery with barrels askew, tanks tumbled sideways by the roadside, but most remembered were the bodies of the German troops who had been caught attempting to escape to the homeland. The putrid smell of death was everywhere along with the miasma of burning rubber, oil, and gasoline.

One officer who witnessed the aftermath of destruction at Falaise remembered the horrific scenes:

> I stood on a lane, surrounded by 20 or 30 dead horses, most of them still hitched to their wagons and carts.... As far as the eye could reach... on every line of sight, there were... vehicles, wagons, tanks, guns, prime movers, sedans, rolling kitchens, etc., in various stages of destruction.
>
> I stepped over hundreds of rifles in the mud and saw hundreds more stacked along sheds.... I saw probably 300 field pieces and tanks, mounting large caliber guns, that were apparently undamaged. I saw no foxholes or any type of shelter or field fortifications. The Germans were trying to run and had no place to run. They were probably too exhausted to dig... They were probably too tired even to surrender.[3]

General Eisenhower described the carnage that he witnessed when he visited the pocket after the battle. "The battlefield at Falaise was unquestionably one of the greatest 'killing grounds' of any of the war areas. Roads, highways, and fields were so chocked with destroyed equipment and with dead men and animals that passage through the area was extremely difficult... It was literally possible to walk for hundreds of yards at a time, stepping on nothing but dead and decaying flesh."[4] But the Allies were unable to completely close the gap, thus allowing as many as 200,000 enemy troops to escape. So why didn't, or why couldn't, they close the Falaise Gap and remove thousands of German troops from the war? As happens in every major battle during the war, there are conflicting explanations and interpretations about why the Allies were unable to inflict a Stalingrad-type defeat on the Germans at Falaise.

Eisenhower wrote in *Crusade in Europe* that the principal reason for the escape of so many Germans was because he and 1st Army commander, Bradley, ordered the Americans to halt at a pre-designated line near the town of Falaise to prevent the Americans, advancing from the south, from crashing into the oncoming British Army coming from the north as the two armies advanced toward each other in the race to close the pocket. Ike and Bradley feared that in the fog of battle the two armies could inflict serious damage on each other before realizing that they weren't German.

Patton didn't buy that reasoning and before the halt order came he sent Haislip's XV Corps advancing towards Argentan, eight miles beyond the demarcation line that Bradley and Eisenhower set as the outer limit of the

American advance toward the British and Canadians at Falaise. "Nothing doing," Bradley told Patton when informed of Haislip's advance. Bradley ordered Patton to get Haislip's corps back to the demarcation line much to Patton's disgust.[5] Patton believed that there were ways to avoid an accidental clash between Monty's and Patton's forces and he bristled at Bradley's order to halt. Patton later asserted that his XV Corps "could easily have entered Falaise and closed the gap…. We had reconnaissance parties near the town when we were ordered to pull back."[6]

Wilmot notes, however, that there were considerable, though severely weakened, German panzer forces on Haislip's front as he moved north to block the enemy. The XV Corps' three divisions may not have been strong enough to advance through to Falaise and hold off as many as 19 trapped German divisions trying to escape. Bradley feared that they would stampede out of the pocket and overwhelm Haislip's few divisions. But the Germans had

French General Jacques Leclerc, commander of the 2nd French Armored Division, on the road to Paris in August 1944.

no cohesive or directed forces; they were attempting to break out in isolated groups. Troops from General Leclerc's 2nd French Armored Division kept confronting individual truckloads of German troops attempting to escape. They were shot to pieces as they drove unwittingly into Allied lines.

We will never know the outcome of the Falaise battle had Patton's 3rd Army's XV Corps, kept advancing to close the Gap that was being constricted by the hour. Some critics blame Montgomery and the Canadians for the slowness of their attack south out of the Normandy bridgehead. Wilmot suggests the Gap could have been closed earlier to trap many more German troops than were taken in the end: "The evidence suggests that the thrust from the north was not pressed with sufficient speed and strength. In the final stages Field Marshal Montgomery had British divisions to spare, but Simonds was not reinforced. Nor were the Canadian attacks as vigorous and venturesome as the occasion demanded. (Simonds was the general in command of the Canadian forces advancing south out of the Bridgehead) ... But in the attacks (by Montgomery) of August 7th and 14th opportunities of exploitation were lost."[7]

Once again, the competition between Patton and Montgomery may have interfered with the conduct of the war. Patton railed against Montgomery's deliberateness and blamed him for the slow advance toward Falaise by the Canadians, believing that his 3rd Army could have sealed the fate of the Germans in the Falaise Pocket. He was not alone in his assessment. General Gavin called the Battle of Falaise "Sicily all over again,"[8] arguing that Montgomery was too slow on the attack while Patton was galloping into the fray. "To military professionals, it (Falaise) was to be a Cannae. If they (the Allies) could have been successful in realizing their objective, it would have saved many Allied lives and almost certainly have ended the war in 1944." Gavin notes that Patton couldn't believe the order not to go beyond Argentan and to Falaise and tried all day on August 13 to have the order reversed so his troops could continue north and close the Gap. Instead 3rd Army's lead corps was instructed to advance west, away from the battle. Gavin cites German General Walter Warlimont, deputy chief of the high command's operations staff: "a good half of the troops thus encircled fought their way out." General Warlimont called the escape, "one of the great feats of arms of this campaign."[9]

Like Sicily, where some 40,000 German troops escaped from the island over the Straits of Messina in 1943 to fight again, Gavin attributes part of the failure at Falaise to a breakdown in the command structure that led to misunderstandings as to whom was in charge: Montgomery, Patton, Eisenhower, or Bradley. At the time Montgomery was in overall command of the land battle in Normandy with Bradley and the Americans taking orders from him. But Eisenhower was supposed to be in charge of both the British 21st Army Group and the newly designated American 12th Army Group under Bradley. Even though Ike was, in theory, the top commander, Bradley, at Falaise, looked to Montgomery for direction. Gavin rendered his opinion: "If there was need for over-all guidance, it should have come from the Supreme Commander, General Eisenhower.... So the battle of Normandy ended on a very bad note."[10]

But, not to be too harsh on the Allies, there were other forces that contributed to the escape of thousands of German soldiers from the pocket. The skill and leadership of the German army and its generals should never be discounted. Many of the top commanders, von Kluge among them, honed their skills of defensive warfare on the Russian front where battles of the magnitude of Falaise were commonplace, with the Germans by 1944 having to save entire armies from encirclement and destruction by the Russian juggernaut. Field Marshal Model, who replaced von Kluge, was considered a master of defensive warfare learned in Russia.

Many of the German troops were veterans of five years of warfare in the east against the Russians. In Normandy, these veterans were up against several "green" or inexperienced Allied divisions – the 80th ID, the 5th AD and the French 2nd AD – that were thrown into the fight. And many of the Allied generals were getting their first real taste of warfare by maneuver of the type that the Germans had perfected early in the war.

On the other hand, the Germans helped create their disaster at Falaise because Hitler and his top generals misjudged the fighting qualities and abilities of the Americans. Wilmot notes, "Both Hitler and the German Command in the West were gravely at fault in their estimate of American strength and skill. The High Command was contemptuous because the American Army had such a small professional core and so little military experience and tradition, but Hitler's scorn had a different source. 'In assessing the military value of the Americans,' says Speer, (Albert Speer) 'Hitler always argued that they were not a tough people.... If put to the test, they would prove to be poor fighters.'"[11]

Their contempt cost the Germans 50,000 men left behind in captivity and 10,000 dead scattered about the Norman countryside. It also cost them hundreds of tanks and thousands of artillery pieces. And the 7th and 5th Panzer Armies were ghosts of their former selves, unable to resist the hard-charging Allies as they pushed the remnants of these two armies to the German frontier. The Germans suffered a stinging defeat that undoubtedly contributed to their ultimate downfall earlier than what might have been had they not lost so much of their 7th and 5th Panzer Armies. General Bradley pegs their losses at some 500,000 casualties since D-Day and "both German armies had been destroyed in all but name."[12] Nevertheless, the Battle of the Falaise Gap calls into question, once again, whether the war in the west would have been shortened even more had the Allies pressed the Germans with greater speed and determination to close the gap and inflict another Stalingrad-type defeat on the Wehrmacht.

CHAPTER 10

Vulnerable Switzerland

Would SHAEF dare to invade neutral Switzerland as a way to trap the German 19th Army and facilitate the destruction of the left wing of the German front line opposite French Alsace and Lorraine? Would Devers' 6th Army Group consider invading Switzerland to destroy the Germans 19th Army before it reached the safety of Alsace and the Rhine? The rapid advance of Devers' 6th Army Group through southern France made such a move unlikely but SHAEF planners did give such a maneuver some thought. Devers' staff also must have eyed a move into Switzerland. General McLean sketched out a possible scenario for an Allied attack on the diminutive nation, but there were no serious plans to invade the country although a rationale could have been found for an invasion. American officials were concerned that the Swiss were trading with the Germans and shipping them what was considered valuable material to be used in weapons production.

That didn't rule out the French, whose 1st Army, under the command of the sometimes impetuous de Lattre, was advancing side by side with the American 7th Army along the frontier of Switzerland. The French on more than one occasion exhibited serious disagreement with the American–British high command. De Gaulle let Eisenhower know that if the Allies by-passed Paris in August 1944 as they advanced rapidly to the German frontier, he would detach General Leclerc's 2nd French Armored Division from the American 1st Army and send it into Paris to quell fighting between Resistance forces and the German occupiers. Later that year de Gaulle also threatened to remove the best divisions in the French 1st Army to maintain order in a liberated France that was convulsed with political unrest in the aftermath of the German occupation. SHAEF could not always control de Gaulle and his armies and while it was unlikely that de Lattre would invade a slice of Switzerland to destroy the German 19th Army fighting for its life to reach the safety of the Belfort Gap and the Alsace Plain, it was not out of the question.

While McLean essentially ruled out an Allied advance into Switzerland, he also believed that a German advance into Switzerland was equally unlikely although he either didn't know of detailed German plans to invade the country and dismissed the likelihood that General Wiese and his 19th Army would encroach on Swiss territory to attack Devers' armies or use Switzerland as a way to escape the Allied net.

The Swiss were always wary of German intentions, and to some extent those of the Allies. The Swiss had feared for years that Hitler would invade this small Alpine nation of just over four million people, as he had overrun Poland, Czechoslovakia, Yugoslavia, Greece, Austria, France, Norway, and Denmark. The German High Command had drawn up sophisticated and detailed plans to invade Switzerland and hundreds of thousands of German troops were occasionally massed along the Swiss frontier with Germany. Prior to the fall of France in 1940 the French High Command warned General Henri Guisan, Supreme Commander of all Swiss forces, that the French anticipated a German attack on France through Switzerland. The Swiss, in turn, feared that the French would strike first and invade Switzerland to attack Germany. They informed the French, as they made it clear to the Germans, that the Swiss would resist to the death any invasion of their territory by any nation.

Fear of German invasion was heightened by a barrage of German propaganda in 1939 and 1940 declaring that Switzerland, with its large German-speaking population, rightfully belonged to the greater Reich, Hitler's rationale for absorbing Austria and the culturally German Sudetenland region of Czechoslovakia. The German newspaper *Frankfurter Zeitung* issued a statement, no doubt approved by propaganda minister, Joseph Goebbels, asserting, "no branch of the German race has the right or the possibility of withdrawing from the common destiny of all Germans."[1] German Field Marshal Herman Goering published a map of the Reich that included most of Switzerland with the German-speaking Swiss described as "exiled citizens of the German Reich." Swiss neutrality was depicted as "a moral defect based or weakness of will."[2]

German military aircraft regularly made incursions in 1940 into Swiss airspace often engaging Swiss fighter planes in aerial combat. On June 1, during the German invasion of France, a flight of 36 German Henkel-111 bombers ranged over Switzerland and were engaged in combat with Swiss Me-109 fighters, German-manufactured aircraft. Two of the German bombers were shot down. The following day another intruding Henkel was shot down. On the news that Germany had invaded the Netherlands and Belgium the Swiss called for a general mobilization and went on a war footing, ordering blackouts against the possibility of aerial attacks.[3] On June 4, 1940, 29 German planes, Henkel-111 bombers and Me-110 fighter-bombers, were engaged by a flight of a dozen Swiss fighters. Two German planes were shot down while the Swiss lost one fighter. It was discovered that the German pilots had orders to lure the Swiss over German territory. Again, on June 8, 15 Swiss fighters engaged 28 Luftwaffe aircraft over Swiss territory. One Swiss bi-plane was downed while two German planes went down.[4]

Hitler used these dogfights as a pretext for a possible land invasion of Switzerland. A German communiqué warned the Swiss, "In the event of any repetition of such incidents, the Reich will dispense with written communications and resort to other means of safeguarding German interests." The Swiss were used to German threats with the Nazi-controlled press regularly issuing warnings of invasion. The German newspaper, *Völkischer Beobachter*, the voice of the National Socialist party, warned in December 1939 that the Swiss press must curb its malign treatment of Germany or otherwise Switzerland would be considered an enemy of the Reich.[5]

The Germans weren't the only threat to Switzerland. The Italians too intended to invade Ticino, Switzerland's Italian-speaking canton, and a reported invasion was scheduled. On June 18, as the French army capitulated and the French government sought an armistice with Germany, Hitler and Mussolini met to discuss the invasion of Switzerland but Il Duce's lust for conquest was tempered by the fact that Italian troops had performed badly in Italy's recent invasion of southern France to reclaim territory that had formerly been part of northern Italy. Even as the French army was collapsing against the German onslaught to the north, it was mauling the Italians in and around Menton in the Alps Maritime. Only France's capitulation to the Germans in June made it possible for the Italians to occupy large sections of the south of France.[6] That occupation ended in the summer of 1943 with Italy's surrender to the Allies. The Germans then occupied all of southern France. Germany's plans to invade Switzerland in 1940 were aborted largely because Germany was occupied elsewhere and was in the planning stages of the attack on Russia that was to take place in the spring of 1941.

The Germans, and anyone else who considered invading Switzerland, including the Americans, were tempered by the Swiss civilian army that numbered upwards of 700,000 troops. The Swiss were prepared for a German attack and an invading enemy force would face horrendous obstacles in the rugged, mountainous terrain and would come up against a well-trained and ready civilian Swiss army that could be called up to fight at a moment's notice. Defensive preparations were extensive:

> All bridges over the Rhine would collapse, and mines would await invaders who tried to cross by rafts or amphibious tanks. The Simplon tunnel that connects Switzerland with Italy, and the St. Gotthard Tunnel that connects two Swiss regions, would be immediately destroyed. Roads, railways, bridges, power stations and air fields would be blown up. Camouflaged tank traps and electric barbed-wire fences would stop many panzers and infantry… The Swiss could use modern technology to cause landslides and avalanches that no infantry or armored divisions could survive.[7]

As the war in western Europe in the summer of 1944 approached Switzerland, Swiss military authorities again feared invasion from both the Allies and the Germans. They believed the Germans might invade to ferry troops and supplies to General Wiese's beleaguered 19th Army retreating from the south of France with its troops passing close to the Swiss frontier in eastern France. Likewise, the Swiss feared the Americans and French might invade their country to facilitate the encirclement of German forces retreating into Alsace. During the fighting around Belfort from September to December 1944 the sound of battle from nearby France was a constant drumbeat.

The Swiss also were victims of aerial attacks by American aircraft. The most serious U.S. bombing raid against Swiss territory came when a flight of American B-24 bombers mistakenly dropped their 500-pound bombs on the Swiss city of Schaffhausen on the Rhine, killing 50 of the inhabitants and seriously wounding more than 150. Landmarks that clearly delineated the community were apparently ignored by the American formation.[8]

The attacks came from American bombers engaged in Operation *Clarion*, code name for broad U.S. aerial attacks on the German transportation system. The Americans assured the Swiss that it would not happen again. However, two weeks later, two more formations of 8th Air Force "heavies" wandered over Swiss territory and bombed the cities of Basel and Zürich, both near the German frontier. The fallout reached all the way to the White House and General Marshall. Marshall signaled Lt. Gen. Carl Spaatz, commander of U.S. Strategic Air Forces in Europe, that "the successive bombings of Swiss territory now demand more than an expression of regret." He ordered Spaatz to travel to Switzerland and to apologize to the Swiss government and its people for the unintended bombing of their territory and the resulting deaths and casualties. Spaatz journeyed to Switzerland to explain to the Swiss the extraordinary lengths to which the 8th Air Force went to avoid such mistakes and promised that no American air raid would take place within 150 miles of Swiss territory in the future. He asked that the Swiss keep this information secret so that the Germans would not take advantage of the sanctuary area. As for any indemnity, the Swiss asked that the Americans provide its air force with a number of P-51 Mustangs, considered the finest fighter in the American aerial arsenal.[9]

The Swiss continued to demonstrate their resolve to repulse an attack from any source, German or Allied, when a German bomber violated Swiss airspace and bombed and strafed a Swiss community. The plane was met by Swiss fighters that shot down the errant warplane. A flight of 13 American bombers overflew Switzerland after an attack on southern Germany. Twelve of the planes obeyed instructions from Swiss ME 109 fighters to land, the pilots aware that if they refused they would be attacked and possibly shot down. The 13th American bomber refused to obey the order and was shot down. The crew bailed out. Overflights by American bombers were not unusual but most were planes that were badly shot up and crippled during bombing missions over Germany and limped into Switzerland. The planes would never have made it back to bases in England or southern Italy. The crews were interned for the duration of the war, however, many interned airmen escaped minimal detention and made their way back to England through Vichy France and then into Spain or Portugal.

Had the Americans, late in the war, carried out a sketchy, proposed SHAEF plan for an end run around German border defenses by attacking through Switzerland into southern Germany, they would have found themselves fighting two armies, the German Wehrmacht and the Swiss defense force. Better not to attack a hornet's nest.

CHAPTER 11

On the Rhine

Strasbourg, Alsace, November 24, 1944

The 7th U.S. Army was on the banks of the Rhine River ready to cross and advance into Germany. This would appear to be an incredible feat, an American army on this strategic river after months of struggle and thousands of casualties to get there. For every American army, Bradley's 12th Army Group, Patton's 3rd Army, and Devers' 6th Army Group, this was the ultimate prize. It was the objective that Eisenhower and SHAEF had laid out for these three and other generals from D-Day onward. Might they now authorize 7th Army to cross with the hope that the Allies would be across the Rhine, the German southern front line could collapse, and the war might be shortened or even concluded?

This most likely opportunity, and possibly the most likely opportunity to succeed, to breach the German Siegfried Line in the fall of 1944, after Wallendorf, Aachen, and Belfort, occurred near Strasbourg, France, in late November. After advancing from the Riviera to Alsace in four months, 6th Army Group was in position to drive the enemy from France and invade the German heartland. Devers' army group was the only Allied army in the west ready to reach the Rhine.

It began at 7:15am, November 23, 1944, as armored columns from General Leclerc's 2nd French Armored Division raced eastward across a snow-covered Alsace Plain towards Strasbourg whose twisting medieval alleys and timbered houses press against the fast-flowing Rhine. In five years of war this day promised to be the sweetest for Leclerc, the day his quest to drive the Germans from his homeland would be realized. With Strasbourg liberated all the principal cities of France would be free and he would drive the hated Boche from French soil over the bridge into the German city of Kehl opposite Strasbourg on the Rhine. Leclerc had vowed in 1941 not to abandon the fight

U.S. troops disembarking from naval transports during the invasion of southern France on August 15, 1944. (U.S. Army)

against Nazi Germany until the tricolors once against flew over his beloved Strasbourg. The red, white, and blue of the French flag was banned throughout the war. Anyone displaying them could be shot.

Jacques Leclerc, the nom de guerre for Vicomte Jacques-Philippe de Hautecloque, was born into an aristocratic family and assumed his wartime identity in exile to protect his wife and family after he left France to fight the Nazis. Graduating from St-Cyr, the French national military academy, in 1924, he made a brilliant reputation in Morocco during the struggle against the nationalist Riffi. Rising quickly through the ranks, he was a general staff officer when World War II began. Captured twice by the Germans in May–June 1940, he escaped both times and in July joined Charles de Gaulle in London.

De Gaulle sent Leclerc to take charge of Free French Forces in French Equatorial Africa where he formed a task force that advanced from Dakar, Senegal, 1,500 miles through the Sahara Desert to attack and capture an Italian garrison in Libya. There under the heat of the North African sun he vowed to return to France and liberate Strasbourg. He then joined forces with Field Marshal Montgomery's British North African armies that drove the Germans and Italians out of North Africa.

After service in Africa Leclerc took his troops to Britain where he commanded the 2nd French Armored "Blindée" Division, considered one of the best armored division in the Allied armies after the D-Day landings. He forged Frenchmen from North Africa, Lebanon, and France, along with Moroccan Tirailleurs (riflemen) into a magnificent fighting machine. The power behind the division was Leclerc himself. Leclerc and his tankers would avenge their humiliating defeat of 1940. Leclerc was known to be brutal with German POWs, executing them out of hand. He once ordered the execution by firing squad of a group of young Alsacian boys who were soldiers in a German SS division.

The 2nd French AD landed in France over the Normandy beaches on August 1, 1944, two months after D-Day and immediately went into combat. Attached to General Wade Haislip's XV Corps in Patton's rapidly advancing 3rd Army, Leclerc's men were the first Allied troops into Paris on August 25 in their American M4 Sherman tanks with French tricolors flying from their turrets and the Cross of Lorraine painted in blue on the sides of their hulls. Leclerc took the surrender of Paris from the German commander.

Beyond Paris Leclerc's tankers, by now known for their élan and courage, as well as their hatred of the Germans, raced east into Lorraine with Patton's

U.S. troops dug in against German counterattacks in the Hürtgen Forest, Germany, November 1944. (U.S. Army)

3rd Army. In late September the 2nd was transferred, along with XV Corps, to Patch's 7th Army that had fought its way into Alsace from the Mediterranean beaches of southern France. Leclerc's troops found the going slow and the fighting brutal in the Vosges Mountains of Alsace but by mid-November the division was poised on the eastern slopes of the Vosges ready to break out towards Strasbourg and the Rhine.

The attack onto the Alsace Plain began November 13, 1944 in blinding rain and snow and with the support of a thunderous artillery barrage as the troops moved out. Leclerc chose to bypass the Saverne Gap, the more direct route out of the Vosges to the Alsace Plain, that he knew would be heavily defended by the enemy. He sent his columns through smaller undefended passes that bisected the mountain range. The enemy fought stubbornly to slow his forces but by November 18 the German defenses were collapsing and Leclerc's troops were driving out of the Vosges onto the plains with Strasbourg and the Rhine only 20 miles away.

Four separate armored task forces from the 2nd charged ahead through enemy territory, the tankers straining to see the spires of the Strasbourg cathedral as they brushed aside roadblocks and pockets of German resistance. Lt. Tony Triumpho, an American liaison officer with one of the assault forces recalled the heady charge. "We went roaring across the plain in our jeep along with four or five light tanks and a few half-tracks of infantry, about seventy men. We passed working parties and groups of German soldiers… they just stood open-mouthed. When they saw it was French troops they were scared to death for they had heard that the French… did not take too many prisoners."[1] Triumpho's tiny task force was too intent on getting into Strasbourg to take time to kill Boches but follow-up French troops would dispatch them along with hated French collaborators.

One American officer described how different the French army was in comparison to the American army. "The First French Army was a whisk to another and brightly colored planet, where the war, if not exactly cheerful, was at least swathed in antiquities that made the whole affair a lot less depressing. French First Army tanks didn't clank or squeak at prescribed speeds, they zoomed like Maseratis in a cloud of fleeing livestock while red pompom sailor hats bounced in the turrets. Officers' messes poured two kinds of wine; smashing Parisian mistresses lounged around regimental headquarters."[2] The racing Task Force (TF) Rouvillois took the enemy by complete surprise as it entered the city at 10:30 that morning. TF Massu, under Colonel Jacques Massu, one of Leclerc's loyalists from the beginning of the war, followed a short time later along with the two other armored columns. Rouvillois' tanks rumbled through the city before startled Germans knew of their arrival and even before the French population realized they had been liberated. As the first tanks and troops stormed into the city the day was beginning like any other for the citizens of Strasbourg who were walking and bicycling along the boulevards and as German officers and French civilians were taking their morning coffee in cafes or waiting at bus stops on their way to work. Suddenly the tanks opened fire on any figure in a German uniform. Wehrmacht officers shopping with their wives were cut down on the streets and strolling Germans were met by machine-gun fire. "It was the most fantastic surprise I ever heard of in the whole war," General Haislip recalled. "The French swept into Strasbourg, going like the wind. The Germans had no idea the French Second Armored Division was within fifty miles of them!"[3]

General Wade Haislip, commander of the U.S. XV Corps, 7th Army. (U.S. Army)

Leclerc's aide, Captain Chatel, recalled the moment the citizens of Strasbourg knew they had been liberated. "I saw the most moving thing – as the townspeople realized we were French many fell to their knees, crying with joy and uttering prayers of thanksgiving."[4] As the French were rejoicing, the Germans, along with French collaborators, were hurriedly evacuating the city over the Strasbourg rail and highway bridges. History records many high-ranking German officers and officials abandoning the city as the French arrived and Wehrmacht soldiers surrendering to Leclerc's troops.

Leclerc's tanks and troops had done what no other American army, including the U.S. XV Corps, had accomplished in nearly six months of bitter fighting through northern France, Belgium and the Netherlands. They had reached the Rhine that flows from Switzerland through France, Germany, and Holland and was the objective of so many battles to the north. Throughout September, October, and much of November 1944, the Germans beat back every Allied attempt to reach the river. Finally, on November 23, Leclerc's tanks captured Strasbourg and Allied troops stood poised on the Rhine's banks and were ready to cross. General de Lattre's 1st Army, that landed on the southern French coast as part of Devers' 6th Army Group, reached the Rhine at Mulhouse several days before Leclerc's troops to be the first Allied soldiers to reach the river.

Once in Strasbourg Leclerc's tanks and troops fanned out to capture bridges over the city's canals and raced to take the highway and railroad bridges that connect Strasbourg with the German city of Kehl on the river's east bank. But some 650 yards short of the Kehl highway bridge Leclerc's men ran into stiff German resistance from defensive positions in nearby apartment houses and in bunkers and antitank barriers at the bridge's entrance. Over the next 48 hours TF Rouvillois made numerous attacks to take the bridges but all attempts failed.

Small bands of enemy soldiers resisted in various parts of the city and German artillery from across the Rhine in Germany opened up. "The big guns of the Siegfried Line began firing sporadically across the Rhine into the center of Strasbourg this afternoon while Brig. Gen. Jacques Philippe Leclerc's armored forces completed the town's liberation by mopping up isolated pockets of Germans in the southern and eastern outskirts," wrote Dana Adams Schmidt of the *New York Times* in an account of the fighting in Strasbourg.[5]

"French tanks meanwhile exchanged fire with German antitank guns across the undamaged road and rail bridges over the Rhine at Kehl. But the Germans still held the bridges and a heavily defended bridgehead of 300 yards on the French side of the river."[6]

With much of the Alsace Plain still contested by both combatants the Germans counterattacked in an effort to cut Leclerc's tenuous supply line that extended through the Vosges into Strasbourg, and to isolate the French armored division from the rest of 7th Army. The Germans came out of northern Alsace in an attempt to encircle Strasbourg and had the misfortune of coming up against the 4th U.S. AD, often considered the best armored division in the American arsenal and commanded by one of the army's fiercest commanders, General John Wood, known as "Tiger Jack" Wood, had led the 4th on a rampage across northern France at the head of Patton's 3rd Army and now was lashing back at the German forces pressuring Strasbourg.

Additional American forces were closing on the Rhine. The 313th Regiment of the 79th ID marched into Strasbourg just behind Leclerc and claimed to be the first Americans to reach the Rhine, while other units of the same division were within eight miles of the river north of the city. One Allied officer who had accompanied Leclerc into Strasbourg described the arrival of the American reinforcements: "We saw the first Americans coming over the hills in single

The 398th Regiment, 100th U.S. Infantry Division advancing in the Vosges Mountains, 1944. (U.S. Army, NARA)

file each side of the road, loping along with that unmistakable long American slouch, how relieved we were! And they continued coming on, all the day long, slouching along, thousands and thousands of them."[7]

Leclerc was being reinforced by troops from the 100th and 103rd U.S. Infantry Divisions and the U.S. 14th AD that had followed the French out of the High Vosges. The new troops fanned out on the plain, the U.S. 36th ID advanced south toward Colmar to support the French drive to the Rhine while the rest of VI Corps moved northeast to cover the right flank of XV Corps which reconnoitered along the west bank of the Rhine to the Soufflenheim–Rastatt area. The Allies had branched out from Strasbourg and now controlled long stretches of the Rhine.

But control didn't mean secure. The troops had to be alert to enemy infiltration across the Rhine that was a regular occurrence and units were posted on the river bank to prevent cross-river attacks. "A few days after arriving in Strasbourg we were detailed to occupy foxholes on the French side of the Rhine River," one infantryman from the 3rd ID remembered. "Facing us on the opposite banks of the Rhine were German pillboxes... From our foxholes we would exchange rifle fire when they strayed into the open from their pillboxes... Behind the German pillboxes was a high pile of coal. Late one afternoon we radioed for artillery and incendiary fire to hit the coal pile. With a few direct hits the pile was in flames. At nightfall, as we left our foxholes, we tried to stay away from the fire's reflection."[8]

In southern Alsace the French 1st Army, which had advanced through southern France on the left flank of 7th Army, scored a huge victory as well. On November 19, three days before Leclerc's tankers reached the Rhine at Strasbourg, General de Lattre's 1st Army reached the river near Mulhouse. In celebration, French artillery lobbed shells at targets in Germany and sent patrols across the Rhine to reconnoiter the enemy's strength and fortifications. De Lattre had long dreamed of reaching the Rhine and pushing across into Germany as the Germans retreated on every front in France. He had more reason than American and British commanders to target the Rhine and Germany. He saw the harshness of five years of German rule in France as his army moved north from the southern invasion beaches and witnessed the enemy's scorched-earth policy in Alsace, burning and pillaging towns and villages as they fell back. Operation *Waldfest* was in retaliation for Resistance fighters' (FFI) attacks on German personnel and caused the destruction of over 7,500 buildings, the execution of 39 captured SAS soldiers (Special Air Service – a branch of the British Army similar to U.S. Special Forces whose members were airdropped commandos sent to assist the Resistance), and death of some 1,500 French civilians. An additional 3,800 civilians were deported as slave laborers to the Reich, two-thirds of whom died.

De Lattre advised Devers of his plan to bypass Belfort and drive on Mulhouse. Devers wrote in his diary: "Then he (de Lattre) could get his army together and force a crossing of the Rhine and drive north through the Black Forest towards Stuttgart." Devers dreamed too. "With a team such as I see here now (French and Americans) I feel sure we will be able to push across the Rhine..."[9]

The French victories in the south of Alsace and the American gains just to the north around Strasbourg confirmed Devers' belief that his army group could continue to roll up the German army in Alsace. He expected the 19th Army to retreat into Germany leaving Alsace completely in Allied hands, and that the French 1st Army, with the help of one or two American divisions, could mop up the remaining German troops west of the Rhine. More important, Devers saw that his next step was to carry out the Supreme

Command's long-standing orders to support 3rd Army in its drive to take the German Saar industrial zone. For Devers this meant crossing the Rhine with the expectation of unleashing Patton's 3rd Army and unhinging the southern end of the German front. Would it bring an end to the war in 1944? Devers thought it just might accomplish that.

Planning

In September 1944, as British and American paratroopers were floating down to do battle in Holland in the disastrous attempt to secure the cross-Rhine bridge at Arnhem, Devers and his staff devised a plan to seize one or more Rhine bridges using paratroopers dropped on the German side. It was a plan that the German High Command feared most, that Allied paratroopers would seize a Rhine bridge long enough for American or British land troops to arrive and hold it. Operation *Market Garden* to seize the Arnhem bridge was the same concept except that the bridge was more than 50 miles behind German lines in an area that was home to several elite German armored divisions.

One element of Devers' cross-Rhine plan was to launch an airborne attack in the Mulhouse–Freiberg area to seize the Rhine bridges and then reinforce it with more powerful ground forces that had reached the west bank of the river.[1] This operation was part of an overall plan being shaped as early as mid-September 1944 by a special board of officers charged with locating the most appropriate location for a cross-Rhine attack by 7th Army. The group studied suitable terrain, climate, and flood conditions, road networks on the German side, and the best environments for communication. Patrols were sent across the Rhine to determine the quality of German defenses and the numbers of enemy troops and had returned with information that the east bank in Germany was lightly defended, if defended at all.[2] Devers, on one occasion, went down to the river's edge in Alsace and greeted a returning patrol to ask about the German defenses on the east bank. "There's nobody in those pillboxes over there, general," was the reply by the patrol leader. From the information brought back by a number of patrols the planning group was able to formulate a viable plan of attack. Engineers would construct pontoon bridges or make use of the foundations of destroyed bridges to erect temporary spans to carry infantry and tanks to the German side of the Rhine.

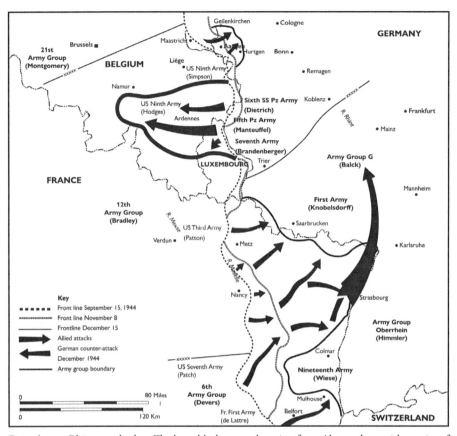

Devers' cross-Rhine attack plan. The large black arrow thrusting from Alsace, along with a series of smaller arrows, depicts the path of 6th Army Group's plan to cross the Rhine at Rastatt and swing in behind the German 1st Army facing General Patton's 3rd Army in Lorraine. Devers, and others, believed that if Devers' attack plan had been approved by Eisenhower, the Germans would have had to contain it with troops allocated to the German armies forming for the German Ardennes offensive, the Battle of the Bulge, thus rendering Hitler's Ardennes offensive moot or dead.

The study group was also planning to employ the French railway system to keep supplies flowing to the troops on the east bank and had organized plans to establish military government in captured German cities.[3] In conjunction with this planning were arrangements with the OSS and 7th Army counter-intelligence to drop agents behind enemy lines to ascertain German strength and the number of combat units located in the area. Included also in the planning were provost marshal groups. It was a solid plan of action that Devers believed would succeed.

By November 23, 1944, Devers was prepared and ready to carry out Ike's orders in previous communiques to his commanders, including Devers, to seize a bridgehead across the Rhine along the southern Allied front line in Alsace. He noted in his diary that once on the east bank with the full force of 6th Army Group a drive "on to Berlin should be easy."[4] His plan was spelled out in great detail in reports to SHAEF planners. Once a sizable force from 7th Army was across:

General Jacob Devers, commander of the 6th Army Group, 1945. (U.S. Army, York, PA. Heritage and Trust)

- North–south movement on the road system "will be fairly easy," and east–west movement would not present problems. Two excellent highways run the length of the Rhine corridor.
- Mechanized units, including tanks should have little trouble maneuvering except at certain narrow bridges.
- There would be some difficulty when encountering swampy land and backwaters and forested areas can be bypassed.
- Observation along the river is generally obscured but local church steeples and some tall buildings will afford good lookouts. A series of hills between Mulhouse and Strasbourg "afford excellent observation."
- The cross-Rhine invading force could face snow to remain on the ground for some time and expect snow to fall three–five days of the month. Summer is relatively hot and dry.

The planning group identified nine locations along the Rhine from Basle, Switzerland, to the area north of Strasbourg that were suitable for landing a corps' size army of American troops. At Huningue–Niffer, Zone A, the southernmost site for the landings, the planning group found that the Germans would have a defensive advantage because of commanding ground overlooking the river. Communications in this zone would be good but cover and concealment for Allied troops would not be good. The one great advantage was that the river is shallowest in this zone.

- Zone A – Huningue–Niffer – Enemy defense of average density. Commanding ground on east bank will increase strength of defenses.
- Zone B – Hombourg–Blodelsheim near Mulhouse would give the enemy commanding ground overlooking the river.
- Zone C – Geiswasser – Mackenheim – Enemy fixed defenses of average strength. Enemy has commanding ground.
- Zone D – Schœnau–Gerstheim – Enemy again has commanding ground. Width of the river plain affords the enemy room for a countcrattack.
- Zone E – Plobsheim–Wantzenau, Strasbourg–Kehl area – Greatest density of fixed defenses.
- Zone F – Gambsheim–Dalhunden – East of Haguenau, greater density of fixed defenses.
- Zone G – Neuhaeusel–Lauterbourg (Rastatt) – Greater density of fixed defenses, enemy has high commanding ground with maneuver room for counterattack, cover is poor and communications not good. However, the zone has the advantage of being the site of a destroyed bridge. Existing caissons (the structures or foundations on which a bridge rests) can be used for a new bridge.
- Zone H – Neuburg–Leimersheim (opposite Karlsruhe) requires two "very difficult" operations.
- Zone I – Sonderheim–Speyer – Tactical considerations are generally as for Zone H.[5]

Some of the materiel required by 7th Army's nine infantry battalions assigned to make the crossing:

(a) three divisional combat engineer battalions (one per division).
(b) four corps combat engineer battalions.
(c) five army engineer battalions, combat.
(d) four army general service engineer battalions.
(e) two heavy ponton bridge battalions.
(f) one Treadway bridge company.
(g) one Bailey bridge company.
(h) four DUKW companies (50 DUKW's each).

The engineering materiel required for the crossing was listed:[6]

    a.   440 M2 Assault Boats with 22 hp outboard motors.
    b.   100 10-man pneumatic boats.
    c.   350 Storm Boats with 55 hp outboard motors.
    d.   2,800 100-foot Heavy Pontoon Bridge units.
    e.   72 infantry support rafts.
    f.   3,440 360-foot Treadway Floating Bridge units.
    g.   350 DUKWs.
    h.   117 130-foot Bailey Bridge sections.
    i.   44 320-foot Bailey Bridge Pontoon units.
    j.   4,000 2-way Fixed Bridge sets.

The stage was set to cross the Rhine and the troops were ready.

CHAPTER 13

Moving Out

There was anticipation in the ranks of the 40th Engineer Combat Regiment the night of November 24, 1944. In the months that the regiment had been on the move the coming day promised to be the most exciting. The regiment was ordered to prepare to move out – to the Rhine. So the rumors were true, the regiment would man the amphibious trucks (DUKWs), string the cables to lead the assault boats across the river, and lay the pontoon bridge and rebuild the existing, destroyed bridge that would carry the jeeps, half-tracks, and Sherman tanks into Nazi Germany. The 40th would lead the way for the fall of the German Reich.

River crossings were not new to the 40th. The engineers had made numerous crossings in North Africa, Sicily, and in Italy. They had cleared ports demolished by the retreating Germans, repaired land bridges for the advancing 7th U.S. Army, and hauled supplies for the fighting men. But never had they relished a job more than what they were about to undertake. The regiment's immediate objective was the area near the French city of Haguenau on the west bank of the Rhine. This was the jumping-off point to the German city of Rastatt across the Rhine in Germany.[1] Rastatt probably was not the best site for a cross-Rhine attack, but it was farther north than most of the proposed crossing spots and closer to the flank of the German 1st Army that was blocking Patton's 3rd U.S. Army from breaching the Siegfried Line and galloping into the Saar industrial zone. Ratstatt also was the center of a road network that would facilitate the American advance.

As the mood at 6th Army Group became more and more positive in October and November because of its advances against the German 19th Army and the cross-Rhine planning, it didn't translate to SHAEF headquarters in Rheims, France. As October turned to November 1944, Eisenhower believed that none of his commanders, Montgomery, Bradley, and Patton, all stalled

U.S. troops look down on dragon's teeth in the Siegfried Line defense along the French border with Germany. (U.S. Army)

at the Siegfried Line, were likely to breach the barrier protecting Germany during the coming winter months. The German army in the west had risen like a phoenix after the devastating battles in northern France in the summer of 1944 where the Germans fell back in disarray to their own border. Allied generals were then taking bets that the German army would collapse in the fall and the war would be over by Christmas. But the enemy bounced back in September, throwing newly formed divisions into the Siegfried Line defenses. Many of the enemy soldiers lacked training, were boys and old men, but a few of them in bunkers and defensive positions could hold up entire battalions.

But Ike would make one last attempt in the fall to break through the German border defenses. He needed to keep the enemy fighting at different points along the line so the Germans couldn't buy time to restore morale and fighting units. Eisenhower also needed to maintain a level of combat in the west for political reasons – to show the American public that the high command intended to end the war as soon as possible and bring the boys home, and to keep the Russians fighting in the east. If the western Allies were to take the winter off the Russians might see it as treachery and make peace with the Germans. Or they might see an opportunity to invade deeper into western Europe and impose Communist government in conquered states. The Red Army was pushing into German territory in East Prussia, was at the gates of Belgrade, and fighting in the city of Budapest, Hungary. Both Finland and Rumania, formerly Allies of Germany, had switched sides and Hungary was not far behind.

Eisenhower planned a series of attacks on the western front in early November in hopes that the Allied armies might still smash through at some point along the Siegfried Line. The objectives were the same, the Ruhr and Saar industrial areas. Devers planned to launch attacks on November 13, three days after Patton began his offensive. The delay was designed to catch the German 19th just as it was shifting reserves to face Patton.

The American attacks in Alsace by 6th Army Group began in the worst possible weather, snow, sleet, rain, and biting cold. Devers described the conditions in a letter to his wife, Georgie. "It was raining cats and dogs and the mud is awful but we have the stuff... The Germans are fighting hard in spots but we are too powerful for them and throw them off balance... I have two breakthroughs, one getting strong and past the difficult mountains (the Saverne Gap) the other just as strong and at the gateway (Belfort). With the blessing of God, we shall do it and bag this terrible world of men called Germans." Devers remained confident that his troops could fight their way to the Rhine and then "jump" the river.[2]

"Our chief problem is to overcome weather," Devers wrote. "If we can do this, we shall break through to the Rhine, clean up, and can then start thinking about how we are going to get across that river. However, always a gambler, I have hopes that we may approach the Rhine so fast that we will be able to get a beach-head over it before the Germans can stop us."[3] And by November 23, after the fall of Strasbourg, Devers' 6th Army Group was ready to cross the Rhine with Haislip's XV Corps at Rastatt and General de Lattre's 1st Army near Mulhouse.

Devers' army was the lone army that made progress that November in horrible weather. Patton's 3rd Army was stalled in Lorraine and 1st Army in Belgium and Luxembourg had also been stopped.

But Eisenhower didn't put much stock in Devers or his army group even as it was now a full-fledged army of some 400,000 men and preparing for a breakthrough. As far as Ike was concerned, 6th Army Group's only job was to protect Patton's right flank. Eisenhower knew that Patch's 7th Army was arguably the best and most combat-tested in the American army with three of the most experienced divisions, the 3rd, 36th, and 45th. It was the French 1st Army, half of 6th Army Group, that Ike considered something of a problem; it didn't always perform well. The 1st Army also had to be equipped and supplied by the Americans and de Lattre was forever complaining that he never had enough gasoline and ammunition to fight effectively. Just about every aspect of the French army was American, they wore American helmets, were clothed in American uniforms, drove in American deuce and a halfs, and fought with American Sherman tanks.

As Eisenhower saw it, 6th Army Group had struggled through the fall of 1944 making slow progress once it neared Alsace. But Eisenhower had to take some responsibility for much of the army group's slow progress. SHAEF in September denied General Truscott's plan to breach the Belfort Gap and advance into Alsace and destroy the German 19th Army. Instead, Eisenhower ordered Patch and Truscott to advance into Alsace through the Vosges, a series of 3,000-foot mountains, forested, rugged, snow-covered in winter, and offering perfect defensive positions for the Germans. It was slogging warfare but Eisenhower believed that if Devers' troops advanced through the Belfort Gap, Patton's right flank would be exposed. He also wanted his armies advancing in a continuous line from the North Sea to Switzerland. If there were to be breakthroughs they would come in the north with Montgomery's or Bradley's army groups. There was also the personal matter to consider, Ike did not like Devers and would never allow Devers the accolades that would come at the expense of Bradley and Patton if 6th Army Group were the first over the Rhine.

Besides, Eisenhower put little stock in 6th Army Group's ability to actually effect a breakthrough and he put even less in its commander. It is unclear exactly why Eisenhower disliked Devers particularly when in the fall of 1944 6th Army Group was advancing, albeit slowly, and all other Allied armies were essentially stuck in place. Several incidents stand out, however, where Devers irritated Eisenhower. When Ike was commander of Allied forces in North Africa in 1943, Devers was the American European commander in London, the position Ike would assume in late 1943 after his command in North Africa. Eisenhower asked Devers for several squadrons of B-24s to be transferred from England to assist in the North African campaign. Devers refused and Ike was furious and never forgave him.

In early 1944, when Eisenhower was Supreme Commander of Allied forces in northwest Europe, based in London prior to D-Day, and Devers was 6th Army Group commander and Deputy Commander in the Mediterranean under General Maitland Wilson, preparing for the invasion of southern France, Ike asked Devers to transfer General Truscott from 6th Army Group in the Mediterranean to the European command to lead a corps in the D-Day landings. Once again Devers refused, knowing that Truscott was universally regarded as one of the best fighting generals in the U.S. Army. Again, Eisenhower was furious.

Tough as the fighting was for 6th Army Group, its troops were on the Rhine by November 23 when the 40th Engineers made ready to advance to the Rhine and send combat troops in to invade Nazi Germany. Excitement about the operation wasn't confined to the engineers. At Devers' 6th Army Group headquarters in Vittel, Alsace, and at Patch's 7th Army HQ, expectation of a cross-Rhine attack was building. At 7th Army a colonel pulled aside Brigadier General Morris W. Gilland and gushed, "I've got fantastic news… We are on the Rhine, we are all prepared and we are going to cross tonight."[4]

"I can hardly believe my ears," the general replied.

CHAPTER 14

Target Rastatt

The 7th Army intelligence was fortunate to interrogate a captured high-ranking German army officer who laid out the best location for the cross-Rhine attack. "He (Lt. Col. Willi Kaiser) claims that there were two logical places to cross, one in the Basle area, a penetration to the East along the Rhine river, subsequently turning north after the Black Forest had been bypassed on the left, and exploiting to the North along the Wutach river axis. The second point of crossing, which he claims to be the better from all points of view, is in the Seltz – Rastatt – Lauterbourg area. This maneuver, which would entail the capture of Karlsruhe and the Maximiliansau beachhead from the South and permit exploitation to the East towards Stuttgart outflanking the Black Forest on the North." This site was chosen for the attack.[1]

Rastatt was also targeted because it controlled a highway network that would facilitate 7th Army's ability to maneuver. But Devers also based his decision on Kaiser's intelligence reports that indicated the German city, and much of the adjacent area along the east bank of the Rhine, was lightly defended or not defended at all. The 6th Army Group was well supplied with information about the enemy around Rastatt derived from Kaiser. But ULTRA also played a role (the breaking of the German code). Like all major U.S. commands, 6th Army Group and 7th Army had an ULTRA officer who disseminated the highly secret information about German positions and strengths derived from the German coding machine named Enigma. The American and British did not trust the French to offer the 1st French Army ULTRA data.

American combat patrols, along with spies sent to infiltrate into Germany, reported about enemy strength on the east bank of the Rhine. General Patch made use of anti-Nazi German POWs who volunteered to parachute into the Rastatt region and report back with information critical to the success of the cross-Rhine attack. According to all reports, the enemy had little on the east bank to stop a determined assault.

Devers planned to send nine infantry and armored battalions across the Rhine with the advanced elements of infantrymen being ferried across in assault boats while the bulk of the attacking force would cross on pontoon bridges constructed by the 40th Engineer Battalion. Devers calculated that the Germans regularly crossed back and forth across the Rhine so it should not be difficult for the Americans to cross back and forth as well.

Once across the American troops were to establish a defensive bridgehead and then advance north along the Rhine from Rastatt to Karlsruhe pushing the enemy back and neutralizing the Siegfried Line that ran along the east bank of the Rhine. At Karlsruhe the Siegfried Line turns sharply west following the edge of the salient where the German Palatinate juts into French Lorraine. The salient was where the German 1st Army was dug in blocking the advance of Patton's 3rd Army.

The 7th Army "could have moved north, advancing up either the west or east banks of the Rhine through Rastatt, Lauterbourg, and beyond, thereby unhinging the German Saar basin defenses and achieving significant operational and strategic goals," (destruction of the German 1st Army and the capture of the Saar industries) write Clarke and Smith.[2]

The chief of staff to SS General Vatterodt, the German commander in Strasbourg, confirmed that a cross-Rhine assault there likely would have seriously disrupted German defenses in the Army Group G sector. Lt. Col. Kaiser stated in a debriefing by 7th Army intelligence officers after his capture that the entire river was virtually unguarded and that opposition to a crossing at any point would be negligible.

But not all the action would take place on the German side of the Rhine. The 6th Army Group's XV Corps would advance up the west bank of the Rhine in Alsace and attack the left flank of the salient to add further pressure on the German 1st Army to retreat, allowing Patton's forces to advance to the Saar.

"The result of a breakthrough as a result of the execution of either or both of these plans, (advance up the Rhine on both banks) and a subsequent exploitation up the valley toward Landau and Germersheim would jeopardize the entire German position to the West," Kaiser reported. "The whole SAAR front would likewise be in the greatest of danger because the important E/W (east–west) communication lines over the Rhine near Karlsruhe, Germersheim, and Speyer would be cut."[3]

Eisenhower and SHAEF also could order the French 1st Army to attack across the Rhine near Mulhouse to draw off more Wehrmacht troops from 7th Army. Devers' forces would also be in position to move south along the east or west banks of the Rhine to help the French 1st Army clear the Alsatian plains around Colmar to eliminate the Colmar Pocket. But Eisenhower had never showed interest in enlisting French support.

Devers' ultimate objective once the German 1st Army was destroyed or forced to retreat was to advance deep into Germany to take Pforzheim and Stuttgart. Continuing this advance, Devers' forces would open the way for an attack into southern Germany and the capture of Nuremberg and Munich.

Kaiser also told 6th Army Group intelligence that a cross-Rhine attack carried tremendous political significance. He noted that the south Germans, particularly in the Black Forest and Baden areas, believed they had been ignored by the Reich's government for years. After the fall of France, the Germans poured tremendous resources into Alsace and the south Germans believed they were poorly treated. South Germany was also largely Catholic and opposed to Nazi rule. To force them to toe the line the government stationed large numbers of SS troops in the region.

"Colonel Kaiser... felt that the crossing of the Rhine in this area would have found South Germany generally sympathetic or at least, apathetic to the operations; and in all probability would have forced a cleavage between North

A U.S. soldier of the 7th U.S. Army being rewarded with a bottle of wine by a French child as he and his unit trudge toward Alsace after the invasion of southern France in August. (US Army)

and South Germany, the consequence of which would have been disastrous to the propaganda pattern of a 'United Germany'."[4]

The Allies had complete control of the air and any cross-Rhine attack could have benefited immensely from tactical air support. Devers had also mustered the necessary supplies for 7th Army and the necessary transport to support the offensive.

CHAPTER 15

Countermanded

As 7th Army engineers were preparing to cross the Rhine, General Eisenhower was visiting his army and corps' commanders on the 6th Army Group front. These trips were fact finders and morale-boosters for the troops. "He was a hero to us," one soldier remembered.[1] Many of the generals, being old friends or colleagues of Ike, also looked forward to these meetings either to renew old ties or to discuss the conduct of the war.

Ike's November 24 tour of the 7th Army front turned out to be more business than social. Fateful, might be the best way to describe Ike's trip into Alsace; it may have had a major impact on the course of the war in Europe. Major Hansen, General Bradley's adjutant, recorded his impressions of the trip as Ike and Bradley made their way first to XV Corps' headquarters to confer with General Haislip:

> He (Haislip) was small and noisy, he greeted us: "For God's sake, sir, … we don't want you. There is a report of an armored breakthrough on the front held by our cavalry." Ike laughed, "Dammit, Ham, you invited me here for lunch and I'm not going to leave until I get it." Brad laughed and Haislip took Ike and him inside.[2]

It was in Haislip's headquarters where Eisenhower was informed of 7th Army's planned cross-Rhine attack. Hansen wrote, Haislip's staff was "busily planning to push their forces farther east, seize beach-heads over the Rhine, and cross into Germany itself." Ike was stunned by what he was told even though for months he had been proposing the exact same operation. Without hesitation he ordered a halt to all the preparations. One major consideration in his mind was that he had just come from a visit to Patton and learned that the 3rd Army commander was stalemated in Lorraine and his lightning advances had been halted by stiff German resistance. According to Clarke and Smith, in *Riviera to the Rhine*, Eisenhower "seemed to have made up his mind that something drastic had to be done to assist Patton."[3]

"Concerned about Patton's flagging offensive, he (Eisenhower) wanted the Seventh Army's axis of attack reoriented from east to the north, through the Low Vosges and against First Army's (German) southern flank. At Haislip's command post, he also issued verbal orders for the XV Corps to change direction immediately and advance generally northward astride the Low Vosges Mountains in close support of the Third Army. Supporting Patton's advance into the Saar basin was to have first priority."[4]

If there was any discussion about Ike's new orders, it went unrecorded and Eisenhower's entourage then moved on to Vittel. Major Hansen continued to record events:

We then mounted again and continued our drive through war torn villages. Everywhere there was evidence of sharp and bitter fighting. The houses were punctuated by bullet holes with gaping boudoirs showing through in holes smashed through the side by cannon fire. Even the road signs announcing the names of the community were punctured by bullets as though French Second Armored had passed through shooting at everything they saw.

Everywhere the rivers were running in swift angry torrents that threatened to wash out our bridges so patiently constructed by engineers who had worked for days in water up to their waists, standing in the chilling river beds with the rains beating in their faces to construct these vital roadways over which we might move our armies to the Rhine.

From the XV Corps we turned down to St. Die, the burned village... of utter desolation. In his retreat or withdrawal the German had applied the torch to the countryside. The town of St. Die was completely gutted, only the empty walls remained with the people huddled in miserable lumps on the street, shielding themselves and their possessions from the driving rain, looking incomprehensible in their square, impassive Alsatian faces.

Once again we climbed into our cars... We drove through the shot-up towns past the trenches the Germans had dug for the winter but never occupied, now standing half filled with water across the rolling hills of that lower section of the front to the resort city of Vittel where Group headquarters is located. Devers lives in the same hotel in which his office is located.

Devers looked happy and boyish as usual and Patch appeared grave, much older and far less jaunty in a Doughboy's uniform with steel helmet, a toga jacket and OD pants. (Patch's son "Mac" had just been killed on the Third Army front.) Last time I saw him (Patch) in England he was a model of uniformity with pink britches and polished boots. There were many photographers about... large groups of them with Devers... including Sid Stoen our old ebullient friend from II Corps.

Brad had a room on the top floor... They had liberal quantities of scotch and we attended a cocktail party where General Frederick, commander of the airborne task force and others were waiting to meet with General Ike. Brad, as usual, clung to the background with his normal great modesty. The party was gay with good conversation and the dinner excellent though without the éclat of our own mess. After dinner, there were wires and whatnot while the Gen. (Bradley) sat up late with Ike and Devers talking late in the wee hours of the morning.[5]

"Talking" is the way Hansen soft peddled this fateful meeting between generals Devers, Bradley, and Eisenhower. The discussions became heated and angry, raised voices could be heard beyond the walls of the conference room. Devers vividly remembered the meeting and the conversation:

> Bradley and Eisenhower came down, had been to my front and looked around, and everybody was pleased with what they saw there. However, they had something on their minds and after dinner we went up on the penthouse of my quarters in the hotel – the Heritage in Vittel – and just General Bradley and General Eisenhower and I were present around that table. In a way, that's unfortunate. I wish I had had another officer there. We talked about the front and pretty soon I discovered Eisenhower wanted me to give up two divisions to Patton's army. He said Patton's army was spread on a thin front and I made some comment. "Well, he's got a tremendous number of troops – and he's in the mud – and he's up against a concrete bastion (Metz). What I'm trying to do here… is loosen this front up so he can move with all those troops he has because I have no reserves of any kind."

"Bradley got into this argument," Devers recalled, "and I got so moved that I let out a secret I had and hadn't told anybody else. I said, 'Well, Ike, I'm on the Haguenau River, moving north. I've got everything in the woods there to cross the Rhine. On the other side there are a lot of pillboxes but they're not occupied. I want to cross the Rhine and go up the other side and come back behind their defenses… We've been up there and saw some of them, we got close up. In that way I will force the Germans to lighten up Patton's front and I think I've got enough that I can hold this corridor. Patton can then move and then I can move. If he can get moving and get across (the Rhine) and going, he's got nothing ahead of him.'"

"Well, I'm thinking of taking two divisions from you and I wouldn't think of crossing the Rhine," Eisenhower replied.

Devers was shocked.

Bradley spoke, "You can't cross the Rhine because those pillboxes are like the hedgerows." Devers knew he was referring to difficulties Bradley's troops had in breaking through the hedgerow country in Normandy just after D-Day. Hedgerows and pillboxes, they weren't the same. Devers knew Bradley was exaggerating.

Devers replied, "Well, Brad, we haven't got any hedgerows. We've got pillboxes and the pillboxes aren't occupied… there's nobody in those pillboxes… The point is that I think we can do this with a minimal force – as a raid, really – and this will cause the Germans no end of trouble because they're in trouble all along my front and at the moment I think I have the initiative."

Devers recalled his anger. "He (Bradley) made me feel that he was attacking my integrity." He turned to Bradley, "Remember, no matter what you think, Brad, I'm not involved with any hedgerows. I'm involved with concrete emplacements and there's nobody in them at this minute."

"How do you know it?" Bradley pointedly asked.

"Because I've been down (to the Rhine) and I saw the patrols," Devers replied angrily. "I talked to some patrols that I found along the river that had just come back from over there (Germany). Also, my intelligence tells me that."[6]

Devers knew that American and French patrols had crossed the Rhine to assess enemy strength. Devers believed that Bradley was finding excuses to deny 6th Army Group the opportunity to cross the Rhine. Bradley had recently been advocating for the invasion of Germany and had stressed the psychological effect of a violation on the German border.

Devers replied to Eisenhower, "Furthermore, Ike, I've always been taught that you always reinforce strength. You never reinforce weakness. This is a basic thing of an aggressive commander. Patch is successful. His divisions are all in good strength. Patton's divisions are under strength. They've had casualties. But we're up to strength – that's the one thing we are."[7]

Eisenhower was angered by the apparent rebuke from a subordinate, particularly from Devers whom he didn't like. But Ike was adamant, no one was going to cross the Rhine at this time.

Devers was stunned as well as infuriated. The 7th Army had an opportunity to cross the Rhine and, if not destroy the enemy's already shattered divisions, force a precipitous withdrawal to relieve the pressure on 3rd Army and unleash Patton. Devers' attack might also force the Germans to withdraw behind the Rhine all along the western front.

Devers later stated. "So I was prepared to do this (cross the Rhine) with a flexible command that we could get back across… anytime we wanted." The 6th Army Group had also prepared its supply services for the crossing.

But Ike refused to budge.

To Devers, Eisenhower's decision was a tragic mistake; he recalled SHAEF's orders: *Advance in zone, secure crossings and deploy in strength across the Rhine.*[8]

These orders applied to all the armies, without exclusion. Post-war official histories confirm the Supreme Commander's commands: "SHAEF directives had provided for the opportunistic seizure of beach-heads across the Rhine during the November offensive by all participants."[9]

The Supreme Command, Forrest C. Pogue's official history of Eisenhower's command in Europe, also agreed with Devers' conclusion; SHAEF orders expected the Allied armies to cross the Rhine if the opportunity arose. "General Hodges was to attempt to establish a beach-head south of Cologne… Meanwhile General Devers' French and U.S. forces were to attempt to cross the Rhine in their sector."[10]

Devers' diary of September 17 reaffirmed his belief in his mission: "General Eisenhower had each of the Army Group commanders give us the situation on his front and then proceeded to discuss the strategy in the future... The Sixth Army Group to be reinforced as soon as possible by at least two divisions and possibly three, to drive across the Rhine and through the Vosges Mountains in order to hold as many troops as possible in the south of Germany..."[11]

An entry two weeks later on October 5: "The Twelfth Army Group is to capture the Ruhr. The Sixth Army Group is to continue its offensive, cross the Rhine and advance to the northeast. All are to push forward to the Rhine River with a view to crossing it at the earliest possible moment."[12]

Devers had every reason to believe that Eisenhower and SHAEF would approve of a forced river crossing. SHAEF directives to 6th Army Group about seizing beachheads were ambiguous as to the exact time and place of a crossing, they were ambiguous to all commanders. They were specific about one aspect nonetheless: *"deploy in strength across the Rhine."*

That is what Devers intended to do. Already the order had gone out to the 40th and 540th Combat Engineer Battalions to begin transporting bridging equipment, assault boats and DUKWs to the Rhine in preparation for an attack across the river. General Patch also wanted to cross the Rhine to forestall possible German counterattacks launched against the west bank from German territory across the river. (Such counterattacks would come five weeks later.)

Devers believed 7th Army was the most aggressive and successful army at that moment on the western front. Patton was "roadbound and nearly halted." The weather was abominable, "flooding, and military traffic were breaking up what few good roads remained passable in Patton's sector, and elsewhere the ground had turned into a sea of mud. Additional factors delaying Patton's troops just to the north of Seventh Army included a high rate of non-battle casualties (with trench foot predominating), lack of infantry replacements, extensive German minefields, a growing shortage of artillery ammunition, and miscellaneous other supply problems." Devers' 7th Army commanders were confident and ready: Haislip "exuberant over the capture of Strasbourg," and "the usually serious Brooks was more relaxed, elated over his success in finally pushing his command over the Vosges and urging all of his scattered forces to continue the pursuit."[13]

"I felt that my army commanders had demonstrated that they were well out in front in carrying out successful operations," Devers wrote. "Both Patch and I were set to cross the Rhine and we had a clean breakthrough. By driving hard, I feel that we could have accomplished our mission."[14]

Clarke and Smith agree. Ike's order meant that "the Seventh Army would lose most of its priceless momentum. Eisenhower's orders required major regroupings within both of the army's corps; as a result, neither corps would be ready to launch another major offensive until 5 December. These delays in turn, would provide the First and Nineteenth Armies [German] with a much-needed respite, during which they would be able to rest and reorganize their units and absorb replacements and materiel."[15]

The 7th Army would remain positioned on the west bank of the Rhine. Patch's army would attack north into the German 1st Army's prepared left-flank defenses in the Siegfried Line. But Devers confided in his diary that he wondered if he and Eisenhower were "on the same team."

Devers believed that Eisenhower should decentralize the command structure to give field commanders more discretion to fight the Germans. Montgomery had often made the same recommendation believing SHAEF was meddling in decisions that should have been made at the division level. Montgomery believed that relations between SHAEF and both General Bradley and Devers were such that SHAEF was now "dealing in detail with the moves of individual divisions inside an army group commander's area, and in telling him in so many words how he should fight his battles," thus "interfering with his prerogatives... The proper method would appear to be that the army group commander should be given a directive and that his conduct of the battle should not be interfered with unless it is seen that his actions are jeopardizing his own or the adjoining armies."[16]

Devers wasn't alone in questioning Ike's strategy. Other high-ranking officers, including Patton, were confounded by Eisenhower's order. Haislip was surprised to learn that the cross-Rhine attack was aborted. "Our orders were to continue across the Rhine and we had all our plans made, all of our equipment ready, and all our materiel on the ground when suddenly, without warning, we were ordered to turn north," Haislip wrote.[17]

Col. Comm, with SOS, Service of Supply, responsible for supplying 7th Army in France, believed the Rhine crossing would have been successful. "There wasn't any great opposition on the other side of the Rhine. There couldn't have been. It was the Black Forest area. I think we could have held a beach-head and then expanded... All I know is that we did not cross the Rhine that night or indeed any other night for a long time to come."[18]

General Garrison Davidson, 7th Army chief engineer, believed a crossing would have been successful and remarked years later:

> On Thanksgiving Day, General Patch had me go to General Haislip's headquarters (XV Corps) at Sarrebourg to outline the plan to him (for a Rhine crossing) and to get his opinion

as to the practicability of such a crossing since his corps is to be given the mission if the idea is approved.

Upon my return to the Seventh Army headquarters that evening (Thanksgiving) I told General Patch that General Haislip considered the idea feasible. The following afternoon Ike, Omar Bradley whom I knew well since he had been tac (cadet company commander) at West Point during my coaching days, then commander of the Twelfth Army Group, and Jakie Devers who had been graduate manager of athletics during my last two years as head coach and then Commander of the Sixth Army Group, and General Patch reviewed the situation with General Haislip at Sarrebourg and after due deliberation Ike decided against trying to cross the Rhine and instead to have Jakie turn the Seventh Army north to help General Patton envelop the Saar.

I wish I could have been in on the high-level meeting for I doubt if anyone there really understood the extent of our engineering preparations and therefore the high probability of a swift crossing in force that could be sustained....

The point of this recitation is that the forethought and planning of the engineer section of the Seventh Army provided the Supreme Allied Commander with an opportunity to depart from his broad front strategy then abundantly apparent to the Germans and make a lightning thrust across the Rhine in the Strasbourg–Rastatt area. Affording him this opportunity seemed to me to be a major contribution to the combat effort.[19]

General Patch also was critical of Eisenhower's decision to halt the Rhine crossing. Patch died in the fall of 1945 shortly after the war ended and never had the chance to explain his thinking about the plan. Patch stated in an article about the operations of 7th Army in France for *Army & Navy Journal*: "Instead of crossing the Rhine north of Strasbourg, for which preparations had been made, the Army was ordered to change directions and advance north astride the Low Vosges and generally parallel to the river."

Patch added, "This change in direction, which forfeited taking a chance on a short cut to the heart of Southern Germany, gave the Germans much needed time; for the breakthrough to Strasbourg had split the German First and Nineteenth Armies and only weak forces were east of the river to contest a crossing."[20]

Patton, who stood to gain from a cross-Rhine attack was surprised at Ike's decision. "I personally believe VI Corps should have crossed the Rhine, but it was stopped by Eisenhower the day he visited Devers."[21] Weigley summed up Patton's attitude, "ever the opportunist, Patton believed that opportunity in war is too rare to be missed."[22]

The 40th Engineer Combat Regiment was waiting for the go-ahead order. Their equipment and the boats were still loaded on trucks. Then came word that the operation was cancelled. "The consensus (among the 40th troops) was that the crossing had been called off. This was confirmed on Monday when the boats were hauled to a rear area dump near Luneville. A PFC quipped that this is where SHAEF should be located."[23]

CHAPTER 16

Ike's Rationale

What was Eisenhower thinking when he countermanded Devers' order to cross the Rhine north of Strasbourg? Devers at that moment was Ike's most successful army group commander having advanced all the way from the Mediterranean to the banks of the Rhine in Alsace. The 6th Army Group had momentum while the rest of the Allied armies along the German frontier were checkmated. Certainly, Patton would have crossed the river and Eisenhower likely would have given him a green light. Patton made it plain that his intention was to cross the Rhine and advance deep into Germany. Patton was aiming at Berlin.

Eisenhower could have taken advantage of the enemy's grave weakness along the Upper Rhine region from Karlsruhe to Basle. The area was suitable for an amphibious assault and it was known to be lightly defended. Ike had earlier stated, "southward, in the Strasbourg region, crossings were practicable." Why not go for the strategic breakthrough and possibly end the war?

SHAEF had been planning for one or more of the Allied armies to breach the Rhine yet Ike rejected Devers' plan out of hand without even considering how it might have been adapted to benefit the Allied cause. He neither asked to see 6th Army Group's plans for the assault nor did he consider talking to 7th Army commanders, including General Patch, and 7th Army chief engineer, Garrison Davidson, both of whom had approved the attack. Ike gave the plan no consideration.

Maj. Gen. F. W. von Mellenthin, chief of staff to German Army Group G commander Hermann Balck, speculated why Eisenhower rejected Devers' planned cross-Rhine attack. "There is no doubt that the Allied strategy was not at a high level at this period of the war; it was rigid, inflexible and tied to preconceived plans. The whole German defense of the Lower Rhine was collapsing, but the Allied leaders would not allow their subordinates to exploit success. Everything had to wait until Montgomery had prepared an elaborate

set-piece attack and was ready to cross the river according to plan. Thus, Field
Marshal Model's (German) Army Group B was given a new lease of life and
the long agony in the West was prolonged for a few weeks." Mellenthin was
referring to Montgomery's Operation *Plunder*, a planned cross-Rhine attack
north of Cologne that included hundreds of thousands of men and vast
quantities of supplies.[1] German General Siegfried Westphal remarked that "a
'Remagen' (the American capture of the Remagen Bridge over the Rhine in
March 1945) in the autumn of 1944 might have landed the Allied vanguard
in a critical position because of the intervention of German divisions which
had been transferred from the Eastern Front at that time, but if the Allied
nerve held, German resistance could have been extinguished in the same year
on both Eastern and Western Fronts."[2]

The *New York Times* shared Devers' belief in the advantages of a cross-Rhine
attack at Rastatt: "The French and Americans will now be able to drive up
the Rhine Valley to threaten the flank of the German armies to the north…
(and) threaten the whole German position west of the Rhine." Why was it
left to journalists to see this possibility?[3]

SHAEF planning was noted for its inflexibility and rigid adherence to
previous planning. General Walter Bedell Smith, Eisenhower's Chief of Staff,
later asserted that the Allied High Command had followed, almost to the
letter, the pre-D-Day plan for the invasion of Europe and Germany's defeat.
"Looking back over the eleven months of fighting which were required to
defeat the German armies, I can say very sincerely that I do not believe a
great campaign has ever been fought before with so little change in its original
strategic plan. The grand strategy for *Overlord* which was agreed upon at
SCAF (SHAEF) before the troops were ever put aboard ship for the invasion
was followed almost without alteration. Tactical changes were made as the
German reaction called for them, but the strategic plan was not changed. I
find no point where I really think it might have been improved in the light
of subsequent knowledge."[4]

But even Smith railed against the supreme command's decisions. "Bedell
Smith… had been struck by the German beach-head across the Rhine at
Strasbourg (during Operation *Northwind*, attack into Alsace in January 1945),
a model of pragmatic assault – pushing a motorized battalion across on barges
and reinforcing it with a division before the Allies could properly react. Why
could the Allies not take a leaf from the German book of warfare and 'if we
find a weak spot in the Siegfried Line we might be able to drive a salient into
the German Line.'" Kay Summersby, Eisenhower's driver and confidant wrote
that Smith complained that "we never do anything bold; there are always at

least 17 people to be dealt with so we must compromise, and a compromise is never bold."[5]

General Bradley got a first-hand look at SHAEF's adherence to the *Overlord* plan after his troops captured the Remagen bridge over the Rhine. Bradley planned to exploit the capture and expand the bridgehead on the east bank. When he announced news of the capture of the Remagen Bridge to General Harold "Pink" Bull, SHAEF's assistant chief of staff, he was stunned by Bull's reaction. "You're not going anywhere down there at Remagen." Bull said. "You've got a bridge, but it's in the wrong place. It just doesn't fit the plan. Ike's heart is in your sector but right now his mind is up north."

Bradley responded angrily. "A bridge is a bridge and mighty damned good anywhere across the Rhine… What in hell do you want us to do, pull back and blow it up?" Bradley asked.[6]

Russell Weigley stated that SHAEF regarded the pre-invasion plan, "as equivalent to inscriptions on tablets of stone…" Ike limited Bradley to four divisions in the bridgehead and advances to no more than 1,000 yards daily to ensure the Americans would not detract from Monty's coming Operation *Plunder* to cross the Rhine in the vicinity of Wesel, some 50 kilometers north of Cologne, for an advance on the Ruhr.

Ike wasn't about to satisfy Devers and 6th Army Group at the expense of his other generals. He saw the Alsace front as a sideshow and explained his thinking in a letter to General Marshall, army chief of staff: "All current 6th Army Group operations are, of course, merely for the purpose of cleaning up Devers' area before turning the bulk of 7th Army northward to undertake, in conjunction with Patton's 3rd Army, 'a converging attack upon the great salient in the Siegfried Line west of the Rhine.'"[7]

Eisenhower also was deterred by international and personal politics and knew instinctively that he had to give Monty and the British a large slice of the glory in winning the war even as their influence waned against growing American might. To unleash Devers would have stolen the thunder from Montgomery and the British but also from Generals Bradley and Patton. The historian Martin Blumenson noted that "Eisenhower favored a broad-front advance with all the Armies continuing to move forward in order to stretch the German defenses and, more significantly, to preserve equal glory for the Allied forces. Triumph had to be shared."[8]

Clarke and Smith speculate that Eisenhower was so worn out refereeing the conflicts between his generals, Monty, the British, Patton and Bradley, that he couldn't deal with Devers taking off on a potentially risky cross-Rhine attack: "Eisenhower may have simply concluded that he was having enough trouble dealing with Montgomery and the British without trying to force through such a major change of direction in the main Allied ground thrust. The political demands of waging a coalition war could not be denied... In the upper reaches of the Allied High Command, there was room for only a few mavericks, like the irascible Patton."[9]

One critical reason why Devers was at odds with Eisenhower related to their concept of how the war should be fought. Devers believed firmly that Eisenhower was too fixated on capturing terrain as a way to end the war rather than destroying the German army. Ike's near obsession with the broad front strategy where all the Allied armies moved in tandem like a giant plow mitigated against bold strikes against the Germans, such as Devers' cross-Rhine attack. The broad front strategy was really one of engaging the enemy in struggles of attrition to grind down the Germans. This was the strategy that played out in the Hürtgen Forest and in much of the action along the Siegfried Line. The overriding intent was not whether the Allies would prevail but how long it would take to achieve victory and how many men would have to die.

Stephen Ambrose noted that "as early as the fourth day of *Torch* (the invasion of North Africa), Eisenhower was showing that as a field commander he would not take chances."[10]

In North Africa Ike was reluctant to attack until he was assured no units would be isolated and cut off. He followed much the same strategy in France where the front moved as one large unit forcing the Germans back. As Ambrose put it, Eisenhower lacked the hard-nosed attributes of a Truscott, "No sonofabitch, no commander." Ambrose added, "At the point of attack, he had shown a lack of that ruthless, driving force that would lead him to take control of the tactical situation and, through the power of his personality, extract that extra measure of energy... He had not forced himself or his subordinates to the supreme effort; there had been an element of drift in the operations he directed."[11]

Ingersoll assessed Eisenhower's leadership qualities. "A Supreme Allied Commander... could have ended the war by Christmas (1944)... But there was no such Supreme Allied Commander. There was no strong hand at the helm, no man in command. There was only a conference, presided over by a chairman – a shrewd, intelligent, tactful, careful chairman."[12]

Eisenhower also had never served in a combat zone and had never experienced combat. To his detractors this was a serious deficiency in that he had never been in the position of a combat commander. Many of his subordinates had been combat tested in World War I. Except for one six-month period between the wars when Eisenhower commanded an infantry company, he served his entire career in administrative positions. It was because he was an excellent staff officer that he was selected to take command in England in 1942 which led to his being named as Supreme Commander in late 1943.

To be fair, Eisenhower had to assume the mantel of political leader as much as commanding general, and it was as a politician that he excelled. In North Africa a substantial portion of his administrative duties was devoted to Allied dealings with the French and in smoothing over animosities between the Americans and British. As Supreme Commander in Europe his abilities as a politician may have saved the British–American Alliance. As American might was in ascendancy as Britain's was in decline, Eisenhower worked assiduously to smooth over the conflicts between the two nations.

Eisenhower had become a creature of the organization and in civilian life he would have been categorized as an "organization man," whose reasoning closely followed the groupthink of the corporation. Many historians have characterized Eisenhower as a CEO rather than the Supreme Commander. The organization had a plan and the plan would be followed. Devers' plan didn't conform to SHAEF's *Overlord* plan and presented Eisenhower with an operation that he saw as thorny with risk. Ike wanted all his armies closed up along the west bank of the Rhine before he authorized any of his generals to establish a beach-head on the east bank.

Was Ike's decision not to allow Devers to cross the Rhine wise and correct? Some would say yes. Other generals, including Devers, Patch, Davidson, Haislip, and even Patton, believed it wasn't. Eisenhower might have ended the war sooner and saved countless American and British lives.

CHAPTER 17

Ike Hates Him

Fate may have also played a role in Eisenhower's decision. Was it providence that Eisenhower was visiting the 6th Army Group that day in November 1944? Or had Eisenhower learned of Devers' planned cross-Rhine assault and timed his visit to thwart his plan? Either way, Devers lost the opportunity to cross the Rhine because Eisenhower disliked him and would not allow him the fame that would follow Devers for being first over the Rhine.

"Ike hates him," Patton noted. "Devers was full of himself… but is a clever man," Patton added.[1] Other generals disliked him as well. General Mark Clark, Devers acknowledged, commander of the U.S. 5th Army in Italy and once subordinate to Devers, "is a bitter enemy of mine." Devers was sometimes described as "clever," but the term was not meant as a compliment, it meant that Devers was considered devious and scheming.

The journalist Ralph Ingersoll said of Devers when he was American European commander prior to Eisenhower: "As an organizer, Devers thought clearly… He had energy, drive, persistence and the courage of his own convictions. He was also naive, unsubtle and inexperienced in high rank…"[2] Eisenhower demeaned Devers' abilities ranking him 24th among a list of 38 generals in the ETO, lower than many of Ike's corps' commanders and Ike had nothing good to say about Devers, asserting that he "was often inaccurate in statements and evaluations… He has not, so far, produced among the seniors of the American organization here [a] feeling of trust and confidence."[3] One problem for Devers was that he was not discreet about his criticisms of Eisenhower's leadership and many of those comments got back to Ike. Ike considered dismissing Devers and replacing him with Patch, but was constrained from doing so for political reasons. Devers was a Marshall protégé and Marshall had followed and encouraged Devers' career from before the war. Devers showed himself to be an able manager of troops and overseeing the development of critical war material. He was largely responsible for the development of the Sherman tank and oversaw the expansion of Fort Knox at the beginning of the war.

Ike and Devers were very different personalities. Ike was rough and tumble growing up, he was not averse to fisticuffs, and he was an outstanding football player at West Point, and today would be considered NFL material. He loved poker, enjoyed his drinks, and did not mind using strong language. He "swore like a sergeant," Stephen Ambrose wrote.

Devers shared none of these traits. He was skinny growing up. The strongest swear words anyone ever heard Devers utter were, "Gol dang it!"[4] He seldom drank and was strongly opposed to the use of bad language.

Patton had nothing good to say about Devers. Patton dismissed him remarking about his lack of combat experience: "Jake, who has at last heard a gun go off in anger, talked in a big way… He now has become a great strategic expert, but he believes everything he is told until someone tells him different." Patton added, "Ike says that Devers is .22 caliber, and I rather concur."[5]

Because 6th Army Group was fighting in the south of France, removed from SHAEF, it was difficult for Devers to establish that trust and confidence from his base. Devers was on the sidelines and this was made clear in a photograph in the army's history, *The Siegfried Line Campaign*, that depicts "The Thirteen Commanders of the Western Front" on October 10, 1944. Devers was one of the top generals yet, symbolically, he is literally out of the picture.

Would Eisenhower have allowed any of his other generals to cross the Rhine in November 1944? Patton would have crossed without telling Eisenhower; Patton believed Eisenhower was a timid commander. Five months later when Patton did cross the Rhine, he did it secretly.

"Brad [General Bradley, Patton's superior], don't tell anyone but I'm across," Patton reported in a telephone call to Bradley on March 2, 1945.

"Well, I'll be damned – you mean across the Rhine?" Bradley asked.

"Sure am," Patton replied. "I sneaked a division over last night. But there are so few Krauts around there they don't know it yet. So don't make any announcement – we'll keep it a secret until we see how it goes."[6]

Eisenhower might have allowed General Truscott to cross had Truscott been in command of 7th Army. He greatly respected Truscott as a military commander and wanted him among his D-Day commanders. But Ike had no such confidence in Devers despite Devers' reputation for proficiency and the obvious successes of his armies through southern France to the German frontier on the Rhine. Truscott and Eisenhower were friends and had previously worked together and Truscott would likely have berated Eisenhower for being too timid.

Eisenhower might have permitted General Patch to conduct a cross-Rhine attack. He respected Patch more than Devers and even considered relieving Devers and replacing him as 6th Army Group commander with Patch.

In the end Devers fell in line; he was the consummate team player once a decision was made and he would carry on without rancor. "I agree we must keep the whole front moving and destroy the Germans west of the Rhine… We shall carry on with energy and drive and force the Siegfried Line…"[7]

But in a letter to Maj. Gen. Persons, on Marshall's staff, Devers implied that Eisenhower should have allowed him to proceed with the attack. "We were poised to dash across the Rhine and then north; and I believe we would have made it for the Germans were completely disorganized; but the weather was so bad that Patton's Third Army had been slowed down to almost a standstill and I think it was wise for us to swing in close to them to break through together."[8]

Devers was confident that he was right and Eisenhower was wrong and that his troops could have destroyed the German 1st Army, had he crossed the Rhine. The German 19th Army would have been forced to evacuate the Colmar Pocket or face being cut off and destroyed as Devers' troops moved south along the east and west banks of the Rhine to interdict their supply lines. But in the army one follows orders. And Eisenhower was the commander.

CHAPTER 18

If Devers Had Crossed

If Devers had crossed the Rhine on November 26, 1944, what would have been the outcome? Would the Germans have contained a 7th Army attack, or would the operation have led to the disintegration of the entire German front from the Netherlands to Switzerland? A team of West Point historians speculated on that very subject.

On the Rhine, opposite the north edge of the Black Forest, Devers was in a position to exploit the most significant gain the Allies had made since crossing the Seine River… Little thought seems to have been given to placing Patton's army under Devers, a logical choice considering how the situation had developed in the south. A speculative question, which requires more scholarly research, particularly in the logistical area, is how a Devers' crossing of the Rhine might have affected events. Even reinforced, 7th Army would have had rough going, but such an advance would have loosened Patton's front and might very well have forced Hitler to unleash the forces he was readying for the Ardennes counteroffensive.[1] Would Patton have been happy if his 3rd Army had been transferred to Devers' 6th Army Group? Surprisingly, he was somewhat amenable to such a move.

Patton may have disliked Jake Devers, but he chafed under Bradley's command. "It would perhaps be a mercy if the latter (Bradley) were gathered (into heaven) – a fine man but not great," Patton wrote in his diary. "I'm not sure that, as the lesser of two evils, it might not be better to be in his (Devers') army group; he interferes less and is not as timid as Bradley."[2]

With or without Patton's 3rd Army, a 7th Army cross-Rhine attack probably would have drawn off German forces from the northern and central sectors of the western front to contain the bridge-head above Strasbourg. When the Americans captured the bridge at Remagen, Hitler stripped forces from other sectors of the front to contain the Americans. The enemy also brought up heavy artillery; aircraft, floating mines, frogmen, and even fired 11 V-2 rockets in attempts to destroy the bridge.[3] Because of the thinning of the German front, Patton broke through farther to the south along the western front and advanced deep into Germany.

Hitler summoned Field Marshal Kesselring to command the German troops attempting to contain the Remagen breakthrough and to drive the Americans back over the Rhine. "Smiling Albert" was an expert in the art of defensive warfare, who had prevented the Allies from advancing out of Italy into Austria and Yugoslavia. But he could not stop the American advance out of the Remagen bridgehead.

Even if Devers' cross-Rhine operation failed, it still would have drawn off thousands of German troops to contain the bridgehead. Devers believed he could easily withdraw his troops from across the river. He reasoned the Germans did it all the time so so could the Americans.

General Patch believed the operation would have offered a short cut into Southern Germany, while unhinging the enemy front. General Davidson certainly believed the attack would have far-reaching impact. "It is interesting to conjecture what might have been the effect of the exploitation of an unexpected crossing of the Rhine in the south in late November or early December and an envelopment of the Ardennes to the north along the east bank of the Rhine. The actual preparation for a crossing in the north provided a perfect cover. (Davidson was referring to Allied plans and German awareness of that plan, to cross farther north to capture the Ruhr.) I have often wondered what might have happened had Ike had the audacity to take a calculated risk, as General Patton would have instead of playing it safe. Perhaps success would have eliminated any possibility of the Battle of the Bulge, 40,000 (80,000 actually) casualties there would have been avoided and the war shortened by a number of months at the saving of other thousands of lives."[4]

Clarke and Smith note "that in the end, Eisenhower's Sarrebourg decision (not to cross) also reinforced Hitler's own plans. First, it confirmed the German leader's decision to adhere to a counteroffensive in the Ardennes instead of switching the main effort to Lorraine and northern Alsace. Second, the decision gave the Germans a free hand to continue the Ardennes buildup, which would proceed without facing the crisis that a Rhine crossing by the Seventh Army would have created."[5]

Devers' cross-Rhine attack would have been a Battle of the Bulge in reverse. Hitler, like Eisenhower, would have had to reinforce the German southern front with troops he didn't have.

A massive Allied war machine was available to support a 7th Army trans-Rhine attack, one, probably two, airborne divisions in reserve, one or two American tactical air forces, and the 8th Air Force Bomber Command with thousands of B-17s and B-24s. The Allies also had thousands of trucks to supply the advance; the same vehicles that poured troops and supplies into the Bulge the weeks later.

The 19th Army's LXIV Corps' commander, General Hellmuth Thumm, noted that "after the fall of Strasbourg I expected a critical danger for the entire upper Rhine front." Thumm feared a cross-Rhine attack and suggested that a lightning attack over the intact Kehl bridges at Strasbourg would have created a "Remagen" in November 1944.[6]

Lt. Col. Kaiser stated that the Americans made a strategic blunder when they failed to take advantage of the Vosges breakthrough to achieve a quick crossing of the Rhine either in the area north of Strasbourg, or north of Basle. He added that Germany's resolve to continue the war would have collapsed if the Rhine had been crossed in November 1944.

A successful attack across the Rhine in November or December 1944 could have galvanized the Russians to increase their attacks to help bring the war to an earlier end. They were determined to reach Berlin before the Allies and any American or Allied advance that threatened to capture the capital was a threat to Russian designs. Berlin was a symbol of Nazi terror and its capture would add to the Soviet's territorial gains in eastern Europe and Germany.

In March 1945 when the Americans captured the Remagen Bridge, Stalin ordered Field Marshal Zhukov to take Berlin immediately to prevent the western Allies from reaching the city first. Zhukov was the commander responsible for seizing Berlin.

"When we were working on the Berlin operation we took into account the actions of our Allies," Zhukov later wrote. He expressed the Russians' fears that "the British command was still nursing the dream of capturing Berlin before the Red Army reached it."[7] The Russians also feared that the Germans would surrender to the Allies or stage a slow retreat in the west to allow the Allies to reach Berlin before the Russians. In March 1945 Stalin demanded of his top generals: "Who is going to take Berlin: are we or are the Allies?" Stalin asked Zhukov and Marshal Konev, both of whom commanded an army preparing to attack Berlin.

"We will," Konev replied.[8]

Negotiations might have been different at Yalta in February 1945 with a successful cross-Rhine attack. A major result of discussions between Roosevelt, Churchill, and Stalin at Yalta was the division of Germany into occupation zones. The final decision of who would get what was not made until February

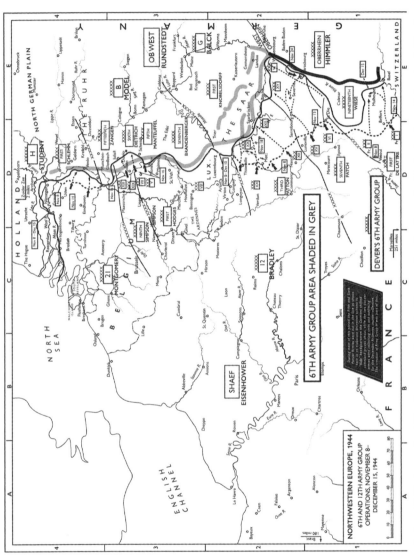

The western front in late 1944 shows the Allies drawn up along the German frontier from the Netherlands to Switzerland. The front would remain virtually unchanged into the late winter of 1944/1945 when the Allied armies finally broke through and charged into Germany to end the war.

1945. Had Devers broken through at Rastatt the western Allies might have controlled more of post-war Germany.

The decision to hold back 7th Army assured that the war of attrition on the western front would continue. The Allies' November 1944 offensives had come to an end with virtually no change in the position of the front line except along the 6th Army Group front in Alsace and on Patton's right flank in Lorraine. The Allies would not start advancing again until late February and early March 1945.

Devers never understood the Supreme Commander's decision. In an entry into his diary on December 19, three days after the Battle of the Bulge began, he wrote, "The Seventh Army was poised to strike across the Rhine in the vicinity of Rastatt, turn north and outflank the Siegfried Line. Events at this moment (the Battle of the Bulge) prove that that maneuver, thoroughly planned and taken boldly, would have been successful."

A quarter-century later Devers was even more convinced of Eisenhower's error in judgment. Asked whether a thrust up the east bank of the Rhine would have cut off the German 1st Army, Devers' reply was terse:

"That's right."

"And wiped out the German Army there?"

"Most of it." Devers asserted also that an attack up the Rhine would have required the Germans "to pull some of those 5th and 6th Armored Armies that were up there (in the Ardennes) and come down and strike us." He then added confidently, "We wouldn't have had the Bulge!"[9]

Lost Opportunity at Valmontone

In May 1944, the war in Italy had reached stalemate. The Allies had landed at Salerno the previous September and advanced north 90 miles to the town of Cassino at the entrance to the Liri Valley through which Highway 6 leads to Rome. At Cassino, however, the Allied advance was halted by the Germans dug in along the Winter Line that was anchored at Monte Cassino, rising 1,700 feet above the valley below. From their vantage point atop the mountain, the Germans observed and blocked by targeted artillery fire all movement in the converging valleys below. The impasse at Cassino was to last five months from January to May with the Americans, British, French, and Polish forces launching a series of failed attack on the German mountaintop fortress.

In an attempt to break the stalemate, in mid-January 1944 the Allies executed an end run behind the German lines in an amphibious landing 40 miles south of Rome near the city of Anzio, and some 90 miles north of Cassino. The objective was to force the enemy's 10th Army positioned around Cassino into a trap. The landing at Anzio by the U.S. VI Corps, that included the British 1st Division, along with a British infantry brigade, however, was quickly contained by the Germans and thus failed to force the hoped-for retreat of the enemy's 10th Army.

The Allied forces tried on several occasions to break out of the Anzio beachhead while the U.S. 5th and the British 8th Armies attempted to break the stranglehold around Cassino by determined and battle-wise German paratroopers. On the fourth attempt, however, in early May 1944, the Allies breached the Winter Line at Cassino and also broke out of the Anzio beachhead. The stage was set for converging Allied armies to trap and destroy the entire German 10th Army as it retreated from Cassino towards the safety of the northern Italy. The 10th was commanded by General Heinrich von Vietinghof, a veteran of the German eastern front against the Soviet Union. As the 5th and 8th Armies drove the 10th northward, VI Corps, commanded by General

Truscott, advanced westward out of the beachhead. Truscott's troops would set up a blocking force to stop the 10th Army where it could be enveloped and destroyed between VI Corps and the Allied forces advancing from Cassino.

The VI Corps, however, failed to spring the trap on 10th Army and Truscott lost a magnificent opportunity to destroy, or at least seriously impair, the 10th's fighting capabilities. The blunder truly was, in many observers' minds, the result of the folly of generals, one general in particular, the commander of the American 5th Army, General Mark W. Clark. As VI Corps positioned itself as the anvil to crush the 10th around the town of Valmontone and await the sledgehammer of the advancing 5th Army, Clark issued a new set or orders ensuring that the 10th would escape destruction.

In late 1943 the Supreme Command under Eisenhower was encouraged to attempt an end run at Anzio because of the success of a similar amphibious attack by British and Canadian troops at the port city of Termoli on Italy's Adriatic coast in October 1943. Designed as a limited, flanking attack, British commandos landed under cover of darkness behind German lines, surprised the enemy, and captured the town and its valuable port. The Germans attempted to throw the invading Brits out but the commandos held with the help of two brigades from the British 78th Division. The assault forced the Germans to withdraw from their natural defense line on the Biferno River and denied them the use of a lateral road running to Naples.

The water-borne assault at Anzio was launched on January 22, 1944, under the command of American Major General John Lucas, with Truscott as his deputy. The operation – code-named *Shingle* – came 10 days after the Allies began coordinated attacks on German lines at Cassino on January 12. The Allied attacks in the south, however, failed to budge the enemy in month-long assaults and resulted in heavy American casualties including the near destruction of two regiments of the 36th ID attempting to cross the Rapido River under withering enemy fire. At the same time an attack out of the Anzio bridgehead by VI Corps also faltered; the troops could not break out and the Germans could not drive the invasion force into the sea. The Allies would try again three more times to breach the enemy defenses in the south and at Anzio before succeeding in May.

Field Marshal Kesselring, who commanded German troops in Italy, was taken by surprise by the Anzio assault. He was so confident that the Allies would not attempt an end-run amphibious landing that he depleted his reserves in the Rome/Anzio area and dispatched two combat divisions to the south to counter the Allied offensive around Cassino. This left a small German force of only one company to guard a nine-mile stretch of coastline around the towns of Anzio and Nettuno. The Allied attacking force came ashore and easily brushed aside the small German garrison as it landed an army of some 36,000 men in the first 24 hours of the assault. The Allied force consisted of the U.S. 3rd ID; the British 1st Infantry Division and 4th Royal Tank Regiment; the U.S. 751st Tank Battalion; the 504th Parachute Infantry Regiment of the 82nd Airborne Division; the 509th Parachute Infantry Battalion; two British commando battalions; and three battalions of U.S. Army Rangers. The U.S. 45th ID and a regiment of the U.S. 1st AD's Combat Command A (CCA), were directed to land as reinforcements once the beachhead was established. By the end of

A German S mine, dubbed "Bouncing Betty" by U.S. troops because when triggered it shot a meter in the air before exploding, often emasculating a soldier.

D-Day at Anzio the assault gave the appearance of a walk through; casualties were almost less than minimal with 13 killed, 97 wounded, and 44 missing.

Kesselring reacted quickly, however, and began sending thousands of troops to encircle the beachhead to destroy the invasion force. By the end of the first week the Allies landed more than 60,000 troops, but their number was matched by the enemy who had gathered at least 70,000 troops to contain the invasion. The German command immediately recognized the threat to communications links to its forces farther south and dispatched the 4th Parachute and Herman Goering Divisions to protect the north–south road systems below Rome. Kesselring also ordered the 3rd Panzer Grenadier and 71st Infantry Divisions to Anzio while Hitler and the German High Command dispatched troops from France, Yugoslavia, and Germany to increase the fighting power of the German forces.

The Luftwaffe was active in support of Kesselring's troops and constantly bombed and strafed the Allied troops and blasted targets of opportunity along the beaches that were packed with supplies. German aircraft also bombed offshore Allied shipping, sometimes sending radio-guided missiles against cargo and combat vessels. Long-range artillery bombarded the Allied troops, some of it coming from massive 11-inch railroad guns, dubbed Anzio Annies, that lobbed shells weighing more than 500 pounds into the bridgehead. No one was safe from the barrages, not even medical personnel treating the wounded several miles from the front.

The Allies answered with fighters and bombers of their own and as many as 2,600 fighter planes, many stationed on the island of Sardinia that had fallen to the Allies in the fall of 1943. The British and American fighters contested the Luftwaffe over the beachhead and flew cover while a fleet of warships provided protective artillery fire and transport vessels delivered supplies to the beaches.

The Allied commander at Anzio, General Lucas, decided as the invasion force landed that prudence was the better part of wisdom against the formidable enemy. He ordered the bridgehead to be expanded and fortified to a distance of some seven miles beyond the coast but that was the extent of the penetration. With no initial enemy opposition, the Allied troops could have advanced farther inland to sever vital enemy rail and road links to the south and advanced into the Alban Hills that overlooked the Allied beachhead and would have deprived the enemy of the panoramic overview of every Allied movement. They might even have advanced to capture Rome, a major transportation hub funneling supplies to Kesselring's troops in the south.

General John P. Lucas

Lucas's decision to delay an advance beyond the Anzio bridgehead was consequential and nearly catastrophic. By the time the Allies were in position to strike out after the landings the Germans had established a ring of fire with troops surrounding the beachhead that Hitler described as the "Anzio abscess." The German troops were part of the enemy's 14th Army of some 70,000 men in 13 divisions commanded by General Eberhard von Mackensen, who had years of command experience in Russia and in Italy. The Germans were notorious for dogged defense regardless of the caliber of the troops and there was little chance an Allied breakout would be successful. When the Allies did attack on January 30, the German defenses were well organized and held.

Kesselring, and Brig. Gen. Siegfried Westphal, Kesselring's chief of staff, were astonished that the Allied Anzio forces had not exploited their unopposed landing with an immediate thrust into the virtually undefended Alban Hills. Westphal later recounted that there were no significant German units between Anzio and Rome, and he speculated that an imaginative, bold strike by enterprising forces could easily have penetrated into the interior or driven straight up Highways 6 and 7 to Rome. Instead, Westphal recalled, the Allies lost time and hesitated. As the Germans later discovered, Lucas was neither bold nor imaginative and he erred repeatedly on the side of caution to the increasing chagrin of both Clark and 15th Army Group Commander, General Harold Alexander.[1]

Lucas had an enviable career in the army compared to several of the top American commanders who had little or no combat or command experience, notably Eisenhower. Lucas graduated from West Point in 1911 and served with the Mexican Punitive Expedition in 1916. In World War I he served with the 33rd Division in France and was severely wounded in 1918. In World War II he initially served as Eisenhower's deputy in North Africa in 1943 when Ike was Supreme Commander of Allied Mediterranean forces. Later he commanded the VI Corps in Italy, the same corps he took to Anzio.

By the end of January Lucas believed he had sufficient reserve forces to initiate an attack out of the beachhead with the ultimate objective of reaching and controlling Highway 6, the roadway 10th Army would take in retreat.

U.S. troops of the 5th Army advance through a destroyed Italian town after the Allied invasion of Italy at Salerno in September 1943. (U.S. Army, NARA)

The 3rd ID launched the attack in the American sector along with the 1st, 3rd, and 4th Ranger Battalions, all advancing against Cisterna, a village about two miles from the Allied perimeter. The 1st and 3rd Rangers were to lead the assault by infiltrating German lines and holding Cisterna until the 4th Rangers and 15th Infantry Regiment, 3rd ID arrived via the Conca–Cisterna Road. At the same time, elements of the 3rd ID advanced on the left to a point above Cisterna while the division's 15th Infantry passed to the right of Cisterna and cut the highway south of town. The 504th Parachute Infantry Regiment attacked along the Mussolini Canal. Unknown to the Americans, their assault was aimed directly at the center of the area where 36 enemy battalions were massing for a February 1 counterattack. After three days of heavy fighting in which the 1st and 3rd Ranger battalions were virtually wiped out, only six men out of a complement of 767 escaped death or capture and made it back to Allied lines. The Rangers were lightly armed and were virtually massacred.

A British attack out of the bridgehead at the same time as the Americans attack ended in failure as well. While initially it gained some success, the Brits, exhausted and stalled by rain-soaked mud, were unable to exploit their successes.

The Germans responded in the first weeks of February with counterattacks that came close to reaching the sea and threatening the existence of the entire bridgehead. The enemy attacks continued until March 4 when their troops had exhausted their ability to continue. The Allies in the beachhead held.

Six weeks of continuous fighting took their toll on the VI Corps' troops who were as exhausted as the Germans. Following the final enemy counterattack on March 4, a three-month lull began and both armies limited their operations to defending their positions while carrying out limited counterattacks and raids. The reinforced German 14th Army, totaling 135,698 troops by March 15, remained on the defensive, awaiting the expected Allied spring offensive.[2]

Lucas's tenure as VI Corps' commander lasted only a month before he was relieved by Clark and succeeded by Truscott. Lucas had been placed in an impossible position at Anzio, given an insufficient number of troops – in his estimation – to advance from the beachhead into the Alban Hills and into Rome, yet told by his superior, General Clark, not to stick his neck out for fear of another Salerno. But Lucas didn't have Truscott's fighting spirit.

Military historian Carlo D'Este wrote: "The square-jawed, rough-hewn Truscott possessed all the qualities needed for success on Earth's deadliest place: the modern battlefield. He had toughness, courage, tactical ability, and professional competence. He also had an intangible [sic] only the best possessed: great leadership under fire – the genius for doing what must be done in the heat and chaos of battle that separates the adequate from the exceptional."[3]

For the next three months under Truscott's command the 6th lived through daily shellings and bombings but the beachhead held in part because Truscott's aggressive and optimistic leadership sustained the Allied forces. Unlike Lucas, who commanded from an underground bunker, Truscott visited every unit under his command, often coming under fire with his troops and he made himself highly visible with his attire, a brown leather jacket, shiny lacquered helmet, and high riding boots. "Looking back upon my experience at Anzio, I think I made my greatest contribution in restoring confidence and morale among all elements of the beachhead," he wrote. "The successful commander must display a spirit of confidence regardless of the dark outlook in any grim situation… And he must patrol the battle area to understand what is happening. Every commander owes it to himself and those under him to be fully informed and acquainted with the terrain and conditions confronting his command, and this necessitates a personal reconnaissance." Truscott later wrote, "Some command posts at Anzio were located in deep caverns or deep shelters insulated from the sounds of battle. These shelters had an unfortunate psychological effect on men who worked in them. Since they depended on situation maps plotted from reports in visualizing any situation, situations often looked much worse than was the case."[4] The underground command post at Anzio was located in a tunnel with a main corridor that ran straight, a quarter of a mile, with a series of ante rooms along the side that housed every conceivable need for the commander, switch board, commanding general's office, and sleeping quarters. The men working in this cavern might as well have been in a stateside headquarters. The war raged above them unseen and unheard.

Anzio became a slugfest that resembled the warfare on the western front in World War I with the troops on both sides living like moles underground and coming into the open only to launch attacks or to go on patrol. Troops took shelter in a crisscross of trenches, in gullies, in canals, and even caves and shellfire-swept rear areas to such an extent that troops often felt safer near the front lines. "What indeed were the Tommy and his comrade-in-arms, the American GI doing in malodorous slots in the ground, fighting for the only time in World War II a battle which, for long weary months, seemed to belong to the trench warfare of World War I; a struggle in the mud, complete with duckboards, trench-raids and patrols in no-man's-land, a miniature Passchendaele in the ear of the Blitzkrieg."[5]

CBS newsman Eric Severeid described life in the bridgehead: "All that the American and British soldiers knew about the history of Anzio-Nettuno was that Nero had been born here and that he had built the original port, whose ruins they glimpsed as they walked from the yawning mouths of their landing craft at the rocky jetty. Many men were apprehensive as they approached the beachhead, for it had an evil name. Soldiers on leave from there had told them frightening stories, and *Life* magazine had informed them that it was unsafe anywhere to pop one's head above ground. This was a considerable exaggeration, for the area was a dozen miles in length and depth, there were many patches of forest, and, while it was true that no spot was immune still the German guns were miles away and smoke screens and haze generally obscured much of our installation."[6] The Allies held the lines but the fighting had been costly – on both sides. The Germans lost an estimated 10,000 men killed, wounded, and missing while the Allied casualties were somewhat less.

The initial failure of the Anzio invasion in January 1944 to break out of the beachhead shattered Allied hopes that the amphibious assault would crack the German defenses and lead to the enemy's defeat in Italy. The man held most responsible for the military failure was Lucas. But Clark must share the blame as well. He was ambivalent about pressing Lucas too hard to immediately advance inland to engage the enemy and move northward to Rome. The crisis at Salerno in September 1943 was well remembered and manifested itself in what has been called the "Salerno Complex," where commanders believed they must construct strong defensive positions before wildly attacking forward.

"Neither General Alexander, nor Clark, put strong pressure on Lucas to press fast and furiously inland – a maneuver which Westphal estimated would have been irresistible on the 23rd. (the day after the landing) All three Allied generals, with the specter of Salerno fresh in their memories, were determined, before all else, to establish a solidly defended beachhead from which they could not be pushed into the sea. Though Clark would speak and send messages to Lucas, calling for aggressive action, he declined, until it was far too late, to impose a sense of urgency upon a subordinate. Had Kesselring been in Clark's place there is little doubt that Lucas would have been made to move inland or make way for his successor."[7] British Prime Minister Winston Churchill, an ardent supporter of the Anzio landings and who had a strong hand in Allied strategy in Italy, expressed his disappointment with Lucas's handling of the operation. "I had hoped we were hurling a wildcat into the shore, but all we got was a stranded whale," he said. Military historian John Keegan pointed out that if Lucas had advanced out of the bridgehead with the intent to capture Rome, his limited force – initially two divisions – might have had some success.[8]

Lucas dismissed Churchill's comments, but other high-ranking Allied military officials, not just the Germans, believed Lucas was too hesitant and should have at least moved into the Alban Hills. One was Devers, deputy theater commander to British General Wilson. Devers visited Lucas on February 16 and "seemed to think that as soon as Lucas was ashore he should have gone on as fast as possible to disrupt enemy communications. He intimated that higher levels thought so and still did."[9]

Lucas disagreed. "Had I done so," he wrote, "I would have lost my corps and nothing would have been accomplished except to raise the prestige and morale of the enemy. Besides," he added, "my orders didn't read that way." He took a swipe at Churchill who followed every detail of the Anzio operation and offered his advice. Referring to Churchill, Lucas wrote in his diary, "the whole affair has a strong odor of Gallipoli and apparently the same amateur was still on the coach's bench."[10] Lucas's reference to "Gallipoli" and "amateurs," was a jab at Churchill who planned and executed the disastrous Allied Gallipoli amphibious invasion of the Turkish Dardanelles in 1915 during World War I.

The Allies always believed the Germans were using the 1,400-year-old Benedictine monastery situated atop Monte Cassino as an observation post to overlook the valleys below. By agreement with the Vatican, neither side would use the monastery for any military reason. The Germans asserted that none of their troops were positioned in the monastery that had been founded in 526 by St. Benedict. St. Thomas Aquinas had once been a monk there. In a tragic mistake, a British intelligence officer is alleged to have misinterpreted an intercepted German radio communication that indicated that the Germans were using the monastery as a lookout post. The mistake was discovered, but too late, as Allied bombers were on their way on February 15, 1943. The planes could not be recalled and the ancient monastery was blown to dust. By one account it was mourned as probably the greatest single aesthetic disaster of the war. Some 250 men, women, and children who had taken refuge in the monastery died in the bombing. The abbot swore ever after that no Germans ever were positioned in the monastery. The irony was that the Germans used the rubble to better effect and held off the Allied attacks for another three months.

During the late winter and early spring preparations were underway on the Allied side for a major offensive that was set to begin in the south around Cassino on May 11 and be joined by the Anzio force, which was ordered to breakout on May 23. The Allied attack in the south began an hour before midnight with a massive artillery barrage along the entire southern front from Cassino to the sea. Then, 25 Allied divisions attacked. The British XIII Corps crossed the Rapido River and established a bridgehead while the Polish Corps assaulted the German redoubt at Monte Cassino. The U.S. 88th Division ran into heavy opposition, but it was the French Moroccan Mountain Division that found an opening in the German defensive line that provoked a gradual

German retreat; the Moroccan advance into the mountainous German defenses threatened the enemy's left flank. Savage fighting ensued along the entire southern front as the Germans were forced back. Faced with encirclement as the Allies progressed, the Germans began a gradual retreat northward, heading into the trap set for them at Valmontone by Truscott's VI Corps.

As the enemy began retreating from Cassino in May to prepared defenses north of Rome the Anzio force began the breakout that was designed by General Alexander's 15th Army Group to strike northwest from the coast and seize Highway 6 that ran north–south and offered the German 10th Army an avenue of retreat from Cassino. If the Anzio troops could cut that escape route the 10th would be trapped between the two Allied forces. Clark confided in his diary at the time: "I believe that if the Eighth Army will attack the Hitler Line in the Pontecorvo region (some 20 miles northwest of Cassino) in the next two days, we hit it north from Pico (10 miles west of Pontecorvo) all-out with all our forces and [from] the [Anzio] bridgehead the next morning, [we] will fold up the German Army in Italy."[11]

The die would seem to have been cast as Truscott thrust his forces out of the Anzio bridgehead confident that he and Clark were on the same page in the operation code-named *Buffalo*, designed to advance west towards Valmontone, reach Highway 6 to cut off the German 10th Army's escape route and force its destruction with Allied ground forces and air power, and as Clark wrote, "fold up the German Army in Italy."[12]

The breakout from the Anzio bridgehead began before dawn on May 23 in an offensive to be carried out in two phases. Phase one was the capture of the town of Cisterna that the Americans had twice failed to capture because of intense German resistance. Situated on a slight rise on the edge of marshland and flat farmland, with its stone buildings and streets, Cisterna was heavily fortified and was surrounded by deep ravines, canals, and irrigation ditches. Extensive caverns lay beneath the town, providing the Germans with ample protection from artillery and aerial bombardment. The town had to be taken and, once neutralized, VI Corps' forces would advance on the town of Cori, then move on to cut Highway 6 at Valmontone.

General Truscott described the opening phase of Operation *Buffalo*:

> Light rain had fallen during the night, but occasional stars now gave promise of a clear day.... We thought we could discern the faint outlines of the Colli Laziali (the volcanic mass known as the Alban Hills) against the northern sky, but we could not be sure. Around us we could see nothing. There was no sight or sound to indicate that 150,000 men were tensely alert and waiting. All was strangely quiet, and in the darkness that precedes the dawn, the whole forward area seemed almost empty.... For better or worse, the die was cast as the minute hands of watches moved slowly towards the zero hour.

0545! There was a crash of thunder and bright lightning flashes against the sky behind us as more than a thousand guns, infantry cannon, mortars, tanks and tank destroyers opened fire. That first crash settled into a continuous roar. Some distance ahead, a wall of fire appeared as our first salvos crashed into the enemy front lines, then tracers wove eerie patterns in streaks of light as hundreds of machine guns poured a hail of steel into the enemy positions.[13]

By the second day of the Anzio breakout VI Corps' forces had cut Highway 7 and neutralized Cisterna, but at a heavy cost. Four hundred seventy-six Americans were killed in the fight for Cisterna that was finally taken May 25. Another 2,321 were wounded and 75 were reported missing. Overall casualties for VI Corps were over 4,000 and the 1st AD lost 100 armored vehicles the first day of the breakout, although many could be salvaged and repaired. The Allies, however, counted 4,838 German POWs, and enemy losses of killed, wounded, and missing soldiers were believed greater than those for the Allies.

The same day, May 25, Allied forces from the south began merging with troops from the beachhead and the pursuit of the reeling Germans was in full force with the enemy 10th Army retreating into preplanned destruction. It was only a matter of time before the Germans would be forced out of Italy, or at least to the Swiss and Austrian frontiers. The war in Italy essentially would be over.

The trap, however, was never closed as originally conceived by both Truscott and Clark and agreed to by General Alexander. Incomprehensively, Clark issued new orders to Truscott in the final hours to turn the bulk of VI Corps to the northwest and march on Rome via Highway 7. Truscott essentially was ordered to abandon the attack toward Valmontone and Highway 6 and forego the destruction of the German 10th Army.

Truscott was "dumbfounded" by the order to change the focus of the VI Corps attack. "I protested that the conditions were not right." He noted that when he and Clark had discussed advancing on Rome through the Alban Hills and Highway 7 it was an option only if the Germans reinforced their forces in the Valmontone area to the extent that the American advance was faltering. But the American thrusts toward the town and Highway 6 were going well. "This was no time to drive to the northwest where the enemy was still strong; we should pour our maximum power into the Valmontone Gap to insure the destruction of the retreating German army," Truscott fumed. "I would not comply with the order without first talking to Clark in person," Truscott wrote in his memoir.[14]

Truscott's observations were confirmed by a later 5th Army history of the events of the day: "Enemy resistance in the Cisterna–Valmontone corridor had collapsed…. Thus far our attack was a superb success."[15] Colonel Hamilton Howze, who commanded an armored task force that led in the attack into the Valmontone Gap, described the chaos and carnage visited upon the Germans by VI Corps on May 25: "There were Mark VI [Tiger] tanks on that road… as well as great quantities of guns and half-tracks. At the head of our column, which was all mixed up with the destroyed German column… there was carnage indeed: bodies and pieces of bodies strewn about among the wreckage and burning vehicles."[16] As a result of Clark's order an army of over 100,000 Germans in as many as 13 panzer, infantry, parachute, and mountain divisions escaped and made their way to safety to fight another day in the defenses of the Gothic Line above Rome. The possibility of a complete victory in Italy was denied – by one man, Lieutenant General Mark Clark.

So why did Clark change the plan when, as Carlo D'Este writes, "Plan Buffalo was succeeding beyond the wildest dreams of its architects. The German defense in the center of the 14th Army (blocking Anzio) had collapsed like a house of cards… The (American) 5th Army was on the verge of a historic victory…. About to win a stunning victory that not only would have gained him the glittering prize of Rome virtually without a fight but have earned him immortality as a great battlefield commander, Mark Clark suddenly dismembered Operation *Buffalo* and in the process sparked a controversy that continues to this day."[17]

Post-war observers maintain that Clark's vainglory lay behind his sudden order to alter the *Buffalo* plan. He wanted to be the first Allied general in Rome. So, instead of continuing the attack east to cut off the enemy's escape route from southern Italy on Highway 6 and then advance on Rome, Clark ordered Truscott to limit the attack toward Valmontone and Highway 6 and pivot large portions of VI Corps to the northwest. This would take the bulk of VI Corps away from Highway 6 and up Highway 7 into Rome, skirting the Alban Hills, strongly defended by elements of the German 14th Army entrenched in there.

Another reason cited for Clark's change of orders was that he was said to be an Anglophobe who frequently questioned the competence of his superior, General Alexander. To boot, Clark feared that the British 8th Army fighting alongside Clark's 5th Army (to form 15th Army Group) in the Cassino region, was in better position to take Rome before 5th Army and to Clark this was intolerable; he was determined that he and the Americans would capture Rome, not the British.

Early in the war Clark was one of General Marshall's favored officers and became one of the most rapidly advanced generals in the U.S. Army – he was skipped two ranks to become a brigadier general in August 1941, several months before Eisenhower and Patton became generals – but he found himself in the spring of 1944 in the sideshow of the Italian campaign. His comrades, Eisenhower, Patton, and Omar Bradley, and numerous other top commanders had departed for England after the North African and Sicilian campaigns to plan for the Normandy invasion. Once the Allies landed at Normandy in June 1944 the world's attention would be on the battles soon to be raging in France and on the generals who led armies and army groups to glory and victory while Italy would be the forgotten campaign.

Clark was also obsessed with the capture of Rome and his image; if the British took Rome before his 5th Army, that image would be tarnished. As a strong practitioner of public relations, he nurtured the persona of a great military leader and he traveled the battle zones with a photographer who knew not to photograph Clark from the right side. All images of the tall general, whom the British nicknamed the American Eagle because of his hook nose, were to be taken from Clark's left side.

D'Este asserts that Clark forfeited his chance at greater military glory because of egotism. "Clark's pride in the Fifth Army and his desire to focus attention on the American contribution to the campaign were one thing, but at a stroke his order to Truscott – an order based more on vanity than military necessity – destroyed any hope of trapping von Vietinghoff's retreating 10th Army."[18]

Truscott also wrote that Clark's vanity and obsession for publicity detracted from his role as a leader of soldiers. "His (Clark's) concern for personal publicity was his greatest weakness. I have sometimes thought it may have prevented him from acquiring that feel of battle that marks all top-flight battle leaders." General Gavin possessed a similar opinion of Clark's leadership abilities. So did German intelligence officers who also perceived a lack of leadership on the part of the "American Eagle."[19]

Despite the evidence of impending victory at Valmontone, Truscott's efforts to change Clark's mind were in vain, he attempted to argue his point in person with Clark but the 5th Army commander made himself scarce and wasn't available either in person or by radio, probably anticipating Truscott's reaction to the change of orders. At a time when his troops were advancing and on the verge of a great victory, it is bizarre, to say the least, that an army commander would not be available to his subordinate commanders for consultation and advice. Reluctantly, Truscott acquiesced to a superior's orders but his subordinate commanders were furious, realizing they were turning away from a stunning victory over the Germans. Truscott later wrote, "Such was the order that turned the main effort of the beachhead forces from the Valmontone Gap and prevented the destruction of the German 10th Army."[20] As D'Este wrote, Clark violated "the military maxim that a commander should always exploit success."[21] Nevertheless, Truscott would have to obey Clark's order or undoubtedly be relieved of his command of VI Corps.

General Alexander also was furious with Clark's change of plan but expressed his anger in typical British understatement:

> When the final battle for Rome was launched the role of the Anzio force was to break out at Valmontone and get across the German main line of supply to their troops at Cassino. But for some inexplicable reason Clark's Anglo-American forces never reached their objectives, though, according to my information later, there was nothing to prevent them from being gained. Instead, Mark Clark switched his point of attack north to the Alban Hills, in the direction of Rome.
>
> If he had succeeded in carrying out my plan the disaster to the enemy would have been much greater; indeed, most of the German forces south of Rome would have been destroyed. True, the battle ended in a decisive victory for us, but it was not as complete as it might have been.
>
> In my plan for the defeat of the enemy I made it clear, in the boundaries I laid down between the British Eighth Army and the United States Fifth Army, that the Americans would enter Rome and the British with their Allies would by-pass it. I had always assured General Clark in conversation that Rome would be entered by his army, and I can only assume that the immediate lure of Rome for its publicity value persuaded him to switch the direction of his advance.[22]

D'Este writes that Clark knew his order to advance via the northwest and Highway 7 was not part of the original plan. To placate Alexander, his superior, Clark instructed his chief of staff, Major General Alfred Gruenther, to inform Alexander that he was making an "aggressive follow-up," of the advance to the Valmontone Gap and Highway 6, but also starting a new attack to the northwest to take Rome. Clark's reasoning was that he was taking advantage of the "impetus of our advance and in order to overwhelm the enemy in what may be a demoralized condition at the present time."[23] Clark could get away with his deception in part because Alexander, at the time, was not fully informed about how well the advance to Highway 6 had progressed. Nor was the British-led Mediterranean command in Africa aware of just how close VI Corps had come to entrapping the German 10th Army. In a cable to the British chiefs of staff, General Wilson accepted the lie that the Valmontone–Highway 6 advance had run into strong resistance from the Herman Goering Division. Truscott had earlier made clear that no such units had arrived at the battle scene.

Clark later defended his decision by asserting that he didn't believe that VI Corps had the strength to carry out its mission to interdict Highway 6 and trap and entire German army – shades of ordering Haislip not to close the gap at Falaise because General Bradley feared Haislip's XV Corps wasn't strong enough to hold off thousands of panic-stricken Germans. Clark also argued that there were too many alternate routes the Germans could have taken to avoid the trap being set by Truscott and his VI Corps. He might have been right. The Germans had an uncanny way of sidestepping disaster and often fought fanatically when the odds against them seemed hopeless.

General Devers, technically Clark's superior as deputy commander of Allied Mediterranean forces and commander of American forces in the region, expressed a negative opinion of Clark in his private diary in September 1944: "Noted two cables received from Clark, [no reference as to the contents] marked personal for me, which show quite well his lack of judgment and tact and indicate definitely that he is not a team player, nor has he the instincts of a fighting general and a gentleman. I shall take no action at this time but my judgment is that I should reprimand him. [Devers was deputy Allied commander in the Mediterranean under General Maitland Wilson.] Both his telegrams are inaccurate and stupid."[24]

It is speculation to assume that the destruction of the German 10th Army around Valmontone would have ended the war in Italy. Nevertheless, it is probable that it could have changed the course of the war there and possibly on the front in France and the Low Countries. The German army was stretched so thin in the west, in Russia, and throughout the Nazi empire, that it is doubtful that the Wehrmacht would have rebounded from the defeat of its 10th Army. A likely scenario is that if the 10th had been destroyed, Kesselring's remaining forces would have withdrawn to northern Italy and the mountain barriers where they would have defended against Allied attacks to reach into Austria and southern Germany. This strategy, of withdrawal to the north, was advanced by Field Marshal Rommel who was charged with developing a plan for the defense of Italy after the Allied landings at Salerno in September 1943. Rommel, as the commander of an army group designed to defend northern Italy, counseled after Italy's surrender in September 1943, that the German army be withdrawn to a defensive line in the northern Apennines with the Austrian Alps as an additional barrier.

Kesselring, on the other hand, favored defending all of Italy, as the Germans did, and Rommel's plan was scrapped in part because Hitler feared that a German withdrawal to Italy's north after Italy's surrender would signal to Germany's reluctant Allies – Hungary, Romania, Finland, Bulgaria, and Slovakia – that they too might see a retreat of German forces from their territory if they surrendered. Retreating from some of the industrial centers in northern Italy would also deprive the Germans of much-needed military materiel. Hitler also knew that a German withdrawal would place Allied air forces within easy striking distance of Germany.

After Valmontone, the war in Italy dragged on for another year consuming men and materiel on the Allied side that might have been useful in other theaters of World War II. With the destruction of the 10th the remainder of German forces in Italy would undoubtedly have suffered severe losses as they retreated north to the safety of northern Italy and the Austrian Alps where they would have taken up defensive positions. To have continued the fight in Italy after such a sound defeat would have required the enemy to gather large formations of hundreds of thousands of troops – men, that after their losses at Stalingrad and Kursk in the east, and in Tunisia in North Africa, they did not have. The Allies could seal the Germans in their mountain redoubts and transfer thousands of Allied troops to France where their numbers and combat experience could have been used to shorten the war by half a year or more. This is what Devers advocated.

On August 21, 1944, six days after American and French troops landed in southern France, Devers wrote in his diary: "As to what should be done insofar as the American troops (in Italy) are concerned, I strongly recommend that they all be withdrawn from Italy as soon as possible. It is a waste of time, effort and manpower. Nothing can be accomplished by arriving on the Po River, whereas a rapid advance in southern France and to the north might well cross into Germany within 45 days." Devers believed that the war in Italy was being poorly managed. Arguing that that the German defenses there were frail "and if they (the Allied command in Italy) had pushed, particularly the 8th Army, as they should have, the Germans would have been disrupted to such an extent that would have had to withdraw all the way into Germany."[25]

Devers realized that Kesselring's strategy, endorsed by Hitler, was to fight a delaying action up the Italian peninsula to tie up hundreds of thousands of Allied troops along with thousands of warplanes and scores of warships to prevent them from being transferred to France, the main theater of war in the west where the fate of Germany would be decided.

Devers and his subordinate, General Patch, were fully aware in August 1944 of the failure at Anzio to immediately break out from the coast and advance inland. Landing near Marseilles on August 15, during the Allied invasion of southern France, Devers' 6th Army Group wasted no time in swiftly leaving the beaches behind and moving miles inland to seize territory and disrupt the enemy's ability to strike back. Unlike at Anzio, 6th Army Group advanced several hundred miles in a month to reach Germany's doorstep.

CHAPTER 20

Escape from *Husky*

Before Arnhem, before Aachen, Wallendorf, Belfort, Rastatt, and before Valmontone, there was Messina. It was at the Strait of Messina, a 2-to-3-mile wide channel between the island of Sicily and the province of Calabria on the Italian mainland, that the British and Americans in August 1943 botched an opportunity to trap and capture thousands of Axis soldiers before they could escape to Italy. Those same elite, combat-tested Germans, along with all of their equipment including tanks and supplies, were ferried across the narrow strait to fight another day as the German 10th Army that nearly threw the Allied landing force back into the sea at Salerno in September 1944. They blocked an Allied advance up the Italian boot and held them for months at Cassino. Had they been captured on Sicily, by their own admission, the Germans would have been forced to retreat into northern Italy. Instead, for nearly two years, they contested every inch of ground from southern Italy all the way to Rome and beyond.

As in North Africa, General Eisenhower was the Supreme Commander of the operation. Could he have taken direct control in Sicily and driven his American and British forces to close off the Messina escape route? The jury is out on this question but there are those who assert that it was in his power to do so.

"The final episode in this (Sicilian) campaign has never received proper attention; partly for want of information, partly because nobody on the Allied side has cared to dwell on it," wrote the eminent naval historian Samuel Eliot Morison in his *History of United States Naval Operation in World War II*. "This is the Axis troops' evacuation of Sicily across the Strait of Messina, an outstanding maritime retreat of the war, in a class with Dunkirk, Guadalcanal and Kiska."[1] Morison, also a retired navy admiral, continued: "Why could not the Allied forces, then absolutely supreme in the air, and with abundant floating gunfire available, have made an all-out effort to stop it?"[2] The reasons are several, among them poor coordination between the various services, ground air and sea, questionable strategic and tactical decisions by the Allied commanders on the ground, the vacillating British General Harold Alexander, growing German experience in retreat in North Africa and in Russia, and British disdain for American combat arms.

The Sicilian campaign began on the night of July 9, 1943 when a British–American armada of 2,590 ships launched a seven-division assault along a 100-mile stretch on the island's southern coast from Licata to the west, to the Pachino peninsula in the east. The Americans landed three divisions around Gela while the British sent in four divisions along with an independent brigade and a commando force farther to the east. Paratroop units from both armies were also dropped inland to help foil enemy counterattacks.

From the outset of the European war and after the successful British and American campaign in North Africa, which ended with the capture of an entire German army of some 275,000 men in Tunis, the Americans opposed any further military actions in the Mediterranean. The Americans, led by Army Chief of Staff Marshall, wanted the Allies to focus their efforts on an invasion in northern France or in northwest Europe as early as 1943, believing that Sicily and the Mediterranean area were sideshows that did little damage to Germany and her Allies.

Prime Minister Winston Churchill in particular, wanted to attack the Germans through the "soft underbelly" of Italy, the Balkans or even through Greece. The Americans believed that in 1943 the British and Americans were not strong enough to go head-to-head with the battle-wise and superbly led German army in France even though France offered the shortest route to Germany. The British also advocated the Mediterranean strategy to maintain the lines of communication with their colonies in Africa, India, and Asia. An Allied thrust through the soft underbelly, likely the Balkans, would also place Allied troops in Eastern Europe to join with Soviet forces pushing east. It might also prevent an expected Soviet takeover of Eastern European nations following the war.

The invasion of Sicily became a compromise hammered out by Churchill and President Franklin D. Roosevelt at the Casablanca Conference in January 1943. The Americans agreed to Sicily as a way to assist the beleaguered Russians by engaging German troops who would otherwise be sent to the eastern front. The operation would also utilize the thousands of combat-tested American troops who had fought in North Africa who would otherwise be idle for many months before being landed in France. But the Americans made it clear they had no interest in invading the Italian mainland afterwards; the focus of the war had to be in France. Thus, Operation *Husky* was born and approved.

The invasion began in the American sector on July 9 with the troops from the 1st, 45th, and 3rd Divisions establishing a beachhead up to four miles deep and 50 miles wide. The following day, however the Americans were severely tested as Italian and German troops, supported by fighter bombers, counterattacked and nearly drove to the sea in several places. The Americans held and the enemy was driven off during fighting so fierce and critical that cooks, clerks, and navy shore personnel were thrown into the breach. Offshore naval gunfire greatly contributed stabilizing the front.

Fearing more enemy counterattacks, General Patton, in command of the American 7th Army, called in 2,000 reinforcements from paratroop units stationed in North Africa who began arriving in C-47 transports on the night of the 11th. Unfortunately, Allied antiaircraft crews on land and at sea in the naval armada mistook the arriving troop carriers as German aircraft and shot down 23 and damaged 37 out of a flight of 144 planes. Some 200 of the paratroopers were casualties, many of them killed or drowned.[3]

Despite this debacle the beachhead was secured and expanded rapidly as the American troops began advancing inland. Because the American 7th Army was regarded by the British as questionable in combat after the ignominious defeat of the 1st ID at Kasserine Pass in Tunisia, the British 8th Army, advancing up Sicily's east coast, took on the bulk of the German forces on the island defending Sicily's east coast and the port city of Messina. Messina was critical to German strategy; it was the port closest to the Italian mainland from which the Axis troops could escape.

The four British divisions in Field Marshal Montgomery's 8th Army found the going up the east coast rough and the advance stalled in the face of German resistance. Montgomery asked General Alexander to permit some of his forces to move westward to broaden attacks on the Germans. Alexander agreed but this meant that the demarcation line between the American 7th and the British 8th Armies had to be moved farther to the west.

The British XXX Corps would move directly across the American 7th Army front while the British XIII Corps would continue the advance along the east coast toward Catania. This would enable the 8th Army to advance on Messina from two directions up the coast and from the interior on the west side of Mount Etna. This meant that the Americans were pushed farther to the west into central Sicily where there was little enemy opposition. To accomplish the repositioning of the 8th Army westward the American 45th ID had to pull up stakes and move to another sector on the American front.

In essence, Alexander was interposing British forces between the Americans and the Germans, allowing the Eighth Army to monopolize the primary approaches to Messina and giving it complete responsibility for the Allied main effort. With its original line of advance blocked, 7th Army was thus relegated to protecting the Eighth Army's flank and rear from possible attack by Axis forces in western Sicily, a distinctly secondary mission.

The change in the front was one of the most important and controversial operational decisions of the campaign. It clearly reflected the British belief that the veteran Eighth Army was better qualified to carry the main burden of the campaign than its junior partner from across the Atlantic.[4]

The change resulted in a loss of momentum for the Allied armies and gave the enemy time to withdraw to a new defensive line between the towns of Catania on the coast, and Enna, inland on the western face of Mount Etna. The German line formed a ring around Etna in rugged, mountainous ground that favored the defender.

General Patton, ever the warrior looking for a fight, was furious with Alexander's new order that would allow the glory of conquering Sicily and Messina to the British. Patton, however, finagled approval from Alexander for a reconnaissance toward the town of Agrigento on the western edge of the American sector. Alexander approved and General Truscott, then in command of the 3rd ID, quickly took the town and was in position to advance northwest towards Sicily's capital Palermo on the island's northern coast. Once Agrigento fell, Patton requested and Alexander approved a 7th Army advance through central Sicily to Palermo and Patton was off and running. Alexander, however, changed his mind and recalled Patton, ordering him to strike due north away from Palermo to protect Montgomery's 8th Army's left flank. Patton received Alexander's new command at 7th Army headquarters but refused to acknowledge it. He replied that the message was garbled in transmission and by the time Alexander cabled a "clarified" message, Patton had advanced through the center of Sicily and captured Palermo. The 7th was ready to strike east along the island's north coast and take Messina before Montgomery and his 8th Army.

With the capture of Palermo a fait accompli, Alexander again altered course and redrew the Allied battle lines that allowed Patton to advance along the north coast. The British 8th Army would continue struggling to dislodge the enemy while advancing up the east coast through Catania. Patton's advance along the north coast would be far more difficult than 7th Army's sweep through central and western Sicily where it met little enemy resistance. To reach Messina the American divisions would have to fight through a series of German strong points built into the rugged Caronie Mountains and Mount Etna's sprawling and fractured terrain.

"Here, in Sicily's rugged northeast corner, the Axis had decided to make its stand. But it was to be only a temporary stand… Berlin had decided to withdraw gradually from the island," writes Martin Blumenson, author of the Army World War history, *Salerno to Cassino*, a history that includes the Sicilian campaign.[5] The Germans fought doggedly along the northern tier of Sicily, buying time for the evacuation. Patton drove his 7th Army with fury to take Messina before Montgomery and show the Brits that Kasserine was behind them and the Tommies weren't the only ones who could fight.

The 7th Army's advance toward Messina was slowed to a crawl at places like "Bloody Ridge," at Santo Stefano and at Troina, a main anchor on the enemy's Etna Line. The battle to take Troina raged for six days on a barren landscape that offered no cover for the attacking troops from the 1st and 9th Divisions. Truscott's 3rd ID also was up against a stubborn enemy at San Fratello. To dodge the defenses there Truscott mounted an amphibious assault to strike behind German lines, but the enemy had largely withdrawn when the Americans landed.

There were reports, never confirmed, that the American Mafia assisted Truscott's amphibious assault on the northern Sicilian coast. As 3rd ID landing craft approached the shore all the search lights ashore went out, one by one, as though they were snuffed out by attackers. Speculation is that members of the Sicilian Mafia doused the lights.

The U.S. Navy reportedly reached out to the American Mafia boss Lucky Luciano to use his Mafia contacts in Sicily to assist in the invasion of the island. The local Mafia reportedly cooperated with American military planners by supplying them with maps of various island harbors and of the coastline. Luciano's deal with the U.S. government was that the mob boss would receive leniency for his assistance. He was serving a 30–50 year prison term for illegal activities. When the war ended, Luciano appealed for a reduction of his sentence, which was granted, but he was exiled to Italy never to return to the U.S.[6]

The American advance ground on, but the prize of Messina would be something of a Pyrrhic victory. The Germans and Italians, commanded by German General Hans-Valentin Hube, had been slowly slipping away from Sicily over the Strait of Messina as an outer ring of combat troops protected the evacuation. On August 17 elements of the 3rd ID entered Messina only to find that the last Axis troops had made their way to the Italian mainland hours before. The fight was over. Nevertheless, for Patton and the Americans the capture of Messina before the British demonstrated growing Yankee prowess and outweighed the escape of the enemy troops to the mainland.

The Americans could now claim equal footing with the British and maybe show them a thing or two.

Was Sicily a win of the Allies? Undoubtedly yes, but with some major caveats. Patton's performance upstaged the British and Montgomery in particular, by driving his 7th Army to Messina before the 8th Army got there. That was an important matter of pride for the Americans after some of their stumbles in North Africa where the British dubbed them "our Italians," comparing them to the poor quality of many Italian troops in that campaign. The Brits conveniently forgot that the Americans were neophytes to warfare in North Africa and were way down on the learning curve. That would change as the war progressed. The British themselves had performed poorly against the Germans in the early days of World War II when the Americans were still neutral. British troops were defeated in France and the bulk of Britain's army barely survived the daring rescue at Dunkirk. The Brits were thrown out of Norway, Greece, and Crete and were nearly defeated by Rommel's Africa Corps in Egypt where American equipment helped turn the tide against Field Marshal Rommel.

In Sicily, the Americans had performed well. The 1st and 9th Divisions had served in North Africa and its troops were now combat veterans. The other U.S. divisions, however, were fresh and untested in battle yet they also performed well. In the first hours of the invasion the Yanks repelled violent counterattacks from a crack German unit and forced the enemy to retreat, later pursuing him over the sunbaked hills and the Americans fought dogged battles to demonstrate that they were a match against the best of the Germans. Ultimately the Americans, along with the British, conquered the island of Sicily.

Sicily proved a training ground for American commanders whose only experience in warfare was in peacetime maneuvers and from book-learning or war college instruction. In Sicily, they learned tactics quickly as well as how to command divisions, corps, and armies. Many of the American generals in Sicily went on to higher commands, Generals Patton, Eisenhower, Middleton, Truscott, Bradley, and Gavin.

Sicily was also a training experience for logisticians and staff planners. "Although overshadowed by the Normandy invasion a year later, Operation *Husky* was actually the largest amphibious operation of World War II in terms of the size of the landing zone and the number of divisions put ashore on the first day of the invasion."[7]

But in Sicily the Allied command failed by not bagging the thousands of Axis troops with all their equipment. "The one great failure of the Sicily campaign – (was) the failure to keep the Germans from successfully evacuating their forces across the Strait of Messina to the mainland." Blumenson writes that an estimated 70,000 Italian troops and 40,000 German troops made their escape along with 10,000 vehicles. (Italy surrendered in August rendering the 70,000 Italian troops useless to the Germans.) Blumenson speculates that had those 40,000 Germans been cut off in Sicily and forced to surrender, the Germans would have probably been forced to retreat to the Pisa–Rimini Line in northern Italy relieving the Allies of months of fighting up the Italian mainland.[8]

The German general who commanded troops on Sicily and later the 10th Army in Italy, Generaloberst Heinrich von Vietinghoff, remarked after the war that the Allies should have entrapped the German troops on Sicily:

> From the German standpoint it is incomprehensible that the Allies did not seize the straits of Messina, either at the same time as the landing [in Sicily] or in the course of the initial actions, just as soon as the German troops were contained. On both sides of the straits, not only in the northeast corner of the island but in southern Calabria as well, this would have been possible without any special difficulty. The battle would then have moved more rapidly and would necessarily have ended with the capitulation of all German and Italian forces on the island.
>
> It has always been regarded by us as a particular stroke of good fortune that this did not happen, and that the German withdrawal across the strait was able to take place without interference. Not only the troops themselves with the full equipment but even a large quantity of Italian motor transport – an item in which the German troops were in dire need – were successfully brought out without material loss.
>
> This fact became of decisive significance to the entire course of the rest of the campaign in Italy. Without the German divisions from Sicily (and they were of especially high combat value), it would have been impossible to put up a continued resistance on the Italian mainland south of Rome.[9]

In short, had the Allies landed in Calabria on the mainland and on the east coast of Sicily around or above Catania, and moved rapidly to control the Strait of Messina, they might have trapped the entire Axis force.

"I cannot avoid the conclusion that the entire *Husky* plan was wrong; that we should have attacked the Messina bottleneck first," Morison writes. "After a severe and prolonged air bombing of both shores, the Western Naval Task Force might have sailed around the western end of Sicily and landed the 7th Army near Milazzo while the Eastern Task Force landed the Eighth Army on both sides of the strait, which was not nearly so strongly defended on July 10 as it eventually became a month later. The enemy, whose dispositions had been made to meet landings elsewhere would have been completely surprised and his communications with the mainland severed. His forces would have been rolled up in western Sicily and forced to surrender, and in less time than it took to push them out of Sicily into Italy, where they lived to fight another day."[10] Morison noted that "more than one" top Allied commander who served in the Mediterranean theater at the time, along with post-war German observers, agreed with his assessment.

But were the American and British Allies ready in the summer of 1943 to risk an amphibious landing near Messina and on the Calabrian coast, and did they have the capabilities to do so? Their German enemies, had they been in the shoes of the Allies, might have carried out such an attack plan with even fewer resources then the Allies had in the air, at sea, and on the land. Field Marshal Erich von Manstein, one of the finest, if not the finest, German general of the war, fought his campaigns on the eastern front and often bested the Russian enemy with inferior forces and equipment but with better tactics. Possibly his greatest campaign was fought in 1942 when he captured the Crimean Peninsula and the city of Sevastapol against a stronger Russian enemy and on a battlefield that offered little protection to his troops. He had no armored forces, the Russians had control of the air and the Black Sea and had troops in greater numbers than the Germans. But von Manstein managed to defeat the Russians nevertheless. Had he been in command of Allied forces in Sicily he undoubtedly would have made a greater effort than the American and British Allies to prevent the Axis evacuation of Sicily. Rommel, in the North African desert, often engaged in risky attacks that paid dividends.

An evaluation of the Sicilian campaign in the U.S. Army history, *Sicily and the Surrender of Italy*, pegs the generals in Operation *Husky* as "cautious and conservative,"[11] hampered by a lack of a unified command; it was led more by a committee from the three services, air, sea, and ground, with Eisenhower as a nominal chairman of the board. Alexander had his headquarters on Sicily, Air Chief Marshall Arthur Tedder was headquartered in North Africa, and Admiral Cunningham maintained headquarters on Malta. "Each of the three services operated independently of the others, doing what it thought best to prevent the evacuation. Since the issue was not presented to the chairman of the board (Eisenhower) the issue remained unresolved and the Germans and the Italians completed one of the most successful evacuations ever executed from a beleaguered shore."[12] The army history notes, in particular, that the Allied air forces in the Mediterranean theater "refused" to work in cooperation with the army and navy during the campaign.

Another example of the lack of coordination between the services was the location of Allied warships. Morison argued that some of the battleships and monitors in the Mediterranean could have fired from protected "over land" positions some 8,000 to 16,000 yards distant from Axis gun positions along the strait. Once these guns were neutralized, cruisers and destroyers could have moved into the strait to silence the remaining guns.

But the Allied navy was absent in Sicilian waters. "The employment of them (Allied warships) during the fortnight when the Strait was swarming with evacuation craft seems, in retrospect, to have been little short of frivolous."[13] A task force was covering Patton's "useless" amphibious end run at Spadafora that came ashore behind enemy lines after the Germans had left. A destroyer was sent to take the surrender of the Aeolian Islands. The U.S. cruisers *Philadelphia* and *Boise* and four destroyers bombarded the towns of Palmi and Gioia Tauro on the strait but failed to interdict Axis ferries heading to Naples. British battleships and cruisers operating in the Mediterranean were in port, and another British cruiser force bombarded targets in the Gulf of Naples. So much fire power trained in any direction but on the Strait of Messina.

Morison speculates that a major deterrent to a bolder plan for the Sicilian campaign was the ghost of Gallipoli, the aborted and disastrous 1916 British campaign in World War I. Its objective was to open a sea lane to its Russian ally and to capture Constantinople (Istanbul), the capital of the Ottoman Empire that had sided with the Germans. Gallipoli was an amphibious attack on the Dardanelles, planned by the then First Lord of the Admiralty, Winston Churchill, and no amount of fire power from offshore British warships could silence Turkish land-based artillery. The British were forced to evacuate their army after suffering huge casualties and severe losses in warships. "The topography of the Dardanelles is roughly similar to that of the Strait of Messina," Morison writes.[14] "Admirals who as junior officers had spent the better part of a year dodging Turkish and German shellfire around the Gallipoli peninsula were not eager to get into a similar scrape again."

The possibility of trapping some 40,000 German troops at Messina in August 1943 offered the Allies an opportunity to seriously damage the enemy in World War II and possibly alter the course of the war. A German retreat to northern Italy would have alleviated the need for a large Allied force on the Italian mainland and thousands of American and British troops could have been transferred to France. The Germans in the winter of 1943 lost over 200,000 men at Stalingrad and another 230,000 troops captured in North Africa that spring. Forty thousand at Messina was not as many but it would have been a serious defeat.

But could Eisenhower have interceded as Supreme Commander and driven his subordinate commanders with an iron fist? A bold Supreme Commander would have done so. Eisenhower's long-time aide, Captain Harry Butcher, claimed, however, that Ike's hands were tied, that the only major decision he could have made was to call off the operation; the day-to-day operations were up to the field commanders.

Field Marshal Kesselring summed up the Sicilian campaign:

> The absence of any large-scale encirclement of the island or of a thrust up the coastline of Calabria gave us long weeks to organize the defense with really weak resources. The slow advance of the main attack and the remarkable dissipation of their other forces over the island allowed the Axis Command to bring sufficient reinforcements into the defense areas as they were threatened. The enemy failure to exploit the last chance of hindering the German forces crossing the Straits of Messina, by continuous and strongly coordinated attacks from the sea and air, was a greater boon to the German Command than their failure immediately to push their pursuit across the straits on 17 August.[15]

CHAPTER 21

Paris Liberated, the War Extended

August 25, 1944, is a day that will be remembered in France for generations, the day Paris was liberated after four years and two months of brutal German occupation during World War II. It was a day for jubilation, for hope and tears; a terrible yoke had finally been lifted. The war now would move through northeastern France and the Low Countries as the Allies pursued the remnants of the German armies that had suppressed Parisians for so long.

It wasn't just Paris that was liberated. Much of France was now free, or would soon be free. Ten days before, American and French armies landed near Toulon and Marseilles in southern France and were advancing rapidly northward up the Rhone Valley to link with the D-Day forces that were driving the Germans back to their own frontier. Vichy France, the German puppet regime that administered much of France south of the Loire River, was finished. Within days, certainly not more than a week or so, the hated Nazis would be driven from most of French soil and France would live again.

It is seldom mentioned – one is reluctant to bring up the issue – but the liberation of Paris had an immense impact of the outcome of the war on the western front, possibly lengthening it by as many as five or six months. But for Paris the war in Europe might have ended in December 1944 instead of May 1945. If that had been the case, thousands of lives would have been saved, American, British, French, and even German. The Americans lost some 57,000 men killed among some 220,000 total casualties from enemy action from December 1, 1944, to the war's end on May 8. Paris's liberation raises an issue to be studied by historians as well as military officers; when engaged in a war against such evil as the Nazis, is it wise to attend to immediate humanitarian needs at the expense of sound military strategy? In short, should Paris have been liberated when it was? Or could it have held out for a few more weeks as General Bradley counseled?[1]

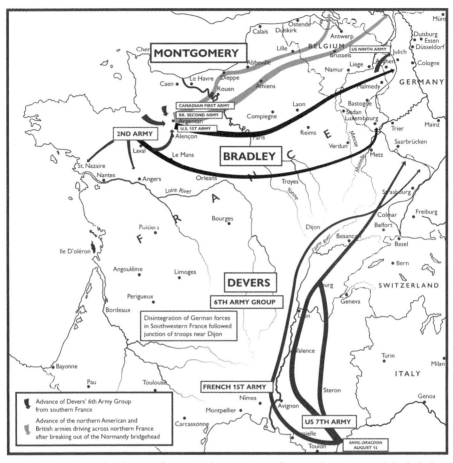

The dark lines depict the advance of Devers' 6th Army Group from southern France while the lighter lines show the advance of the northern American and British armies driving across northern France after breaking out of the Normandy bridgehead.

From the D-Day landings on June 6 until late July 1944, the liberation of Paris and of France was not a certainty. The German 7th and 5th Panzer Armies in Normandy contained the Allies in a narrow bridgehead and the American and British forces struggled fruitlessly to gain ground. Only after seven weeks of struggle were the Americans able to break the German stranglehold and only after the Americans used thousands of heavy bombers and fighter aircraft to pulverize a section of the German front line. The aerial attack, code-named *Cobra*, blew open a section of the German front line and American troops and armor began pouring through into Brittany and eastward towards Paris and the German frontier. Then came the Battle of Mortain and the Falaise Pocket ensued. This was a stunning defeat for the Germans who were forced to retreat in complete disarray leaving as many as 50,000 German soldiers dead, wounded, missing, or prisoners of war. After Falaise the Americans and British had an unimpeded path to Germany.

For weeks in June and July, Parisians waited expectantly for liberation, each day becoming more desperate as their sources of food were cut off in northern and western France as the war raged through these regions. The deprivation caused by the Germans throughout the occupation became worse and there was concern in the Allied camp that the city's residents would face starvation.

It was more than the threat of famine that concerned the Allies. The city was the symbol of France, and for the French, particularly General de Gaulle, as leader of the Free French forces, Paris could not be bypassed. He demanded that the Allies move quickly and drive the Germans out and threatened that if they refused he would order General Leclerc's French 2nd AD, operating with Patton's 3rd U.S. Army, to take matters into its own hands and advance to take the city.[2]

The Allies also feared that the fighting that had broken out in Paris between the Germans and French resistance forces in late August would threaten not only the citizens but much of the splendid architecture and ambiance that makes the city so great and beloved.

SHAEF and Eisenhower were in a quandary over how to deal with Paris. Liberating the city was not part of the Allied High Command's strategic plan; their intent for the British and American armies was to bypass the city and continue the advance towards Germany. The German armies had been so badly defeated that they hardly deserved the name of armies and they would be easy to defeat; they were more a collection of dispirited and decimated units without artillery, tanks, or air cover from the Luftwaffe. The German troops were racing to the Siegfried Line where they hoped to make a stand.

The pursuing Allies were advancing so rapidly across northern France that they surpassed pre-D-Day projections as to where the front would be located in France on certain dates. The Allied armies crossed the Seine River in August, an objective SHAEF planners predicted they wouldn't reach until September. They did not expect to be positioned on the German border until May 1945, by which time the Allied armies had overrun the Reich and the war was ended.

Because the Allied armies were moving so fast and as one huge mass, supplying the troops became a major problem. The Germans held the ports along the English Channel and along the coast in Brittany so all the supplies had to be unloaded over the D-Day invasion beaches in Normandy. As the armies advanced farther and farther from their Normandy base, the more difficult it became to supply them with gasoline, ammunition, medical supplies, and rations. The American army turned to a seat-of-the-pants creation, the Red Ball Express, to deliver supplies to the troops. Red Ball trucks operated on a one-lane loop route out to the front lines and back to Normandy where they would reload for another trip. The Air Force also enlisted C-47 transports and B-24 bombers in the supply efforts, thus diverting entire bomb groups from their primary mission, destroying the enemy's war-making facilities in Germany.

Whether or not to divert supplies for the advance and send vast quantities to the people of Paris after its liberation was a major conundrum. Ike was against it as were many other top American commanders. To supply Paris with food and fuel would divert thousands of gallons of gasoline, and tons of food and other supplies from the front. SHAEF's primary objective was to defeat the German army in the west and force the enemy to surrender and not to feed the French. Bradley as 12th Army Group commander expressed his reservations about supplying Paris after the war.

"I feared that the liberation of Paris might cause our supply lines to snap. Each ton that went into that city meant one less for the front, and G-5 (civil-military operations) of Army Group had estimated the Parisians would require an initial 4,000 tons per day. If Paris could pull in its belt and live with the Germans a little longer, each 4,000 tons we save would mean gasoline enough for three days' motor march toward the German border."[3] Bradley acknowledged a growing food crisis in Paris but added, "In spite of the danger of famine in Paris, I was determined that we would not be dissuaded from our plan to by-pass the city. If we could rush the Siegfried Line with tonnage that might otherwise be diverted to Paris, the city would be compensated for its additional week of occupation with an earlier end to the war."[4] Bradley had the support of SHAEF logisticians who suggested that the supply situation was so critical that the Allies should wait until October before liberating Paris.[5]

> The capture of Paris ahead of schedule aggravated the entire supply and transportation shortage, for the relief requirements of 2,400 tons per day in the days immediately following the city's liberation cut deeply into Allied resources. The needs of Paris presented the 12th Army Group commander with a difficult decision, for with him rested the determination of priority between military and civil supplies. On 27 August he allocated 500 tons of the available airlift to meet the city's relief requirements. Two days later the army group requested the Communications Zone to take action at once to meet at least 2,000 of the 2,400-ton requirement for Paris, and authorized the diversion of 500 tons at the direct expense of military supplies.[6]

By the second week of September the supply situation for 3rd Army remained problematic. Delivery of daily rations, for example, fell below requirements for the men with daily receipts totaling 152,580 rations against the needs of 265,000 men. The shortage was relieved somewhat by the use of captured food stocks the enemy left behind in their hasty retreat, canned and frozen meat and flour for baked goods. Among the captured loot was canned fish that the Americans found tasteless and which army cooks were unable to transform into an acceptable meal.

Aggravating the relief efforts for Paris was that great quantities of the food being shipped in found its way to the Black Market, affordable only by wealthier Parisians. "Black-marketing was regarded as a patriotic enterprise under the German occupation and tended to linger on after the liberation in many parts of France."[7] Additionally, it was discovered that the people of Paris were not in the dire condition that the Allies expected to find once the city was liberated. More important was the restoration of law and order and the return of civil government. Once the Germans left, the city was rife with murder of suspected collaborators.

As the Americans raced on in early September it became impossible to supply every division along the front and gasoline supplies were running low. Six days after the liberation Patton's tanks were running out of gas as they approached the Meuse River in eastern France.[8] Patton began "bellowing like a bull."[9] "I was sure it was a terrible mistake to halt even at the Meuse because we could continue to the Rhine in the vicinity of Worms," Patton wrote.[10] The supplies earmarked for Paris were enough to keep his army advancing. "In addition, Montgomery's 21st Army Group was ordered to deliver 5,000 tons of supplies a day to the city in military vehicles…. Seventy thousand precious gallons of gasoline a day was going to be the price of that effort, one million gallons during the next two vital weeks in the race across France."

So why did Ike and SHAEF relent and agree to supply Paris? It came down to French pride, fear of famine in the city, and the possibility of a bloodbath. De Gaulle had been urging Eisenhower to send forces to liberate the city to stave off bitter fighting between French resistance forces and the German occupiers, and the future French president was concerned about a starving public. But above all, Paris was the center of France and to bypass it would be unthinkable. The Allied command relented and altered its planning and ordered Leclerc's 2nd AD to be the first Allied division into Paris. The American 4th ID followed.

Did the liberation of Paris extend the war by three to six months beyond Christmas 1944? It certainly didn't help. It was the opinion of many high-ranking officers in the late summer of 1944 that the Germans were finished and it was just a matter of time before the western Allies finished them off.

For a variety of reasons the Allies failed to follow through for the kill. Lack of supplies, principally gasoline, is often cited as a reason. The need to rest the armies that had been fighting without reprieve for three months is another. A broad front strategy made it impossible to supply all the needs of all the troops.

With enough gasoline could the Allies have breached the Siegfried Line and advanced to the Ruhr and the Saar and ended the conflict in the west? Enough gasoline was being consumed in the operation to feed and supply Paris that Patton might have been able to make good on his planned objective to drive to the Rhine and cross the river into the heart of the German Reich. Patton made that clear.

Paris' liberation opened something of a Pandora's Box or, more accurately, provided a magnet for the further diversion of critical supplies and materiel from the front lines. At the end of August General John J. C. H. Lee, who commanded SHAEF's supply services in Europe (also known as COMZ, for Communication Zone), ordered his vast headquarters comprising nearly 30,000 service troops – 8,000 officers and 21,000 men – to move from the Normandy sector to Paris, a transfer that required hundreds of trucks and thousands of gallons of gasoline to complete. Once in Paris the supply troops took over accommodation in nearly 300 city hotels. SHAEF headquarters, also situated in Paris, required 25 hotels to house its staff. Lee's organization was larger than a standard American Infantry division, several of which were idle in the Brittany area because they had been stripped of all their transport that was assigned to the Red Ball Express that operated from September to November 1944.

Paris also became the center for the black market that thrived once the war passed by the French capital. Trainloads of supplies were raided and sometimes entire box cars were emptied as devious supply troops routed gasoline, cigarettes, and rations to Parisians who had gone without for five years. At one point in the fall of 1944 front-line troops were receiving only the worst brands of cigarettes; the standard ones like Lucky Strike, Camel, and Chesterfield disappeared into the black market. As winter set in many troops were without adequate winter clothing because of supply debacles. Pilferage was so rampant from trucks, trains, and supply dumps that 12th Army Group assigned five battalions of infantry to act as guards with "shoot to kill" authority. Five battalions equal between 3,500 and 4,000 troops that could have been used on the front lines.[11]

If the liberation of Paris had been delayed by several weeks, the war in Europe might have ended months earlier.

CHAPTER 22

Reserves

By September 1944 the German Army had suffered 3,744,890 casualties in dead, missing, and demobilized soldiers. The ratio of combat effectives in the Wehrmacht's 41 divisions stationed in the west facing the Americans and the British was 2 to 1, favoring the Allies.[1] The enemy's front line protecting the German frontier was stretched to breaking point and in some areas the Siegfried Line was undefended. The ranks of Germany's combat units were filling with older men and boys, some as young as 12, and the country was facing converging Allied armies of millions of men from the east and west with superiority in just about every category. Yet the German High Command seemed always to find new resolve and adequate reserve forces to counter and stave off American attacks along their frontier from Aachen to Metz. What the Germans called the "Miracle in the West," when the U.S. V Corps withdrew from the Schnee Eifel in September 1944 after advancing seven miles into Germany, was pulled off by a motley collection of German reserve forces hastily rounded up and sent into action against the Americans. In contrast, the Americans never seemed able to assemble reserve regiments or divisions to reinforce their potential breakthroughs on the western front. Or if the Allies did dispatch reserve forces to contested areas they were sent to the hopeless fight in the Hürtgen Forest or to the highly risky airborne attack on the Rhine bridge at Arnhem.

At Aachen where the Americans had breached the Siegfried Line the Germans were reeling from the blows of General Collins' attacks into the Stolberg Corridor. In response, the German High Command rushed its 12th ID to the Aachen sector on September 16 to shore up German forces attempting to hold off the Americans. The division had a venerable combat record in Poland and Russia but was destroyed with the bulk of its men killed or captured during the Russians' summer offensive of 1944. The reconstituted division arrived in the west fully equipped with a strength of 14,800 men, "young, healthy, well-trained soldiers," many of them combat veterans.[2]

German General Gerhard Engel, 12th ID commander, was aware of the precarious situation around Aachen when his division arrived: "The Siegfried Line between Stolberg and Zweifall was lost," he later reported. "There yawned a deep gap, of which the Corps did not know any details. Small American task forces had set foot in the pillbox line at Stolberg. There was no connection with Aachen… The equipment as well as the morale of some of the troops flooding back from the West were not in the best of conditions – most of the troops had no fighting qualities at all."[3] The arrival of the 12th ID in the Stolberg Corridor did not assure a halt to the American offensive in the corridor. Engel's men ran into stiff resistance and took terrible casualties in their first two days in combat. In one instance a company-size unit from the 12th was caught advancing in an open field. Observed by an American patrol the Germans were hit by well-directed American artillery, machine-gun, and mortar fire that left 200 enemy troops on the ground either dead or wounded. After four days in the Aachen sector General Engel reported "murderous" losses.

Nevertheless, the arrival of the 12th altered Collins' plan to push through the Stolberg Corridor. "On the American side Collins had noted that the advent of a fresh German division had changed the situation materially. Though the Germans had gained ground in only isolated instances, he recognized that as long as his adversary had reserves and he had none further large-scale advances were impossible."[4]

What would a sizable reserve force the size of Engel's 14,800-man 12th ID have done for the Americans in the Aachen sector? It might have led to a breakthrough to the Roer River and eventually the Ruhr industrial area. General Engel believed the Americans missed an opportunity to advance through the Stolberg Corridor to the Rhine on September 15.

In the V Corps' sector around Wallendorf the situation was much the same as at Aachen. The Americans had no reserves to reinforce the breakthrough by 5th AD and the 28th ID while the Germans, battered and thin as they were, were able to muster enough reserve forces to harass the American advance to the point where U.S. commanders became intimidated and called a halt to their attacks into enemy territory.

As the advance of the 5th AD and the 28th ID carried them to within a few miles of the German communications center at Bitburg, the enemy command realized the severity of the situation, that unless stopped, the American would plow on to the Rhine. After some reluctance to act, Field

Marshal von Rundstedt ordered two infantry battalions and an antiaircraft regiment with 11 antiaircraft batteries to reinforce the LXXX Corps that held that sector of the Siegfried Line. General Otto von Knobelsdorff, the German 1st Army commander, likewise ordered a regimental combat team from the 19th Volksgrenadier Division to bolster the defenses with the remainder of the division to reach the area a day or two later. Knobelsdorff also shortened the LXXX Corps' front to allow greater concentration of the corps' troops in the fight against the Americans.

The reason most often given by the Americans for failure to turn the limited penetration at Wallendorf into a major breakthrough was the lack of supplies, principally gasoline and artillery ammunition, to keep the advance moving forward. Yet V Corps' tanks were reasonably well supplied before the start of the action; they had halted for two days in Luxembourg to restock before attacking into Germany. General Gerow also asserted that the original plan, as outlined to 1st Army commander General Hodges, was for a reconnaissance in force and if it ran into stiff resistance the troops would be called back. The violent German counterattacks were such that Gerow believed 5th AD and the 28th ID could not sustain their advances.

The lack of adequate supplies to keep the advance moving was largely created by SHAEF and Eisenhower's strategy to keep all the divisions and armies moving in a single mass formation. Thus, when a breakthrough did become a possibility, there weren't enough nearby troops and supplies that could be concentrated at any given point to sustain the attack. Gerow had no reserves to turn to other than the divisions in his corps, already in the action, and the bulk of the reserve force he might have requested from SHAEF was, at that very moment, tied up in Operation *Market Garden* and the attack against Arnhem or involved in peripheral action miles away in Brittany.

The Germans on the other hand, were able to scrounge up, literally, odd units here and there to reinforce the thin line of German troops in the Wallendorf sector. "You must realize that the complete confusion of the armies withdrawing from France rendered them useless to us," noted German Major Herbert Buechs, Luftwaffe aide to Generaloberst Alfred Jodl, Chief of the Operations Staff of the Armed Forces High Command. "Therefore, we rushed up all sorts of miscellaneous units deep within Germany. There were fortress battalions, security companies, everything but organized units." And with the German operational philosophy to continually counterattack, those reserve forces were able to halt the American advance and prevent the Allies from penetrating the Wallendorf sector for another six months.[5]

In Lorraine in eastern France in the last days of August 1944, Patton's 3rd Army was racing toward the German frontier with an eye to breaching the Siegfried Line and penetrating all the way to the Rhine. In early September, however, Eisenhower ordered a halt to Patton's fast-moving advance that had driven from Brittany into Lorraine in little more than a week's time. The reason for the halt was a lack of adequate supplies, principally gasoline, to keep 3rd Army tanks rolling. Massive efforts to maintain adequate supplies with truck transport and air delivery from diverted 8th Air Force B-24s proved insufficient.

Nevertheless, it was the Lorraine sector that most worried the German High Command and it was there that they heavily reinforced the front line. If any army was to breach the Siegfried Line the Germans calculated it would be led by Patton. His reputation for lightning advances in Sicily and France preceded him and the enemy began massing reserve troops to meet and stop 3rd Army. The three- or four-day lull in the fighting imposed by Allied supply shortages gave them time to beef up their defenses on the Lorraine front.

"The German High Command made a herculean effort to organize resistance at the scene of the crisis in Lorraine. Reinforcements rushed in from as far away as northern Italy and Denmark, and local commanders worked miracles in reconstituting units that had been cut to pieces in Normandy and during the retreat across France."[6] The German Lorraine front was initially manned by troops of the enemy's 1st Army that had been whittled down to a force consisting of only nine infantry battalions, two artillery batteries, 10 tanks, three Flak batteries and 10 antitank guns after it retreated across France to the Meuse River in late August.[7] If the German 1st Army was going to stop the American 3rd, it needed reinforcements and they began arriving during the first days of September. Advance detachments of the 3rd and 15th Panzer Grenadier Divisions arrived from Italy to be hurriedly thrown into the action. Advance sections of two new Volksgrenadier divisions and a panzer brigade began arriving on September 1. Also dispatched were the 553rd Volksgrenadier Division and the 10th Panzer Brigade with new Panther tanks. The bloodied 17th SS Panzer Grenadier Division that had been pulled from the line for rest and refitting was summoned back to the action when two of its battalions set up an outpost line west of Metz.[8]

The shortage of supplies on the 3rd Army's side gave the Germans a few days' respite from the American advance and gained the enemy valuable time to reset their defenses. "The ensuing lull, as American pressure eased in the first days of September, permitted the 3rd, 15th, 553rd, and the 559th to complete their assembly and assume positions along the 1st Army front."[9]

When Patton's troops resumed their offense in early September they found the going much tougher.

The Germans had halted the Allied advance all along the Siegfried Line in the first weeks of September 1944 and it is safe to say that judicious use of the few reserve forces remaining to the enemy saved their day. The reserves were thrown into the fray in the nick of time and blunted the American advances such that U.S. commanders pulled back into defensive positions. Three months after the battles along the Siegfried Line the Germans put together a quarter of a million men to attack the Americans in the Battle of the Bulge. This, while still maintaining their front all along their lines in the west, while stationing thousands of troops in their occupied territories, and while struggling to contain Russian advances in the east. A month after the enemy attacked in the Bulge another army of at least five corps struck the American and French armies in Alsace in the German operation dubbed Operation *Northwind*. Like the attacks in the Bulge, the Germans were repulsed with severe losses, but how did they manage to find those reserves? Possibly their high command had to be more flexible and imaginative as the war turned against them.

The question remains, why couldn't the Americans, with their abundance of manpower on the continent, release a few battalions or regiments to neutralize the enemy's reserve forces at Aachen or Wallendorf? Some would argue that the Americans were stretched thin all along the western front and had few if any reserves to throw into the fight. But that argument is specious. There were thousands of available troops that SHAEF could have called upon for duty. There were three divisions tied down confining German garrisons in Brittany's ports. Another two divisions, the 6th AD and the 83rd ID were protecting 3rd Army's right flank that stretched from Brittany along the Loire River to Lorraine. These two divisions were guarding against an improbable attack by the German LXIV Corps retreating from France's Atlantic coast and struggling to reach the safety of the Vosges Mountains and the protection of the German 19th Army. Patton wanted those two divisions on his front facing the Germans in Lorraine, not guarding against an improbable attack from the south. Besides, the American air force was monitoring the LXIV Corps from the air to warn the Allied command if the enemy corps was preparing to attack Patton's southern flank. All the while, American fighters bombed and strafed the LXIV along its route of escape.

"Called General Bradley to ask that the 83rd and the 6th AD be moved east and let the Loire take care of itself," Patton wrote in his diary on September 8, 1944. "No supply line runs near it and any enemy who is fool enough to cross it would have to walk. As it is, we have two divisions doing nothing [there] and our future south of Toul is in danger due to the absence of these two divisions. But Bradley said, 'I can't take the risk.' And by saying so takes a much worse risk."[10]

There were other reserve forces that SHAEF might have called on. Even discounting the three airborne divisions earmarked for Operation *Market Garden* and the Arnhem Bridge, there remained two additional airborne divisions still in England, the British 6th AB, and the newly arrived American 17th AB. The 17th arrived in Britain on August 26, 1944, and would have been available for use as a reserve force at Aachen, Wallendorf, or in the Metz sector. The division was considered for use in Operation *Market Garden* but was passed over because it had just recently arrived in the United Kingdom and was considered not yet ready to see action. Nevertheless, it contained the 507th Parachute Infantry regiment that was battle-tested in Normandy, and the division was being held in reserve in case it was needed in *Market Garden*.

Some would say that many of these possible divisions had not seen combat, their troops were green and would have been ineffective if prematurely sent into the front lines. That belies reality. As the war in Western Europe progressed, America's manpower reserves were dwindling to the point that by late 1944 the majority of the new infantrymen were as young as 18 and many arrived in the ETO without adequate training. The same thing was true for the Germans. Yet these young troops on both sides were thrown into the fray. The 106th ID, the Golden Lions, that manned a sector along the front line in the Ardennes just weeks before the Battle of the Bulge, was the first U.S. division manned largely by 18-year-olds. The Germans had resorted to drafting youths as young as 14 as infantry replacements.

Allied casualties mounted as the Allies advanced against the Third Reich and the high command culled service units, antiaircraft units, United States Army Air Force units, and recruited heretofore segregated African-American troops to fill the ranks of the infantry. None had infantry training or had been in combat. It was not uncommon for new recruits sent to infantry units in late 1944 and 1945 as individual replacements to be unfamiliar with infantry weaponry, some, it was reported, who had never fired or mastered the mechanics of an M-1 rifle, the standard American infantry weapon. Thousands of young recruits in officer training at colleges and universities in the U.S., enrolled in the Army Specialized Training Program (ASTP), were pulled from their classes and shipped to Europe as ordinary infantrymen. ASTP was created to draw better educated men into the ranks, mostly infantry, where the level of intelligence lagged behind other branches. Manpower needs late in the war basically ended the program. A future US Secretary of State, Henry Kissinger, trained in the ASTP program.[11] The Germans were able to come up with reserves even after nearly five years of war and millions of casualties. Why couldn't the Americans?

When Eisenhower finally authorized a concentration of forces, it was the ill-conceived *Market Garden* plan with the starting point miles from the penetration point. The Germans were habitually amazed that the Allies never concentrated their forces at a weak point in the German front line.

Hubris undoubtedly played a part in the Allied failure to end the war in 1944. The Allies believed the Germans were defeated and incapable of rebuilding their defenses after their rout in France. In September Allied generals were taking bets about how much longer the Germans could hold out. Gerow, departing on September 18 for Congressional hearings in Washington on the Pearl Harbor disaster, told his men that the war would probably be over by the time he returned to his command in several weeks' time. There was no urgency among Allied generals to force a breakthrough. There was no need to, the Germans would collapse.

Ultimately, the Americans lacked the manpower commensurate with the size of its population because of a strategic decision at the start of the war to limit the size of the army ground forces to about seven and a half million men and number of combat divisions to 90. Those divisions would have to be allocated to a two-front war and most would go to the European Theater. Many would not be fully trained until 1944 and 1945 when American divisions were still arriving in Europe from the U.S. only weeks before Germany's surrender. One armored division served in combat for just one day and several others were in the fight no more than a month or so.

The American army was not much larger than the German army at its height. This as the population of Germany was around 80 million while the population of the U.S. was around 140 million. The thinking among American military and political leaders was that much of the American war effort would go to manufacturing the tools of war: guns, planes, tanks, trucks, and the whole panoply of combat.

CHAPTER 23

Brittany

The Allies may have forfeited a golden opportunity to win the war in 1944 by maintaining large ground forces in Brittany throughout the summer and fall of 1944. Prior to D-Day, Allied invasion planners selected the Breton ports, notably Brest and Quiberon Bay, as sites where the Allies could unload supplies for their armies fighting in the Normandy region. The battle for France was expected to take months before the enemy was driven back to the Seine River and the Brittany ports were chosen for their proximity to the expected battle zones and crucial to the Allied effort to defeat Nazi Germany in the west.

By the second week in September, however, the Allies had advanced across northern France and the Breton ports remained in German hands but were no longer needed. They were farther from the front than the Normandy beaches where all Allied supplies were being offloaded. General Eisenhower canceled the plan to use the ports on September 7 and the Allies turned their attention to capturing and opening the port of Antwerp, some 400 miles from Normandy and the Cotentin peninsula.

An enemy force of nearly 150,000 men was stranded and trapped in the various Brittany ports after the rampaging American armies sealed the peninsula and the various port cities and turned east towards the German frontier. The German troops left behind in Brittany had orders from Hitler to fight to the death to prevent the Allies from gaining their use. Ten thousand German troops remained in St. Malo, 40,000 at Brest, 35,000 at St. Nazaire, 26,000 in Lorient and 22,000 in La Rochelle.

The question for the American command was how to deal with those enemy troops, contain them or attack and destroy them? While numerous, the enemy didn't constitute too great a threat, being spread out in various locations, isolated and lacking effective communication, and immobilized with no tanks and few vehicles. Nevertheless, Generals Bradley and Patton believed they had to carry the fight to the end with several divisions of American troops for reasons of American prestige. General Patton later wrote, "We (Patton and Bradley) agreed that, when the American Army once put its hand to the plow, it should not let go. Therefore, it was necessary to take Brest." Bradley also made the capture of Brest a priority equal to that of 1st and 3rd Armies reaching the Siegfried Line. His order of September 8, 1944, stated: "The Armies will have equal priority in supply *except that the capture of Brest will have first priority.*"[1]

One infantryman who served three months with the 94th ID in the line containing the Germans in Lorient wrote that no one in the division expected the enemy to break out and cause havoc in the Allied rear. "The problem was that there were about 25,000 Germans in Lorient and 35,000 in St. Nazaire." He noted sardonically, "with a successful breakout they might be able to reach a fuel dump, and possibly some badly overcrowded POW enclosures. The danger wasn't great because cornered Germans were not organized combat units."[2]

To deal with these enemy troops an entire U.S. corps, the VIII, commanded by General Troy Middleton, continued the fight to capture Brest and the additional ports at Lorient, St Malo, and Quiberon Bay rather than seal them off and allow them to die on the vine. Thus, some 80,000 Americans in four divisions of General Middleton's corps were engaged in Brittany and unavailable to help force a possible breakthrough at the German frontier.

Generals Bradley's and Patton's decision to continue the fight on the Breton Peninsula did not sit well with some generals. General John P. Wood, commander of the 4th AD, believed that the thousands of veteran American infantrymen and tanks allocated to the capture of Brittany would have been better used to pursue and destroy the battered German 7th and 5th Panzer Armies, then in full retreat from Normandy. Once at the German frontier the Allies, with these additional troops, could smash through the Siegfried Line before the Germans had time to organize a defense. Wood wrote in 1954, "In my opinion, the decision of the high command to move the two armored divisions (the 6th and Wood's 4th) away from the pursuit of a disorganized enemy for the purpose of driving toward the fortress of Lorient and Brest was one of the great mistakes of the war. A rapid move toward Chartres at this time would have been of immense value and I believe it would have greatly shortened the time it took us to arrive on the Rhine."[3] General Middleton, Wood's commander, refused to permit a combat command from Wood's 4th AD to join the pursuit across northern France and ordered him instead to keep his division fighting in Brittany. Middleton later wrote: "I said (to Wood during a visit to the 4th AD headquarters) 'Where's your division?' He said,

'I've got one combat command south of Rennes and another in Chateaubriant [about 20 miles in the direction of Paris]' He had no orders at all to go in that direction. So I had to get him back on track and get him started toward Lorient – much to his disgust. Maybe he was right – I am inclined to believe he was – but those weren't the orders we had had from General Bradley."[4]

The Breton campaign might have been a rare instance where Patton seemed out of character when he refused to let his best armored division commander go for the jugular. Patton wrote in his diary, "'P' Wood, 4th Armored, got bull headed and turned east (towards Paris) after Rennes and had to be turned back to his objectives, Vannes and Lorient. He wasted a day." General Wood would have argued that his boss wasted a day, maybe even a week or months.[5]

General Middleton later questioned the decision of his superiors, Generals Bradley and Patton: "I do know this," Middleton wrote to General Wood after the war, "… Ike and General Bradley could have left a corporal's guard (a small detachment commanded by a lowly corporal) at Rennes (in Brittany) and followed you to Paris, Belgium, etc., and the Battle of the Bulge would never have happened. I presume, however, they felt it was imperative to secure Brest as a port."[6]

Major General Hobart Gay, General Patton's chief of staff, wrote to Wood after the war: "I also remembered the time when I came up to see you in Rennes and you were convinced you were headed in the wrong direction (into Brittany). History proved that you were correct, but alas, wars are not fought on history."[7] The battle for Brittany involved at one time or another five infantry and two armored divisions in what might best be described as Indian fighting and "dragging sieges." Initially the 6th AD was sent racing for Brest to take the city and its port before the Germans could consolidate their defenses in and around the city. The Americans arrived too late and it took a month of siege warfare, infantry attacks, artillery barrages, and aerial attacks to break the enemy's will. The Germans surrendered the city on September 18. In the rest of Brittany American forces surrounded the port cities and clashed here and there with German patrols and infantry units attempting to reach the safety of one of the ports.

The great irony of the battle for Brittany was that once the Germans in Brest surrendered on September 17, 1944, the city and the port were so badly damaged from artillery fire and aerial bombing that the port was declared useless by the Allied High Command and never used for the delivery of supplies. The fighting cost the Americans nearly 10,000 casualties and vast supplies of ammunition, artillery shells in particular, while Patton was urgently demanding more shells for a potential breakthrough of the Siegfried Line some 200 miles to the east. Middleton's VIII Corps was eventually moved to the Siegfried Line area, Brittany continued to tie up U.S. forces until the end of the war, first the 94th ID and later the 6th AD, all ordered to contain German troops at Lorient and St. Nazaire.

The fighting in Brittany also tied down truck companies that could have been better used to supply the armies moving across France to the Siegfried Line. Landing craft (LSTs) and DUKWs (ducks) also delivered tons of ammunition over Brittany beaches that could have been delivered, along with gasoline, to beaches along the Channel coast in the wake of the Allied advance through northern France to supply the Allied armies. The 19th Tactical Air Force was also tied down in Brittany strikes in close support of the ground troops.

In later years, even General Bradley also questioned his decision to expend so much blood and materiel in the fight to take Brest. "We might have been well advised at this point to give up the good fight and let Brest remain in German hands, contained by our newly arriving green infantry divisions or by the French Forces of the Interior, which had ably assisted General Patton's run through Brittany."[8]

If there was good that came out of the Brittany campaign it was that a vast army of German troops numbering nearly 100,000 strong, even after the surrender of Brest, was not available to the enemy to stop the Allied advance from Normandy to the Siegfried Line. In fact, the Germans intentionally left behind some 200,000 men in the various Breton and Channel ports, the British Channel Islands, and ports in Belgium and Holland.

The British military historian B. H. Liddell Hart said of the Breton campaign: "Only a few scattered German battalions lay in the 90-mile wide corridor between that point (Brittany) and the Loire. So American spearheads could have driven eastward unopposed. But the Allied High Command threw away the best chance of exploiting this great opportunity by sticking to the outdated pre-invasion programme, in which a westward move to capture Brittany ports was to be the next step."[9]

Whose decision was more ill-advised, SHAEF for expending so much blood to capture the Breton ports, or Hitler's to tie up enough troops left in the Breton and Channel ports to form a complete army?

CHAPTER 24

Lorraine: Patton's Supply Dearth – Myth or Reality

Could Patton have breached the Siegfried Line attacking from Lorraine in September 1944, crossed the Rhine and advanced to capture the Saar industrial area, then turned east and drive deep into Germany? Historical interpretations relating to this possibility are confusing and often contradictory because of the multitude of orders, verbal and written, issued at the time, and by the differing recollections of the various American army commanders, General Bradley, Field Marshal Montgomery, General Walter Bedell Smith, Eisenhower's chief of staff, and Eisenhower himself. And, of course, Patton offered his perspective on the controversy.

The standard explanation for 3rd Army's failure to reach the Saar in September 1944 is that 3rd Army's rapid pursuit of the enemy into Lorraine in Eastern France was halted for several days in late August and early September by the scarcity of gasoline. There was plenty of gas, ammunition, and equipment in the Normandy area where supplies were building up but because the Germans controlled the Channel ports, all supplies until the fall of 1944 came over the D-Day beaches and had to be trucked to the ever-expanding and distant front.

Patton blamed Ike for diverting his much-needed gasoline to Montgomery's 21st Army Group and the American 1st Army advancing north of the Ardennes. Patton knew that the high command's aim was to carry the advance into Germany along a more northerly axis through Belgium and Luxembourg and to supply Operation *Market Garden*, the attack on Arnhem. The principal objective of the Allied advance from the beginning of the campaign was the Ruhr industrial area, north of the Ardennes, while Patton's zone of operation was south of that forested region. Histories of the war often suggest that had Patton been given the green light and a greater abundance of gasoline, he would have advanced deep into the Reich and possibly ended the war. The

Germans were in total disarray all along the Siegfried Line and an advance to the Rhine and beyond seemed possible, even likely.

Probably no one will unravel all the facts about Patton's failure to advance to the Rhine during the period from late August 1944 to mid-September on the western front. Orders relating to supplies were issued, altered, countermanded, sabotaged, and ignored. Patton himself may have exaggerated his plight with an eye to prodding Eisenhower to allocate more gas to 3rd Army. The historian Chester Wilmot, whose book *The Struggle for Europe* remains one of the most respected works on the war in the west, lays much of the blame for not breaching the Siegfried Line and advancing to the Rhine in September on Eisenhower's leadership and his broad front strategy. (Wilmot covered the war in the ETO as a correspondent for the London *Times*.) But command leadership at army, corps, and division level also played a part as did international politics, and Ike's inability to stick with one set of orders and control the man many consider his best general – George General Patton.

In his book, *War As I Knew It,* published posthumously in 1947 – Patton died in December 1945, from injuries received in an auto accident – Patton wrote that August 29, 1944, was "one of the critical days in this war," the day when the Allied High Command withheld 140,000 gallons of gasoline from 3rd Army as it advanced at a rapid pace toward the German frontier and the Saar. Patton argued his case for more gasoline to Eisenhower and his lieutenants but to no avail. He claimed that depriving 3rd Army of much needed gas was "the momentous error of the war."[1]

The furious Patton complained that B-24 bombers that had been airlifting gasoline to his fighting troops were being diverted from military to civilian use to supply food and supplies to Parisians. He asserted also that C-47 transport planes that had been carrying gasoline supplies to 3rd Army were also being diverted for planned airborne operations in late August and early September.

An added thorn in Patton's side was Com Z, the supply service for American army operations in France. "Finally, the last straw," Patton complained, "Com Z used several truck companies to move their Headquarters from Cherbourg to Paris at this very date."[2] The move to Paris for some 80,000 Com Z personnel used thousands of gallons of gasoline that would have benefited Patton's advance.

By the end of August 1944 Patton's 3rd Army had crossed the Marne River northeast of Paris and the advance did not seem to be overly hampered by a shortage of gasoline. The airlift kept him supplied. But when the airlift ceased on August 30, 3rd Army received only 32,000 gallons of gas, not enough to maintain the advance; 3rd Army's normal allocation was to have been 400,000 gallons. This was the day when Patton found his tanks running out of gas and he ordered his corps' commander, General Eddy, to drive them until they ran out of fuel and then order his men get out and advance on foot, which they did.[3]

Bradley warned Patton that 3rd Army would have to hold in place for a time awaiting 1st Army to catch up and come abreast on the left flank with Patton's fast-moving legions.[4] But Patton would have none of a pause and persuaded Bradley to allow him to continue attacking the retreating Germans by calling his advance a reconnaissance in force.

It appears that even without adequate gasoline in the last days of August and the first days in September, the 3rd continued a partial advance into eastern France south of the Ardennes. Wilmot notes that Bradley's acquiescence for Patton to continue operations beyond the Marne, couched as reconnaissance, was "an act of defiance," against Eisenhower's and SHAEF's orders. With Patton's continued advance south of the Ardennes and toward the Saar, Bradley would have no choice but to continue to supply 3rd Army at the expense of the operations that SHAEF gave priority – the offensive into Belgium, north of the Ardennes.

To deal with the supply shortage the Americans organized the Red Ball Express to carry supplies from the Normandy beaches to the front lines in eastern France and into Belgium and Luxembourg. The Americans were also constructing POL pipelines to carry gasoline to the front although the construction lagged well behind the armies' advances. The 1st Army also commandeered trucks from antiaircraft and artillery unit, ordnance, quartermaster, signal, and chemical warfare units to haul needed supplies to the front.

On September 1, 12th Army Group received 7,000 tons of supplies of which 2,000 tons were allocated to Patton. The next day Eisenhower ruled that 1st Army had priority over the 3rd and that Patton's troops would have to go on the defensive. Again, Patton complained that his cavalry patrols had reached the Moselle River while his main force had been halted for two days because of a lack of gasoline. He asked permission to send reconnaissance patrols across the Moselle and once again Eisenhower relented and granted Patton permission to continue. At the same time Ike gave Patton the green light to continue, he authorized Bradley to reposition V Corps from the center of the 1st Army line to the right where it would be in position to protect 3rd Army's left flank.

In authorizing Patton to send "patrols" to the Moselle, Ike was sabotaging his own plan to focus the Allied attacks north of the Ardennes. All Patton needed was Ike's approval and his army would follow the reconnaissance patrols over the Moselle and keep on advancing toward the Meuse River. Where was he to get the gasoline to continue the advance? Sneaky Patton apparently neglected to inform Ike that his 3rd Army on August 29 or 30 had captured a large store of German gasoline that he could combine with the 3rd Army fuel allotment to keep his forces moving.

Could Patton have been exaggerating his paucity of gasoline, in order to receive a greater allocation from the high command? He was not above stealing gas from other Allied armies so why not exaggerate his situation with Bradley and Ike. Certainly, by September 4, 3rd Army had enough gas to continue its advance, receiving an allotment of 240,000 gallons "and during the following three days almost 1.4 million gallons, more than it usually used."[5]

By September 4, 3rd Army was receiving half of the supplies allocated to 12th Army Group plus an additional allotment designated to V Corps, operating on Patton's left. The 3rd was also reinforced by the addition of two divisions to the XV Corps on 3rd Army's right flank.[6] The approved reinforcements did not speak of an army that was expected to dig in and hold in place until the gas shortage subsided. On September 5, Patton's army resumed a whole-hearted offensive towards Germany. And the gasoline shortage was subsiding: "… by September 10 the period of critical shortage was ended."[7]

Was General Patton's plight as difficult as he made it out to be? He told Eisenhower that his men could "eat their belts," but the tanks "gotta have gas."[8] But Patton conveniently failed to include the captured gas from a German supply dump. The amount captured is often pegged at 110,000 gallons. Or was it a million gallons? Bradley asserted in his memoir *A Soldier's Life*, General Patton's troops had captured "a million gallons of low-grade but usable German gasoline."[9] Patton confirmed that amount in his diary on August 30, "Also I captured about a million gallons [of German gas]; it is poor gas but runs a hot engine."[10] Was it a million gallons or 110,000? A million gallons would have made a huge difference. The Army's official history, *Logistical Support of the Armies*, Volume 1, notes that during this critical period of the gasoline shortage, August 29 to September 2, 3rd Army made use of hundreds of thousands of gallons of captured German gasoline. Where is the truth? It probably will never be known. "The XII Corps (in 3rd Army) alleviated its shortage to some extent by the fortuitous capture of about 115,000 gallons of enemy gasoline in the region of Châlons on 29 and 30 August, and 3rd Army utilized a total of nearly 500,000 gallons of captured fuel."[11] Where did all that gas come from and did Patton's army capture more gas than the 110,000 gallons that is usually reported in the history books?

Additionally, high-ranking 3rd Army officers were commandeering gasoline trucks destined for 1st Army and delivering them to 3rd Army, with Patton's tacit and admiring approval. Ranking 3rd Army officers donned 1st Army patches and directed gasoline convoys into 3rd Army areas of operation where the trucks were often stripped of every drop of gas, so much so that sometimes the vehicles didn't have enough gas to return to their base.

The 3rd Army sent spotter aircraft aloft to search for Red Ball convoys whose trucks were often overloaded with Jerrycans of gasoline. Once spotted 3rd Army pirates closed in and confiscated the gas that was destined for 1st Army.

Bradley wrote that Patton had been hoarding gasoline: "To the south of the Ardennes, General Patton, after stockpiling gasoline, jumped off from his Meuse bridgeheads on September 5."[12] Bradley interpreted Eisenhower's constantly changing orders to Patton about farther advances, even as reconnaissance, as affirmation of the broad front strategy in which 1st and 3rd Armies would move in tandem. Could it be that Bradley was helping to position 3rd Army in its race to the Saar in hopes that Patton would breach the Siegfried Line before Montgomery did at Arnhem? The testy international politics of the war in the ETO suggest that Bradley may have hoped to trump the Field Marshal.

Patton noted in his diary how easy it was to persuade Bradley. "Omar (General Bradley) is O.K. but not dashing. All that I have to do (I do) over protest. I just pushed on a lot and will be warned of over extension when the phone works. Luckily it is out for the time [being]."[13]

The curse of the politics of the war may have meant that Eisenhower could not and would not stop the rampaging Patton who had become a hero to the American people as he chased the Germans through France at a faster pace than Montgomery. Ike believed in the importance of public relations and to order Patton to stop altogether would have created a furor back home. The American people were tired of hearing about Montgomery's exploits. It was time to hear about daring American advances and Patton was the man of the hour in the U.S. To reign in Patton in favor of the ever-whining Montgomery would have tarnished Eisenhower's image and possibly his career.

For Patton in the second week of September things were looking up. In an entry in his diary dated September 15 he noted, "It was decided that we had enough supplies to get to the Rhine and force a crossing." He told his XII Corps' commander, General Manton Eddy, that he should form a flying column of divisions and push through the Siegfried Line into Germany and secure a bridge over the Rhine at Worms.[14] Patton couldn't have suggested such an advance without being supplied or expecting to be supplied. By September

20, he was even more certain that with adequate supplies and manpower he could push to the Rhine. "I was convinced then, and have since discovered I was right, that there were no Germans ahead of us except those we were actually fighting. In other words, they had no depth."[15]

Eisenhower's chief of staff, General Smith, told Montgomery on September 12 "that General Patton's drive to the Saar would be stopped,"[16] that the bulk of General Bradley's 12th Army Group's supply resources would be given to 1st Army (so that 1st Army could cover Field Marshal Montgomery's flank in *Market Garden*). He added that three American divisions in the ETO would be grounded and their vehicles allocated to deliver supplies for *Market Garden*.[17] But Smith wasn't telling the whole truth. The 3rd Army wasn't completely grounded and the three American divisions that also were supposedly grounded, were likely the ones in Brittany under 3rd Army command that were idle anyway. They were newly arrived divisions in Normandy and Brittany whose transports had been commandeered for the Red Ball Express. Those divisions didn't need any supplies. Nevertheless, Patton called the news that supplies were to go to 1st Army "heartbreaking." Then came September 23, "one of the bad days of my military career," Patton wrote.[18] Bradley informed General Patton he would lose the 6th AD and "assume a defensive attitude along his entire front, owing to lack of supplies."[19]

A blow, yes, but by the last week in September Patton's chances of breaching the Siegfried Line and advancing to the Saar and the Rhine were drastically diminished anyway. Patton was a victim of his own hard-charging reputation. The Germans regarded him as the Allies' best general and feared him the most to breach their shallow border defenses. They responded by concentrating the bulk of their reserves in the 3rd Army sector to blunt his advances. By mid-September the Germans had mustered a force opposite Patton that was nearly equal in size and combat experience. Even in the most critical period of 3rd Army's gasoline shortage in the last days of August and first days of September, the enemy was bolstering his defense along 3rd Army's front.

> While it was true that the Third Army encountered relatively weak delaying forces as it forced crossings of the Meuse on the last day of August, captured documents later revealed that the enemy had already begun building up substantial forces along the Moselle. Certainly the deceleration of the advance occasioned by the gasoline shortage gave the Germans additional time for these preparations, but the formation of the Moselle defenses had already proceeded farther than was realized by U.S. forces.[20]

There would be no walk through by the 3rd to the Rhine or the Saar. Had the Allied High Command chosen to reinforce the Aachen sector or the Wallendorf bridgehead, the Germans would have been forced to respond with greater reserve forces to those areas, thus weakening the German 1st Army front facing General Patton.

Shortages of gasoline weren't the sole reason for Patton's failure to reach the Rhine in September. There were many other shortages as well and not just in 3rd Army. Patton's troops, as well as many of the troops on the Western Front, were without adequate warm clothing for the approaching winter. Shoepacks that kept the soldiers' feet dry were issued without the accompanying liners so the troops had to improvise and lined these boots with strips of standard issue army blankets. Critical shortages continued in raincoats, field jackets, and sleeping bags. Rations were in short supply and many troops were fed from captured German food stocks, much to their disgust. Front-line bakeries used captured German flour to bake bread. Upon hearing of the food shortages Patton raged: "Goddamn! SHAEF is not only hog-tying us but trying to starve us to death as well."[21]

A more serious shortage was ammunition. "The weekly ammunition allocation amounted to only about one-third of a unit of fire per day for all calibers of artillery guns. The situation became so critical that orders were issued to hold all fires to observed fire so as to conserve shells".[22] (A unit of fire per day was an estimated amount to be fired over a 24-hour period.) The situation reached such a critical point that 3rd Army artillerymen resorted to employing captured guns, Russian 76.2mm and German Schneider 155mm howitzers.[23]

The ammunition shortage was to plague U.S. forces till the end of the war in the ETO. A *New York Times* article dated February 3, 1945, reported that commanders in the field "hammered home," the need for greater quantities of ammunition. For some reason, the *Times* reported that the nation's ammunition program was cut back in the spring of 1944.[24]

The rapid advance across France in the summer of 1944 exacerbated the supply problem. "The hard driving of August created even more critical shortages in major items such as tanks and general purpose vehicles, and a severe maintenance problem demanding greater quantities of tires, tank motors, and other spare parts. The Communications Zone was fully aware of these shortages and many of the items needed in the combat units were available in the rear depots or in ships lying offshore. Because of transportation limitations and unloading difficulties, however, equipment could not be laid down at the point where it was needed."[25] Combat losses contributed to the shortage of critical supplies. Eisenhower highlighted the losses, "in the first seventy days of operations more than 2,400 BARs, (Browning Automatic Rifles) 1,750 ¼-ton trucks (jeeps), 1,500 mortars, 2,000 planes, and 900 tanks had been swallowed into the maw of battle, and emphasized the imperative need for more and more trucks of all kinds and sizes."[26]

General von Mellenthin argued that the overall broad front strategy limited the Allies' options, and was as responsible for the inability of the Americans and British to drive to the Rhine in early September. The German General Herman Balck, commander of Army Group G that faced Patton's 3rd Army, recalled his battles against Patton and downplayed Patton's reputation as a great field commander. "Within my zone, the Americans never once exploited a success. Often General Friedrich Wilhelm von Mellenthin, my chief of staff, and I would stand in front of the map and say, 'General Patton is helping us: he failed to exploit another success.'"[27]

Von Mellenthin later wrote about a specific missed opportunity by 3rd Army to plunge through the weak German 1st Army defenses and advance all the way to Sarrebourg within striking distance of the Rhine. By mid-September 1944, 3rd Army had breached the German Moselle line and was poised to continue advancing into Germany. The German reaction was violent; they understood the significance of the breakthrough and they had few reserves to stop the Americans. "General Wood, champing at the bit, wanted to keep pushing along the Marne–Rhine Canal to Sarrebourg. General Patton agreed and on 16 September, he ordered the XII Corps to drive rapidly northeast into the Darmstadt area and establish a bridgehead across the Rhine."[28]

But the advance was halted not by a lack of gasoline, but by General Eddy who ordered Wood to "tidy up," the battlefield before advancing any farther. He also ordered Wood to divert some of his tanks to the rear to help the 35th ID that was advancing behind Wood's 4th AD. The 4th was some 15 miles ahead of 3rd Army's main body and eager to keep on advancing. Von Mellenthin noted the lost opportunity: "the Americans failed to exploit a fine opportunity for a rapid advance to the Saar…. General Eddy, the commander of the XII Corps, turned down a request from the 4th Armored Division, whose commander realized that ….[the German] 1st Army had no reserves and could not resist a bold thrust along the Marne–Rhine Canal to Sarrebourg."[29]

As September progressed the Germans were able to mass veteran combat units against the 3rd Army front as it reached and crossed the Moselle Line and the advance was stalled as Wood's 4th AD was hit by a series of "furious armored counterattacks." Hitler called on one of his best panzer generals, Hasso von Manteuffel to attack Wood's flank and wipe out the 4th AD's bridgehead across the Moselle. The battles raged for nearly a week as Manteuffel's mammoth Panther tanks, with their high-velocity 75mm high velocity guns, drove into the 4th AD to be challenged by Wood's Shermans with their low-velocity 75mm guns. There should have been no contest, the Shermans were no match in firepower and armor for the much larger Panthers but the American tankers had learned their lessons on how to take on the Panthers. Vulnerable to head-on attacks, the Shermans scooted here and there using their greater speed and agility and shooting at the Panther's vulnerable sides and tracks. Dug-in American M36 Jackson tank destroyers waited for the Panthers almost until the last minute before opening fire. The Americans were aided by artillery and air support.

When the smoke cleared the Germans limped off with heavy losses; by September 22, Manteuffel had lost 150 tanks. The enemy withdrew to try again but was repulsed once more. But the battle was something of a Pyrrhic victory for the Americans. It was September 23, and General Eisenhower issued his order to halt. "The rampaging 3rd… was to regroup, beef up its supply lines, clean up pockets of German resistance and get its wind for another push."[30]

"The 3rd U.S. Army received categorical orders to stand on the defensive," von Mellenthin wrote. "It certainly simplified our problems [and] gave us a few weeks' grace to rebuild our battered forces and get ready to meet the next onslaught."[31]

Was Patton hampered by a lack of supplies, particularly gasoline? Most certainly he was, but the question is, how serious was the problem and how did he get so far without adequate stocks of gasoline? Gas was available, albeit not at first in great quantity, but there was enough to carry General Patton and the 3rd to the Moselle where, with the support and clairvoyance of the high command, it might have jumped off and possibly breached the Siegfried Line and reached the Saar.

The gasoline crisis peaked in the last days of August and the first two or three days of September when no American army had reached the German frontier. The V Corps would not close on the German border at Wallendorf for another ten days and VII Corps did not reach the Aachen area until around September 12. Generals Gerow of V Corps and Collins of VII Corps were also hampered by a lack of gasoline and supplies. At the end of August, Patton was farther from the Siegfried Line than either Gerow or Collins. There was a gap of 50 to 100 miles between 3rd Army and the German frontier and Saarbrucken, depending on which route Patton took. On September 3, Patton wrote that he was in the process of reaching and taking Metz but in late August the Germans were stiffening the defenses around this fortified city and would hold out against the Americans for weeks. On September 12, Patton confided in his diary that 3rd Army had enough gas for its tanks to drive to the Rhine. And where did Wood get his gas to fend off Manteuffel's furious panzer attacks that went on for a week in late September?

But if a shortage of gasoline hampered the 3rd, it was hindered even more by the high command. SHAEF and Eisenhower should have been prepared to focus the Allied attack on one feasible breakthrough area, whether it be Patton in Lorraine, Gerow at Wallendorf, or Collins at Aachen. As the Germans have attested, the Allies failed to concentrate at any one point and continued to advance as one mass that could be blunted at any one point on the line. The Allied command ignored Napoleon's dictum that a commander must concentrate his forces at the point of attack while reducing strength on his flanks. When the high command did decide to concentrate, it was on the risky and ill-advised attack on Arnhem where the broad front strategy contributed to the failure of *Market Garden*. Because of the supply shortages at the front, 1st Army could not assist *Market Garden*'s right flank and Monty had to rely on the resources allotted to 21st Army Group, thus sidelining the British VIII Corps in the *Market Garden* attack that might have hastened XXX Corps' advance to Arnhem. Lack of gasoline appears to be a convenient excuse for faulty tactical and strategic planning.

There are several versions and interpretations to the story of Patton in Lorraine struggling to cross the Rhine and capture the Saar. Some say Patton could have succeeded if given adequate supplies and encouragement while others say it was Allied strategy that restrained 3rd Army's advance.

The official Army history, *Logistical Support of the Armies*, notes in retrospect: "Although the gasoline shortage was a decided handicap in pressing the pursuit with full vigor, therefore, it is certain, in the light of developments on the enemy side of the hill, that the American forces would have encountered increasing resistance regardless of the fuel situation."[32]

The 3rd Army also was stretched across a wide front and might not have been able to concentrate for a fatal blow against the Germans. Colonel Robert S. Allen, a member of Patton's staff in the ETO, noted that 3rd Army was "spread out paper-thin over a 474-mile embattled zone." Hardly a prescription for a massed blow against an enemy, particularly one as formidable as the Germans.

Another interpretation of Patton's chances for a breakthrough was given by the military historian S. L. A. Marshall who asserted that General Patton's army was too small to fight its way through increasing German opposition to the Saar: "That army (the 3rd) was spread out from the Moselle to the Brest Peninsula (the entire VIII Corps was engaged in containing the enemy garrisons holding the Breton ports.). It was in no shape to attack. It was not just short of fuel; it was short of everything. It was short of concentration for one thing, and the Germans were in strength across the Moselle. …My deputy [Hugh M. Cole] was historian of the 3rd Army at that time… His conclusion was there wasn't a chance for the 3rd Army to even get across the Moselle."[33]

CHAPTER 25

Other Lost Opportunities

Horrocks at the Albert Canal

The Americans weren't the only ones driving across France and the Low Countries in the late summer of 1944. Field Marshal Montgomery's 21st Army Group, operating along the Channel coast on the left flank of General Bradley's 12th Army Group, was also racing toward the German frontier and on August 29 Horrock's XXX Corps set out on a drive that some conclude might have altered the course of the war. Spearheaded by the British 11th AD and Guards AD, XXX Corps seized a bridgehead over the Somme River at Amiens, France, and then charged 55 miles through driving rain in the dead of night through scattered German opposition. "For six days and nights five armored divisions and five armored brigades tore in a furious crescendo through towns and villages that had known only the Nazi invader for four years…. The British armor had broken lose…."[1]

The XXX Corps had advanced some 250 miles through northern France and into Belgium where they captured the strategic port of Antwerp virtually without a fight. Then, with seeming compliance with biblical dictates, on the seventh day the exhausted troops and tanks halted and rested. In so doing, XXX Corps and 21st Army Group may have forfeited an opportunity to drive on to breach the Siegfried Line and "bounce" to the Rhine.

Horrocks admitted as much. "Had we been able to advance that day we could have smashed through… and advanced northward with little or nothing to stop us. We might even have succeeded in bouncing a crossing over the Rhine… if we had taken the chance and carried straight on."[2] "There were no significant German forces between Horrocks and the Rhine. But instead of ordering Horrocks onward, on September 4 Monty halted him."

At the same time 21st Army Group failed to push beyond the port of Antwerp to isolate the German 15th Army positioned in the Walcheren region on the eastern bank of the Scheldt River. As long as the 15th survived intact it controlled the 60-mile-long river estuary and could block all shipping sailing up river from the sea to the port of Antwerp. It could also threaten the flanks of the Allied armies driving into the Siegfried Line.

General Bradley lays the blame for both oversights on Field Marshal Montgomery. "Having achieved this striking gain, (across France) Monty now committed two tactical blunders that must rank among the costliest of the war. Once again, he failed to exploit his opportunities – go for the jugular...."[3] Ironically, the same could be said of General Bradley for failing to pursue breakthroughs at Wallendorf and Aachen in the same days of September 1944.

Bradley criticized Montgomery for not "dashing" over the Albert Canal and advancing down the Walcheren road to capture the German coastal batteries situated along the Scheldt that prevented shipping from reaching Antwerp and delivering critical supplies to the Allied armies massing along the German Siegfried Line. The Germans quickly took advantage of Monty's failure by sending in heavy reinforcements to the Walcheren area. It took 21st Army Group more than two months to clear the region of enemy troops.

Bradley wasn't the only critic of Montgomery's leadership. The British military historian, R. W. Thompson, who was an intelligence officer with the British Army in World War II, also lays the blame for his army's failure to exploit the German defeats with the field marshal. "At the crucial hour leadership was lacking, the kind of leadership and decision only Field Marshal Montgomery could have exercised, and which the hour demanded. It was not a time for planning operation into a future that was unknown, but for seizing options and opportunities."[4]

Thompson was referring to Operation *Market Garden*, then in the planning stages; the assault on Arnhem took place two weeks later. Thompson suggests that Montgomery was so dazzled by the lightning advances of his armies and believing, as other commanders did, that the Germans were on their last legs, and that a coup de grace at Arnhem was all that was needed to end the war. On the contrary, Thompson asserts in using Haislip's words: "It was the moment of truth, the moment when commanders needed to 'push all personnel to the limit of human endurance.'"[5]

Philip Warner, author of *Horrocks: The General Who Led From the Front,* is particularly hard on the Horrocks for his failure to continue the advance when it was known that he could have smashed through shattered German defenses and a demoralized enemy army to reach the Rhine. Warner notes the excuse for not bullying ahead – the lack of supplies – but dismisses that rationale for failing to push the advance: "One cannot but think that had Rommel been in command of XXX Corps instead of Horrocks he would have failed to receive the order to halt, and crashed on.... There was only a single, low grade (German) division ahead of Horrocks on September 4. It was spread over a fifty-mile front along the Albert Canal. Horrocks believed that this could have been brushed on one side and XXX Corps could have gone on to cross the Rhine."[6]

Another Breach – Another Retreat

In early February 1945, troops of the U.S. XVIII Airborne Corps assaulted the Siegfried Line near the towns of Udenbreth and Neuhof on the northern edge of the German penetration during the Battle of the Bulge. The objective was to drive the enemy back to the point on the Reich's frontier where the Germans had launched their attacks against the Americans in the Ardennes on December 16, 1944. General Mathew Ridgway, XVIII Airborne Corps'

U.S. troops line up for chow in the midst of a blinding snowstorm along the German–Belgian frontier, January, winter 1944–1945. (U.S. Army, NARA)

commander, expected "extremely heavy going,"[7] when he sent the 82nd Airborne Division and the 1st ID against the Siegfried Line defenses, a "double line of tremendous obstacles – concrete pillboxes, wire, and dragon's teeth." The fight, however, was less arduous than Ridgway expected as the 1st and the 82nd "smashed through the first zone and moved well inside."[8] His troops had "momentum," Ridgway said of his veteran combat troops. But would he push them deeper into Germany? The answer was "no!" as it seemed frequently to be the case on the Allied side.

Ridgway wrote in his memoir, "and there (through the Siegfried Line) they were stopped, not by the enemy, but by orders from First Army."[9] These magnificent veteran troops were being reassigned by Generals Eisenhower, Bradley, and Hodges to join the fight to take the Ruhr dams. To do so, the 82nd would fight its way through the Hürtgen – once again – where so many Americans had died in that forest. After the dams were taken, Ridgway's troops would be sent to support Montgomery's 2nd British Army attack across the Rhine later in March.

Would Ridgway's Airborne Corps' troops have been able to push all the way to the Rhine once they were through the Siegfried Line defenses? Maybe, if they were reinforced, which was unlikely. Once again, the high command was relying on a massive assault by Montgomery – Operation *Plunder* – set to get underway on March 23, to cross the fabled river. Ridgway was not critical in his assessment of the high command leadership. That's left to the reader. He wrote matter-of-factly, "So ended the Battle of the Bulge, and the breakout thereafter."[10]

Gerard M. Devlin noted in his book, *Paratrooper,* that before the 82nd was ordered to the Hürtgen, the division was preparing to advance all the way to Bonn. "The way was now clear for the First Army to attack up and down this massive ridge line all the way to Bonn."[11]

Leclerc and the Colmar Pocket

Politics, national, international, and personal, are very much a part of warfare. In World War II one thinks of the disputes that raged between the Americans and British about war policy and strategy, particularly the date and place for D-Day. Then there was the feuding between General Patton and Field Marshal Montgomery about who would lead the decisive drive to Berlin.

But the feuding wasn't confined to the Anglo-Americans in the western alliance. Disputes arose between the Allied High Command and General de Gaulle and the 1st French Army. On several occasions de Gaulle threatened to remove the French 1st Army from the Allied line to engage in security duties through liberated and politically divided France. He also threatened to leave the alliance and send the 1st Army into Strasbourg to prevent it from falling into German hands during Operation *Northwind*, the German attack into Alsace – the Little Battle of the Bulge – in January 1945.

Bad blood between two French generals in the fall of 1944 had a serious impact and may have extended the war by allowing the Germans to solidify their positions in Alsace, in what became known as the Colmar Pocket. This salient into the Allied front line, connected to Germany by Rhine River bridges, consumed large numbers of French and American soldiers and vast quantities of materiel. Had the pocket been encircled and cut off as planned by Devers in September 1944, the remaining 50,000 or more Germans from the 19th Army entrenched there would have been taken prisoner or forced to flee across the Rhine to the safety of Germany.

In November 1944 6th Army Group's XV Corps, that included General Leclerc's 2nd French AD, broke through German defenses in the Vosges and captured Strasbourg. But much of the Alsace Plain south of Strasbourg to the city of Mulhouse along the Rhine remained in German hands. General Devers, whose earlier plan to cross the Rhine at Rastatt in Germany was rejected by Eisenhower, then ordered Leclerc to drive the 2nd AD south along the river's west bank through German-held ground towards Mulhouse where the French 1st Army had gained a foothold along the river. If Leclerc's advance were successful, his division would link with French forces commanded by 1st Army commander, General Jean de Lattre de Tassigny. The German 19th Army, pressed into a pocket around the city of Colmar after its retreat from the south of France, would be encircled and cut off from the Rhine where intact bridges provided it with reinforcement and supplies. The 19th would have been faced with annihilation.

But Leclerc did not advance along the Rhine to cut off the hated German enemy. He hated de Lattre as much as he hated the Germans and he failed – refused – to carry out Devers' order to link with de Lattre's forces. Had he done so and had the German 19th Army been trapped the effects might have been catastrophic on the entire German front line. Thus, for the next three months, a 70-mile stretch of Alsace along the Rhine, the base of the Colmar Pocket, remained in German hands and was a threat that drove Eisenhower crazy. Ike feared the Germans could use the pocket to spring an attack against the rear of the Allied front line.

Ironically, Eisenhower created the Colmar Pocket by refusing to allow Generals Devers and Truscott to advance through the Belfort Gap in September to cut off and entrap the German 19th Army before it could reach the safety of the Alsace Plain and Germany across the Rhine. By ordering 6th Army Group to forgo the attack through the Gap and instead, advance north along the western slopes of the Vosges to protect the right flank of Patton's 3rd Army farther north in Lorraine, 19th Army was spared.

Devers later noted that in late November after 7th Army had captured Strasbourg and stretches of the Rhine to the north, the French 1st Army didn't have the resources to destroy the pocket in the south without additional support. "The idea was that they (2nd AD) would push south along the Rhine and cut the Germans off, which this armored division could do. I got hold of Leclerc and told him he had to move south to join the other French army, but he refused. This was the only failure in command I ever had in war," Devers wrote.[12] Leclerc argued that because of water-saturated ground, canals and streams, the zone for the attack was "no place for an armored division to operate with any hope of success."[13] Devers, to no avail, pointed out that the Germans successfully operated armor there, but Leclerc would not budge. Devers decided to send him and his 2nd AD back to XV Corps where they had performed magnificently.

Leclerc later confided to the French-speaking Haislip, who had spent several years in Paris as a young officer, that he refused because of his dislike of de Lattre and his army. Leclerc's division was made up of dedicated volunteers, many of whom had escaped German-occupied France and fought in North Africa and in the drive across France after D-Day. Leclerc perceived de Lattre's army as comprised of defeatists and a hodgepodge of soldiers, former Resistance fighters with little military training, North African tribal men who wore colorful ankle-length robes and traveled with their wives and mules, and old-line soldiers from the old French army that was so roundly defeated by the Germans in 1940.

To Leclerc, de Lattre represented the old French army with its aristocratic and medieval traditions. American visitors to French 1st Army headquarters sometimes remarked on the rigid formality with which the headquarters was conducted that included high-ranking officers in immaculate dress uniforms with colorful ribbons and sashes. To Leclerc, who dressed in rumpled American-supplied uniforms, de Lattre represented "the bad old France."[14]

Marc Bloch, a junior officer in the 1940 French 1st Army, and later a member of the resistance who was executed by the Germans, noted that what that army needed were a few young Turks, the kind that Joffre appointed during World War I. "But by 1940 they were elderly men, weighed down with honors and spoiled by a lifetime of office work and easy success." In 1940 Bloch served in

General George Marshall, U.S. Army Chief of Staff, left, confers with French General Jean de Lattre, center, and General Jacob Devers, 6th Army Group commander during Marshall's visit to the army group in the fall of 1944. (U.S. Army)

an army headquarters and recalled the commanding general remark that there wasn't much use trying to stop the German onslaught. Bloch said, "at that time it was only 26 May, and we had the means, if not of saving ourselves, at least of putting up a long, heroic, and desperate resistance as whole islands of men had done in 1918 when they were surrounded on the Champagne front and so of containing and exhausting large numbers of German divisions."

An added problem for Leclerc was that de Lattre had served more years as an officer in the Vichy "Armistice Army," after the fall of France than time spent commanding the 1st French Army in 1944 and 1945. Under the Vichy regime he served in various regional commands and later as commander-in-chief of Vichy troops in Tunisia. He was later arrested for refusing to declare that he would not fire on German troops after the Allied invasion of North Africa. He later escaped to the Allied cause. Leclerc regarded de Lattre's service for Vichy as treasonous.

The hatred remained and Bloch remarked, "There is an old (French) army saying about the mutual feelings of any two officers who happen to be traveling together up the ladder of promotion. 'If they are Lieutenants, they are friends: if Captains, comrades: if Majors, colleagues: if Colonels, rivals: if Generals, enemies.'" Leclerc told Haislip that if forced to carry out Devers' order, he would pack up his division and he and his men would go home.[15]

One wonders what might have been if Leclerc's armored division had obeyed Devers and proceeded to cut off the German 19th Army or forced it to retreat into Germany. In November, the 19th Army was still smarting from its wounds and retreat having lost thousands of men and much of its equipment. The Allied failure to immediately destroy the 19th when it was in disarray, enabled the Germans to restore some of the army's fighting power. The Germans held two bridges over the Rhine that Allied bombing had failed to destroy and could continue to supply their troops in the pocket. It would not be until early February 1945, that the pocket was finally destroyed and the German 19th, what was left of it, retreated back into the Reich. Trapping that army in November could have collapsed the German southern front. If nothing else, it would have freed up large numbers of French and American troops involved in the fight to destroy the Colmar Pocket. It wasn't reduced until early February 1945.

Lessons Learned?

Wallendorf, Stolberg, Belfort, Operation *Diadem*, and the breakout from the Anzio beachhead were all lost opportunities to shorten the war that were the result of command failures at the highest levels in World War II. That great conflagration secured America's place as the most powerful nation on earth and left a legacy of national invincibility and military astuteness. Our vast military, backed by even more massive industrial power, swept across the globe to vanquish Nazi Germany and imperial Japan and we came home victorious and largely unscathed. Because of that overwhelming victory we seldom cast a critical eye on the errors by our military leaders that lengthened the war and led to many more casualties. The majority of the narratives about the war tell of heroic actions by our soldiers and their commanders, the blood and guts of battle. We even turn defeats such as the Battle of the Bulge, the Hürtgen Forest, and Operation *Market Garden*, into heroic struggles of Olympian proportion, without much questioning as to why these actions had to be fought in the first place.

The thrust of *The Folly of Generals* has been to shed light on some of the major tactical and strategic mistakes by General Eisenhower, the supreme commander in Europe in 1944–1945, and some of his commanders. In too many instances he lacked the insight, flexibility, and boldness of a superior commander. Some of the nation's best fighting generals were relieved from their commands because they were "tired," while other generals of less competence were retained. Yet the divisions these "tired" generals commanded were considered the best led in the army. Among these men were Major General Terry Allen and Major General John Wood. Allen commanded the 1st Infantry Division and forged it into a magnificent fighting machine. The same was for Wood who turned the XX Armored Division into a deadly force. These men were bold and agile in their thinking, yet they were sent home.

222 • THE FOLLY OF GENERALS

Lucian Truscott was of a similar mold, and while not totally forgotten, he isn't among the stars that we think of today as great generals of World War II. Truscott was imaginative, aggressive, and willing to take risks, yet he was often thwarted by high command. The same can be said of General Devers who drove his 6th Army Group through southern France and was prepared to invade Germany, possibly to end the war sooner than it ended.

One might argue, "so what," we won the war, didn't we? Every commander makes bad decisions no matter what army or nation he serves. True, but the Germans seemed to have to knack to make fewer; they had reserves of competent generals. It was their leader, Adolf Hitler, who made the grievous errors by forcing them into battles they knew they couldn't win, such as leading them into the Falaise Pocket or the disastrous defeat at Stalingrad.

It is also true that the American military had little training in the command of large formations and the intricacies of modern warfare; they had to learn as the war progressed. The Germans often remarked that the American commanders in World War II sometimes acted as though they were still fighting Native American tribes in small skirmishes on the American frontier. They didn't seem to understand the basics of strategy and tactics. Only late in the conflict did the Germans perceive that the Americans had learned how to fight like a modern army.

One could argue that it is unfair to criticize Eisenhower and SHAEF for the mistakes outlined in *The Folly of Generals*. True. The Americans were new to massed, modern warfare, or had forgotten the Civil War and had to learn the lessons of war all over again through defeats and missteps. (The U.S. involvement in heavy fighting in World War I was less than a year and only in the final months were there enough American troops to form a large army.) The generals in World War II also relied heavily on our overwhelming superiority in materiel – thousands more tanks, combat and transport aircraft, ships and men – to subdue the enemy. This advantage reduced the need for well-conceived tactics and strategy. Vietnam is proof of that. The generals there threw massive amounts of ordinance at the enemy to no avail.

It is also true that it is important to acknowledge the mistakes that were made not only for the sake of honest and accurate history but to acquaint modern military and political leaders with the past so that there is less chance of their being repeated in future wars. It may be that they won't learn – armies are always fighting their last war – but at least they should be made strongly aware of the challenges of the past.

Bibliography

Adams, John A. *The Battle for Western Europe, Fall 1944, An Operational Assessment.* Bloomington, IN: Indiana University Press, 2010.

Adams, John A. *General Jacob Devers: World War II's Forgotten Four Star General.* Bloomington, IN: Indiana University Press, 2015.

Allen, Robert S. *Drive to Victory (Lucky Forward): The History of Patton's Third Army.* New York: Berkley Publishing, 1947.

Ambrose, Stephen. *Eisenhower, Soldier and President.* New York: Simon & Schuster, 1968.

Atkinson, Rick. *An Army at Dawn.* New York: Henry Holt and Company LLC, 2002.

Atkinson, Rick. *Guns at Last Light: The War in Western Europe, 1944–1945.* New York: Henry Holt & Company LLC, 2013.

Baldwin, Hansen. *Tiger Jack.* Johnstown, CO: Old Army Press, 1979.

Bancroft, Mary. *Autobiography of a Spy.* New York: William Morrow & Company, 1983.

Barnett, Correlli, ed. *Hitler's Generals.* New York: Quill/William Morrow, 1989.

Beevor, Anthony. *The Fall of Berlin.* New York: Viking Press, 2002.

Beevor, Anthony. *Ardennes 44. Hitler's Last Gamble.* New York: Viking Press, 2015.

Blumenson, Martin. *Breakout and Pursuit.* Washington, DC. Center for Military History, United States Army, 1961.

Blumenson, Martin. *Salerno to Cassino.* Washington, DC: Center for Military History, 1969.

Blumenson, Martin. *The Battle of the Generals: The Untold Story of the Falaise Pocket: The Campaign that Should Have Won World War II.* New York: William Morrow, 1993.

Blumenson, Martin. *The Patton Papers.* Boston: Houghton Mifflin Company, 1974.

Blumenson, Martin. *General Lucas at Anzio.* Washington, DC: Center for Military History, 1990.

Bonn, Keith E., *When the Odds Were Even: The Vosges Mountain Campaign, October 1944–January 1945.* Novato, California: Presidio Press, 1994.

Bradbeer, Thomas G., Lieutenant Colonel (ret). "Major General Cota and the Battle of the Huertgen Forest: A Failure of Battle Command?"(PDF). United States Army Combined Arms Center. Archived from the original (PDF) on December 10, 2010.

Bradley, Omar N., *A General's Life.* New York: Simon and Schuster, 1983.

Bradley, Omar, *A Soldier's Story.* New York: Henry Holt and Company LLC, 1951.

Bryant, Arthur. *Triumph in the West: History of the War Years Based on the Diaries of Field Marshal Lord Alanbrooke, Chief of the Imperial General Staff.* New York: Doubleday, 1959.

Bryant, Arthur. *The Turn of the Tide: History of the War Years Based on the Diaries of Field Marshal Lord Alanbrooke, Chief of the Imperial General Staff.* New York: Doubleday, 1957.

Caesar, Julius. *The Gallic War and Other Writings.* New York: Modern Library, 1957.

Clark, Mark W. *Calculated Risk.* London: George G. Harrap & Co, 1951.

Clarke, Jeffrey J., and Smith, Robert Ross. *Riviera to the Rhine.* Washington, DC: Center for Military History, 1993.

Cole, Hugh M. *The Lorraine Campaign*. Washington, DC: Center for Military History, 1950.

Colley, David P. *Decision at Strasbourg*. Annapolis, MD: Naval Institute Press, 2008.

Colley, David P. *The Road To Victory*. New York: Warner Books (paperback), 2000.

Combat Study Institute Battlebook. *Remagan Bridgehead*. Fort Leavenworth, Kansas, Jan. 30, 1986.

Cross, Robin. *Operation Dragoon: The Allied Liberation of the South of France, 1944*. New York: Pegasus Books, 2019.

Crosswell, D. K. R. *Beetle: The Life of Walter Bedell Smith*. Lexington, KY.: University of Kentucky Press, 2010.

D'Este, Carlo. *Fatal Decision: Anzio and the Battle for Rome*. New York: Harper Perennial, 1992.

Davidson, Garrison H. *Grandpa Gar*, self-published, 1974, U.S. Military Academy/U.S. Army Military History Institute.

de Tassigny, Jean de Lattre. *The History of French First Army*. London: George Allen and Unwin Ltd, 1952.

Devers, Jacob. *Devers' Diary*. York, PA.: Historical Society and Museum. 1944–1945.

Doubler, Michael D. *Closing with the Enemy: How GIs Fought the War in Europe 1944–1945*. Lawrence, KS: University Press of Kansas, 1994.

Eisenhower, Dwight D. *Crusade in Europe*. New York: Doubleday, 1948.

Ellis, Major L. F., Warhurst, Lt Col. A. E. *Victory in the West, Vol II The Defeat of Germany*. London: Her Majesty's Stationary Office, 1968.

English, John A. *Patton's Peers*. Mechanicsburg, PA: Stackpole Books, 2009.

Ethint 27: Siegfried Line, By Generalmajor (Waffen SS) Fritz Kraemer; 4 pp; 29 Nov. 1945.

Fussell, Paul. *Doing Battle: The Making of a Skeptic*. New York: Little Brown and Company, 1996.

Garland, Albert N. and McGraw Smyth, Howard, assisted by Martin Blumenson. *Sicily and the Surrender of Italy*. Washington, DC: Office of the Chief of Military History United States Army, 1965.

Gavin, James M. *On to Berlin, Battles of an Airborne Commander 1943–1946*. New York: The Viking Press, 1978.

Giziowski, Richard. *The Enigma of General Blaskowitz*. New York: Hippocrene Books, 1996.

Goerlitz, Walter. *History of the German General Staff*. New York: Barnes & Noble, 1995.

Gray, Glen J. *The Warriors: Reflections on Man in Battle*. New York: Harper Torchbooks, 1959.

Greenfield, Kent Roberts, Editor. *Command Decisions*. Washington, DC: Office of the Chief of Military History United States Army, 1960.

Guderian, Heinz. *Achtung-Panzer!: The Development of Armoured Forces, Their Tactics and Operational Potential*. London: Octopus, 1999.

Guderian, Heinz, *Panzer Leader*. Boston, MA: Da Capo Press, 2001.

Halbrook, Stephen. *Target Switzerland: Swiss Armed Neutrality in World War II*. Boston, MA: Da Capo Press, 1997.

Hamilton, Nigel. *Master of the Battlefield: Monty's War Years 1942–1944*. New York: McGraw Hill, 1983.

Hart, B. H. Liddell. *History of the Second World War*. New York: G.P. Putman's Sons, 1970.

Harvey, Ferguson. *The Last Cavalryman: The Life of General Lucian K. Truscott Jr*. Lawrence, KS: University of Kansas Press, 2015.

Hillery, Vic and Hurley, Emerson. *Paths of Armor: The Fifth Armored Division in World War II*. Independently published, 2016.

Hinman, Major Jade, Monograph: *When the Japanese Bombed the Huertgen Forest: How the Army's Investigation of Pearl Harbor Influenced the Outcome of the Huertgen Forest. Major General Leonard T. Gerow and His Command of V Corps 1943–1945*. CreateSpace Independent Publishing Platform, 2014. Kindle Edition.

Hirshson, Stanley P. *General Patton: A Soldier's Life*. New York: Harper Perennial, 2002.

Hogan, David W. *A Command Post at War: First Army Headquarters in Europe 1943–1945*. Washington, DC: Center of Military History U.S. Army, 2000.

https://www.ibiblio.org/hyperwar/USA/ref/Casualties/Casualties-1.html, accessed November 2017.

https://allhands.navy.mil/Stories/Display-Story/Article/1840565/the-planning-of-operation-husky/, accessed July 10, 2018.

Ingersol, Ralph. *Top Secret*. New York: Harcourt Brace, 1946.

Irving, David. *War Between the Generals*. New York: Congdon and Latte's and St. Martin's Press, 1981.

James, D. Clayton. *A Time for Giants – The Politics of the American High Command in World War II*. New York and Toronto: Franklin Watts, 1987.

Jeffers, Paul. *Comand of Honor, General Lucian Truscott's Path to Victory in WWII*. New York: New American Library, Caliber, 2008.

Keegan, John. *Six Armies in Normandy: From D-Day to the Liberation of Paris*. New York: Penguin, 1983.

Keegan, John. *The Second World War*. New York: Penguin Books, 1989.

Kemp, Harry M. *The Regiment Let Citizens Bear Arms, A Narrative of an American Infantry Regiment in World War II* (Hardcover). Austin, Texas: Nortex Press, 1990.

MacDonald, Charles B. *The Mighty Endeavor*. New York: Oxford University Press, 1969.

MacDonald, Charles B, *The Siegfried Line Campaign*. Washington, DC: Center for Military History, U.S. Army, 1990.

Macksay, Kenneth. *Kesselring: The Making of the Luftwaffe*. New York: David McKay, 1978.

Maule, Henry. *Out of the Sand*. London: Odham Books, 1966.

Mets, David R. *Master of Airpower: General Carl A. Spaatz*. New York: Presidio Press, 1997.

Military History Online, The battle for the seaports: https://www.militaryhistoryonline.com/wwii/articles/battleforseaports.aspx, accessed June 13, 2019.

Miller, Robert. *Division Commander, A Biography of Major General Norman D. Cota*. Spartanburg: Spartanburg Publishers, 1989.

Morison, Samuel Eliot. *History of United States Naval Operations in World War II, Vol. 9, Sicily–Salerno–Anzio, January 1943–June 1944*. Boston: Atlantic Monthly Press Book – Little, Brown and Company, 1954.

Newton, Steven. *Hitler's Commander, Field Marshal Walter Model, Hitler's Favorite General*. Boston: Da Capo Press, 2005.

Patton, George S. Jr. *War As I Knew It: The Battle Memoirs of "Blood 'N Guts."* New York: Bantam Books, 1983.

Paul, Jeffers, H. *Command of Honor: General Lucian Truscott's Path to Victory in World War II*. New York: New American Library, CALIBER, 2008.

Persico, Joseph E. *Roosevelt's Secret War, FDR and World War II Espionage*. New York: Random House, 2001.

Pogue, Forrest C. *Organizer of Victory 1943–1945: George C. Marshall*. New York: Viking Press, 1973.

Pogue, Forrest C. *Pogue's War, Diaries of a WWII Combat Historian*. Lexington, KY: The University Press of Kentucky, 2001.

Ridgway, Mathew B. *Soldier: The Memoirs of Mathew B. Ridgway*. New York: Harper & Brothers, 1956.

Ruppenthal, Roland G., United States Army in World War II, The European Theater of Operations: *Logistical Support of the Armies*, Volume 1, Washington, DC: Office of the Chief of Military History, Department of the Army, 1953.

Sevareid, Eric. *Not so Wild a Dream*. New York: Alfred A. Knopf, 1946.

Simon, Murray. *My Journey, Memoirs by Murray Simon*. Self-published, 2010.

Standifer, Leon. *Not In Vain: A Rifleman Remembers World War II*. Baton Rouge, LA: LSU Press, 1992.

Stout, Mark & Yeide, Harry. *First to the Rhine*. Minneapolis, MN: Zenith Press, 2017.

Sylvan, William C. & Smith, Francis G. *Normandy to Victory*. Lexington, KY: The University Press of Kentucky, 2008.

Taaffe, Stephen R. *Marshall and His Generals: U.S. Army Commanders in World War II*. Lawrence, KS: University Press of Kansas, 2011.

Thomas, Wynford Vaughan. *Anzio*. New York: New York Public Library, 1962.

Thompson, R. W. *Montgomery: The Field Marshal*. New York: Charles Scribner's Sons, 1969.

Van Creveld, Martin, *Supplying War: Logistics from Wallenstein to Patton*. Cambridge, UK: Cambridge University Press, 1977.

Von Manstein, Erich. *Lost Victories*. Chicago: Henry Regnery Company, 1958.

Warner, Philip. *Horrocks – The General Who Led From The Front*. Barnsley, South Yorkshire: Pen and Sword, 2006.

Weigley, Russell F. *Eisenhower's Lieutenants*. Bloomington, IN: Indiana University Press, 1981.

Westphal, Siegfried. The *German Army in the West*. London: Cassel and Company, 1951.

Whiting, Charles. *Bloody Aachen*. New York: Stein and Day, 1976.

Wilmot, Chester. *The Struggle for Europe*. Hertfordshire: Wordsworth Edition, 1997.

Wilson, Heefner. A. *Dogface Soldier: The Life of General Lucian K. Truscott Jr*. Columbia, MO, and London, UK: University of Missouri Press, 2010.

Young, Desmond. *Rommel: The Desert Fox*. New York: Harper & Brothers, 1950.

US Army Foreign Military Studies, 1945–1961

WWII Foreign Military Studies, 1945–54, Chapter 2 – A-Series manuscripts A-891, The Battle of the Huertgen Forest

WWII Foreign Military Studies, 1945–54, Chapter 1 – European Theater (ETHINT)ETHINT-37, Defense of the West Wall

WWII Foreign Military Studies, 1945–54, Chapter 1 – European Theater (ETHINT) ETHINT-19, Invasion of Southern France

WWII Foreign Military Studies, 1945–54, Chapter 2 – A-Series manuscripts A-997, Battles in the Aachen Sector (Sep.–Nov. 1944)

WWII Foreign Military Studies, 1945–54, Chapter 2 – A-Series manuscripts A-892, Questions for Consideration and Reply Page 4, Generalmajor Freiherr R. von Gersdorff

WWII Foreign Military Studies, 1945–54, Chapter 2 – A-Series manuscripts A-989 to A-995, The Battle of the Aachen Sector (Sep.–Nov. 1944), Page 44

WWII Foreign Military Studies, 1945–54, Chapter 2 – A-Series manuscripts A-886, The Retreat from Southwestern France (19 Aug.–15 Sep. 1944)

WWII Foreign Military Studies, 1945–54, Chapter 3 – B-Series Manuscripts B-308, (includes B-344, B-633, B-672, B-718), B-308 OB West: Command Relationships (1943–45)

WWII Foreign Military Studies, 1945–54, Chapter 3 – B-Series Manuscripts B-237, Activities of the 157th Reserve Division in Southern France

WWII Foreign Military Studies, 1945–54, Chapter 3 – B-Series Manuscripts B-514, Nineteenth Army (15 Aug.–15 Sep. 1944)

WWII Foreign Military Studies, 1945–54, Chapter 3 – B-Series Manuscripts B-270, German Strategy During the Italian Campaign

WWII Foreign Military Studies, 1945–54, Chapter 3 – B-Series Manuscripts B-787, Nineteenth Army (1 Jul.–15 Sep. 1944)

WWII Foreign Military Studies, 1945–54, Chapter 5 – D-Series Manuscripts D-116, Overall Situation in the Mediterranean

WWII Foreign Military Studies, 1945–54, Chapter 5 – D-Series Manuscripts D-169, Battle for Rome and Retreat North

WWII Foreign Military Studies, 1945–54, Chapter 3 – B-Series Manuscripts B-781, Nineteenth Army (15 Sep.–18 Dec.)

WWII Foreign Military Studies, 1945–54, Chapter 3 – B-Series Manuscripts B-440, Army Group G (May–Jul. 1944)

WWII Foreign Military Studies, 1945–54, Chapter 3 – B-Series Manuscripts B-237, Activities of the 157th Reserve Division in Southern France

Endnotes

Chapter 1

1. Cornelius Ryan, *A Bridge Too Far* (New York: Touchtone Books, 1995), 217.
2. Charles MacDonald, *Siegfried Line Campaign* (SLC) (Washington, DC: Center For Military History U.S. Army, 1990), 41.
3. Roland Ruppenthal, *Logistical Support of the Armies Vol. 2, May 1941–September, 1944* (Charleston, SC: Nabu Press, 2011), 4–7.
4. Military History On Line, *The battle for the seaports,* https://www.militaryhistoryonline.com/wwii/articles/battleforseaports.aspx.
5. AP News, *Soldiers' General, Hero of North Africa and Normandy Dies,* January 8, 1985.
6. Ryan, *A Bridge Too Far,* 123.
7. Ibid, 69.
8. Ibid, 84.
9. Ibid, 160.
10. Ibid, 187.

Chapter 2

1. MacDonald, *Siegfried Line Campaign,* 41.
2. Ibid, 43.
3. Ibid, 44.
4. Ibid, 57.
5. Ibid, 58.
6. Ibid, 59.
7. Ibid, 61.
8. Ibid, 61.
9. Ibid, 62.
10. Richard S. Gardner, *Paths of Armor* (Nashville, TN: Battery Press (digital edition)), 148.

Chapter 3

1. MacDonald, *Siegfried Line Campaign,* 46.
2. Ibid.
3. Ibid, 46, 47.
4. Robert Miller, *Division Commander, A Biography of Major General Norman D. Cota* (Spartanburg SC: The Reprint Company, 1989), 105.

5. Heinz Guderian, *Achtung-Panzer!: The Development of Armoured Forces, Their Tactics and Operational Potential* (London: Cassell, Illustrated edition, 1999).
6. Thomas Bradbeer, "Major General Cota and the Battle of the Huertgen Forest: A Failure of Battle Command?" (PDF). United States Army Combined Arms Center, 10.
7. MacDonald, *Siegfried Line Campaign*, 50.
8. Ibid, 52.

Chapter 4

1. MacDonald, *Siegfried Line Campaign*, 619 (digital edition).
2. Ibid, 65.
3. D. K. R. Crosswell, *Beetle: The Life of Walter Bedell Smith* (Lexington: University Press of Kentucky, 2010), 715.
4. Generalmajor (Waffen SS) Fritz Kraemer (Ethint 27: Siegfried Line, 29 Nov. 1945). 4 pp.
5. MacDonald, *Siegfried Line Campaign*, 63.
6. Major Jade Hinman, Monograph: *When the Japanese Bombed the Huertgen Forest: How the Army's Investigation of Pearl Harbor Influenced the Outcome of the Huertgen Forest. Major General Leonard T. Gerow and His Command of V Corps from 1943–1945.* Kindle Edition, 8.
7. Hinman, Monograph, 8.
8. Forest Pogue, *Organizer of Victory 1943–1945: George C. Marshall* (New York: The Viking Press, 1973), 430.
9. Hinman, Monograph, 8.
10. Ibid.
11. Sylvan & Smith, *Normandy to Victory* (Lexington: University Press of Kentucky, 2008), 127, 128, 129.
12. Ibid, 129.
13. Ibid, 130.
14. Ibid, 128.
15. Heinz Guderian, *Panzer Leader* (New York: Ballantine Books, 1965), 140.
16. Ibid, 164.
17. Bradbeer, "Major General Cota and the Battle of the Huertgen Forest: A Failure of Battle Command?" (PDF), 10, 11.
18. Ardennes, *Hitler's Last Gamble, 1944* (New York: Viking Press, 2015), 57.
19. Stephen Taffe, *Marshall and his Generals* (Lexington: University Press of Kentucky, 2011), 169.
20. Ibid, 57.
21. FMS # 447, May 14, 1946; Seventh Army (1 Sept. 1944 – 25 Jan. 1945).
22. Ibid.
23. Generalmajor Rudolf Frhr von Gersdorff (Ethint 53: Seventh Army; Siegfried Line—Defense of the Siegfried Line, 24 Nov. 1945), 5.
24. Ibid.
25. Ibid.
26. Siegfried Westphal, *The German Army in the West* (London: Cassel and Company, 1951), 172.
27. Westphal, *The German Army in the West.*
28. Robert Miller, *Division Commander*, 105.
29. Omar Bradley, *A General's Life* (New York: Simon and Schuster, 1983), 320.
30. Pogue, *Organizer of Victory*, 382.
31. Sylvan & Smith, *Normandy to Victory*, 129.

32. Blumenson, *Patton Papers*, 527.
33. Combat Study Institute Battlebook: *Remagan Bridgehead* (Fort Leavenworth, Kansas: Combat Studies Institute, Jan 30, 1986), 48.
34. *Germans Facing V Corps*, Sept. 1944–May 1945, NARA RG 319, R-Series, 45.
35. Ibid.

Chapter 5

1. Chester Wilmot, *The Struggle for Europe* (Hertfordshire, UK: Wordsworth Editions, 1997), 496.
2. MacDonald, *Siegfried Line Campaign,* 71–72.
3. Ibid, 76.
4. Ibid, 77.
5. Ibid, 80.
6. Ibid, 83.
7. Ibid, 86.
8. Ibid, 95.
9. Colley, Interview with Walter Lipina, WWII Hürtgen veteran, 1998.
10. Ethint 27.
11. MacDonald, *Siegfried Line Campaign*, 94.
12. Ibid.
13. Weigley, *Eisenhower's Lieutenants* (Bloomington, IN: Indiana University Press, 1981), 365.
14. MacDonald, *Siegfried Line Campaign*, 365.
15. Ethint 27.
16. Ibid.
17. FMS MS # B-308.
18. John A. Adams, *The Battle for Western Europe, An Operational Assessment* (Bloomington, IN: Indiana University Press, 2010), 168.
19. FMS MS # A-997, Chap 2.
20. Wilmot, *The Struggle for Europe,* 495–496.

Chapter 6

1. Ryan, *A Bridge Too Far*, 11, 12.
2. Mathew Ridgway, *Soldier* (New York: Harper & Brothers, 1956), 109.
3. Ryan, *A Bridge Too Far*, 211.
4. Ibid, 246.
5. Ibid, 247.
6. Ibid, 228.
7. Ibid, 228.

Chapter 7

1. Ryan, *A Bridge Too Far*, 142.
2. Ibid, 146.
3. Ibid, 142.
4. Ibid, 89.

5. Ibid, 132.
6. Ibid, 597.
7. R. W. Thompson, *Montgomery: The Field Marshal* (New York: Charles Scribners Sons, 1969), 183.
8. Thompson, *Montgomery: The Field Marshal*, 183.
9. Ibid.
10. Ibid, 184.
11. S. Ridgway, *Soldier*, 111.

Chapter 8

1. Carlo d'Eset, The History Net, https://www.historynet.com.
2. Audie Murphy, *To Hell and Back* (New York: Bantam, 1983), 170.
3. Lucian Truscott, *Command Missions* (New York: Presidio Press, 1990), 426.
4. Truscott, *Command Missions*, 427.
5. Harry Yeide, Mark Stout, *First to the Rhine* (London: Zenith Press, 2007), 79.
6. Murphy, *To Hell and Back,* 187.
7. Future operations report SHAEF, Record Group, 121 Box 121, NARA.
8. Richard Giziowski, *The Enigma of General Blaskowitz* (New York: Hippocrene Books, 1997), 336.
9. Truscott, *Command Missions,* 442.
10. Blumenson, *Patton Papers,* 505.
11. Jacob Devers, *Devers' Diary,* September 3, 1944.
12. Devers, *Devers' Diary,* September 15, 1944.
13. Truscott, *Command Missions,* 442.
14. Ibid.
15. Ibid.
16. Devers, *Devers' Diary,* September 9, 1944.
17. Clarke & Smith, *Riviera to the Rhine,* 232.
18. FMS MS # B-518.
19. Harry Yeide and Mark Stout, *First to the Rhine,* 166.
20. Ibid.
21. Ibid.
22. FMS MS # 787, 30.
23. FMS MS # B-084.
24. David Colley, *Decision at Strasbourg* (Annapolis, MD: Naval Institute Press, 2008), 38.
25. FMS MS # 518.
26. Westphal, *German Army in the West,* 172.
27. Truscott, *Command Missions,* 445.
28. FMS MS # B-518.
29. Jeffrey J. Clarke, Robert Ross Smith, *Riviera to the Rhine* (Washington, DC: Center for Military History, U.S. Army, 1993), 64.
30. Clarke and Smith, *Riviera to the Rhine,* 64.

Chapter 9

1. John Keegan, *The Second World War* (New York: Penguin Books, 1989), 394.
2. Ibid, 403.

3. Blumenson, *Breakout and Pursuit*, 558.
4. Dwight D. Eisenhower, *Crusade in Europe* (New York: Avon Books, 1968), 314.
5. Bradley, *A General's Life*, 298.
6. Wilmot, *Struggle for Europe*, 419.
7. Ibid, 424–425.
8. James Gavin, *On to Berlin* (New York: The Viking Press, 1978), 128.
9. Ibid, 130.
10. Ibid, 130, 131.
11. Wilmot, *Struggle for Europe*, 425.
12. Bradley, *A General's Life*, 304.

Chapter 10

1. Stephen Halbrook, *Target Switzerland* (Sarpedon, 1998), 47.
2. Ibid, 47.
3. Mary Bancroft, *Autobiography of a Spy* (New York: William Morrow, 1983), 17.
4. Halbrook, *Target Switzerland*, 108.
5. Ibid, 57.
6. Ibid, 110.
7. Ibid, 20.
8. Ibid, 203.
9. David R. Mets, *Master of Airpower, General Carl A. Spaatz* (New York: Presidio, 1997), 277.

Chapter 11

1. Charles Whiting, *Forgotten Army* (New York: St. Martin's Paperbacks, 2001), 89.
2. Brendan Phibbs, *The Other Side of Time, A Combat Surgeon in World War II* (Boston: Little Brown and Company, 1987), 101.
3. Henry Maule, *Out of the Sand* (London: Odhams, 1966), 254.
4. Ibid, 252–255.
5. Dana Adams Schmidt, "Strasbourg Rocks Under Shellfire" *New York Times*, November 25, 1944.
6. Schmidt, "Strasbourg Rocks Under Shellfire."
7. Maule, *Out of the Sand*, 258
8. Murray Simon, *My Journey, Memoirs by Murray Simon* (self-published, 2010).
9. Devers, *Devers' Diary*, September 19, 1944.

Chapter 12

1. 6th Army Group diary, USMA, September 25, 1944, 264.
2. 6th Army Group, Special Study: *The Assault Crossing of the Rhine from Basle to Mannheim*, 5–23.
3. 6th Army Group diary, September 1944.
4. Devers, *Devers' Diary*, September 20, 1944.
5. 6th Army Group, Special Study: *The Assault Crossing of the Rhine from Basle to Mannheim*, 5–23.
6. Alexander French, *History of the 40th Engineer Combat Regiment in WWII*, 9.

Chapter 13

1. French, *History of the 40th Engineer Combat Regiment in WWII,* 9.
2. Devers' letter to Georgie (wife), November 8, 1944, York Heritage Trust Library & Archives.
3. Devers' letter to Vice Admiral A. G. Kirk, November 13, 1944, York Heritage Trust Library & Archives.
4. Griess interview with Edward D. Comm, tape 67, side 2, p. 35 of typed manuscript, York Heritage Trust Library & Archives.

Chapter 14

1. Memorandum, Headquarters 7th Army Office of the A.C. of staff, G-2, December 22, 1944, folder 1007-0.3.0 RG427, box 2571, NARA.
2. Clarke and Smith, *Riviera to the Rhine,* 563.
3. 7th Army intelligence report re December 22, 1944, re Lt. Col. Willie Kaiser.
4. Memorandum from Col. William W. Quinn, Headquarters 7th Army, Office of the A.C of S, G-2 December 22, 1944.

Chapter 15

1. Author interview with Paul Fussell, 2005.
2. Chester B. Hansen papers, U.S. Army Military History Institute.
3. Clarke and Smith, *Riviera to the Rhine,* 436, 439.
4. Ibid, 439.
5. Hansen papers.
6. Griess interviews with Devers, tape 29 p. 35 box 88, tape 42 side 1 box 89, York Heritage Trust Library & Archives.
7. Ibid.
8. Official diary for the Commanding General, Seventh Army, USMA Archives/Library, 268. A History of headquarters 6th Army Group.
9. Clarke and Smith, *Riviera to the Rhine,* 439.
10. Forest Pogue, *The Supreme Command* (Washington, DC: Center for Military History, U.S. Army, 1970), 310.
11. Devers, *Devers' Diary,* September 17, 1944.
12. Devers, *Devers' Diary,* October 5, 1944.
13. Clarke and Smith, *Riviera to the Rhine,* 438.
14. Devers, *Devers' Diary,* October 9, 1944.
15. Clarke and Smith, *Riviera to the Rhine,* 445.
16. Nigel Hamilton, *Monty: Final Years of the Field Marshal* (New York: McGraw Hill, 1986), 329.
17. Wade Haislip, *Corps in Combat,* Wade Haislip Papers, USAMHI.
18. Griess interview with Comm, tape 67, side 2, box 91.
19. Gen. Garrison Davidson, *Grandpa Gar* (Military Academy/U.S. Army Military History Institute), 95.
20. Alexander MacCarrell Patch file, cu 5187, box 6, USMA Archives/Library.
21. Blumenson, *Patton Papers,* 583.
22. Weigley, *Eisenhower's Lieutenants,* 407.
23. French, *History of the 40th Engineer Combat Regiment in WWII,* 97.

Chapter 16

1. Gen. F. W. Mellenthin, *Panzer Battles* (Stroud Gloucestershire, UK, Spellmount, 2008), 415.
2. Westphal, *The German Army in the West*, 176.
3. *New York Times*, The French and the Rhine, Nov. 21, 1944, 24.4
4. General Walter Bedell Smith, *Eisenhower's Six Great Decisions* (Longmans, Green, 1956), 21, 211, 213.
5. Hamilton, *Monty: Final Years of the Field Marshal*, 329.
6. Bradley, *A Soldier's Story*, 511.
7. Clarke and Smith, *Riviera to the Rhine*, 445.
8. Blumenson, *Patton Papers*, 527.
9. Clarke and Smith, *Riviera to the Rhine*, 443.
10. Stephen Ambrose, *Eisenhower, Soldier and President* (New York, Simon and Schuster, 1968), 210–211.
11. Ambrose, *Eisenhower*, 227.
12. Ralph Ingersoll, *Top Secret* (New York, Harcourt Brace and Co., 1946), 219.

Chapter 17

1. Blumenson, *Patton Papers*, 565.
2. Ingersoll, *Top Secret*, 33.
3. David Irving, *The War Between the Generals* (London: Focal Point Publication, 210), 323.
4. Ambrose, *Eisenhower*, 267.
5. Blumenson, *Patton Papers*, 414.
6. Bradley, *A Soldier's Story*, 521.
7. Devers, *Devers' Diary*, November 24, 1944.
8. Devers' letter to Major General Wilton Parsons, Office of the Chief of Staff, Nov. 30, 1944, York Heritage Trust Library/Archives.

Chapter 18

1. Thomas E. Griess, *The Second World War, Asia and the Pacific* (West Point, NY., West Point Military Series, 2002), 364.
2. Blumenson, *Patton Papers*, 588.
3. Ken Hechler, *The Bridge at Remagen* (New York, Ballantine Books, Inc., 1957), 181–183.
4. Typescript of the Seventh Army from the Vosges to the Alps, *Army & Navy Journal*, August 2, 1945, Patch File USMA.
5. Clarke and Smith, *Riviera to the Rhine*, 445.
6. Interview with General Hellmuth Thumm, U.S. Army Military History Institute.
7. John Toland, *The Last 100 Days* (New York, Random House, 1966), 243–262.
8. Ibid, 243–262.
9. Griess interview with Devers, tape 21, side 1 p. 54 of typed manuscript, York Heritage Trust.

Chapter 19

1. Clayton D. Laurie, *Anzio 1944*, Center for Military History online: https://history.army.mil/brochures/anzio/72-19.htm, 17.
2. Ibid, 20.
3. History Net, *The Man Who Knew No Fear: General Lucian K Truscott*. https://www.historynet.com/man-knew-no-fear-general-lucian-k-truscott.htm.
4. Truscott, *Command Missions*, 546.
5. Ibid, 538.
6. Eric Sevareid, *Not So Wild a Dream* (Columbia, MO: University of Missouri Press, 1995), 392.
7. Kenneth Macksey, *Kesselring: The Maker of the Luftwaffe* (New York: David McKay and Co. 1978), 201.
8. Laurie, *Anzio 1944*.
9. Martin Blumenson, *General Lucas at Anzio* (https//history.army.mil/books), 346.
10. Ibid.
11. Carlo D'Este, *Fatal Decision* (New York: Harper Perennial, 1991), 353–354.
12. Ibid, 354.
13. Trucott, *Command Missions*, 371.
14. Ibid, 375.
15. D'Este, *Fatal Decision*, 364.
16. Ibid, 362.
17. Ibid, 364–365.
18. Ibid, 370.
19. Thomas Ricks, *The Generals, American Military Command from World War II to Today* (New York: Penguin Random House, 2013), 67.
20. Truscott, *Command Missions*, 375.
21. D'Este, *Fatal Decision*, 369.
22. Earl Alexander of Tunis, *The Alexander Memoirs, 1940–1945* (London: Frontline Books, 2010), 127.
23. D'Este, *Fatal Decision*, 371.
24. Devers, *Devers' Diary*, August 21, 1944.
25. Ibid.

Chapter 20

1. Samuel Elliot Morison, *History of United States Naval Operations in World War II*, vol. 9 (Boston: Little Brown and Co., 1957), 209.
2. Ibid, 216.
3. Bradley, *A Soldier's Story*, 133.
4. Albert N. Garland, Martin Blumenson, Howard Smyth, *Sicily and the Surrender of Italy* (Washington, DC: Center for Military History, U.S. Army, 1993), 14.
5. Martin Blumenson, *Salerno to Cassino* (Washington, DC: Center for Military History, U.S. Army, 1969), 24.
6. The Planning of Operation Husky, https://allhands.navy.mil/Stories/Display-Story/Article/1840565/the-planning-of-operation-husky/
7. Ibid.

8. Ibid.
9. Morison, *History of United States Naval Operations in World War II*, vol. 9, 218, 219.
10. Ibid.
11. Garland, Blumenson, Smyth, *Sicily and the Surrender of Italy*, 419.
12. Ibid, 420 421.
13. Morison, *History of United States Naval Operations in World War II*, vol. 9, 217.
14. Ibid, 219.
15. Ibid, 221.

Chapter 21

1. https://www.ibiblio.org/hyperwar/USA/ref/Casualties/Casualties-1.html.
2. Weigley, *Eisenhower's Lieutenants*, 250.
3. Bradley, *A Soldier's Story*, 386–387.
4. Ibid, 386, 387.
5. Martin Van Creveld, *Supplying War: Logistics from Wallenstein to Patton* (Cambridge: Cambridge University Press, 1977), 217.
6. Roland Ruppenthal, *Logistical Support of the Armies Vol. 1, May, 1941–September, 1944* (Charleston, SC: Nabu Press, 2011), 116.
7. Ibid, 132.
8. General George S. Patton, Jr., *Patton, War As I Knew It: The Battle Memoirs of Blood 'N Guts* (New York: Bantam Books, 1983), 120.
9. Ibid, 227.
10. Ibid, 121.
11. Rick Atkinson, *The Guns at Last Light* (New York: Henry Holt and Company, 2013), 241.

Chapter 22

1. Hugh M. Cole, *The Lorraine Campaign* (Washington, DC: Center For Military History, U.S. Army, 1950), 3.
2. MacDonald, *Siegfried Line Campaign*, 86.
3. FMS MS # A-971, Chap 2 A, p. 3, *1st Battle of Aachen*.
4. MacDonald, *Siegfried Line Campaign*, 89–90.
5. Ethint 37 (ML-1034), Defense of the West Wall, Source, Maj. Herbert Buechs, Luftwaffe aide to Genobst Jodl, 28 Sept. 1945.
6. Michael D. Doubler, *Closing With the Enemy: How GIs Fought the War in Europe, 1944–1945* (Lawrence, KS: University Press of Kansas, 1994), 127.
7. Cole, *The Lorraine Campaign*, 47
8. Ibid.
9. Ibid.
10. Blumenson, *Patton Papers*, 545.
11. The Army Specialized Training Program, http://www.marshallfoundation.org/100th-infantry/wp-content/uploads/sites/27/2014/06/ASTP_The_Army_Specialized_Training_Program_and.pdf.

Chapter 23

1. Wilmot, *Struggle for Europe*, 492.
2. Leon C. Standifer, *Not in Vain: A Rifleman Remembers World War II* (Baton Rouge, LA: LSU Press, 1998), 128.
3. Stanley P. Hirschon, *General Patton, A Soldier's Life* (New York: Harper Perennial, 2003), 509.
4. Ibid, 508.
5. Blumenson, *Patton Papers,* 499.
6. Hirschon, *General Patton, A Soldier's Life,* 510.
7. Ibid, 509.
8. Bradley, *A General's Life*, 285.
9. B. H. Liddell Hart, *History of the Second World War,* 557.

Chapter 24

1. Wilmot, *Struggle for Europe*, 473.
2. Patton, *War As I Knew It,* 116.
3. Wilmot, *Struggle for Europe*, 469.
4. Patton, *War As I Knew It,* 120.
5. Hirschon, *General Patton,* 536.
6. Wilmot, *Struggle for Europe*, 484.
7. Cole, *The Lorraine Campaign,* 52.
8. Wilmot, *Struggle for Europe*, 473.
9. Bradley, *A General's Life*, 321.
10. Blumenson, *Patton Papers*, 531.
11. Ruppenthal, *Logistical Support of the Armies Vol. 2*, 505.
12. Bradley, *A General's Life*, 325.
13. Blumenson, *Patton Papers,* 517.
14. Patton, *War As I Knew It*, 128.
15. Ibid, 130.
16. Wilmot, *Struggle for Europe*, 492.
17. Ibid.
18. Patton, *War As I Knew It*, 135.
19. Ibid, 136.
20. Ruppenthal, *Logistical Support of the Armies Vol. 2*, 515.
21. Col. Robert S. Allen, *Drive to Victory* (New York: Berkeley Publishing, 1947), 97.
22. Ibid.
23. Ibid, 101
24. Harold Denny, "Engines Hardy in Bridging Erft," (*New York Times*, Feb 3, 1945), 3.
25. Ibid.
26. Ibid.
27. Harry Yeide, *Fighting Patton: George S. Patton Jr. Through the Eyes of his Enemies* (Duluth, MN: Zenith Press, 2014), 321.
28. Hanson W. Baldwin, *Tiger Jack* (Johnstown, CO: Old Army Press, 1979), 84.
29. Ibid, 86.
30. Ibid.
31. Ibid.

32. Ruppenthal, *Logistical Support of the Armies Vol. 2*, 516.
33. Hirschon, *General Patton*, 534.

Chapter 25

1. Thompson, *Montgomery: The Field Marshal*, 170.
2. Ibid.
3. Bradley, *A General's Life*, 319.
4. Thompson, *Montgomery, The Field Marshal*, 171.
5. Ibid.
6. Philip Warner, *Horrocks: The General Who Led From the Front* (Barnsley, South Yorkshire: Pen and Sword, 2006), 111.
7. Ridgway, *Soldier*, 128.
8. Ibid.
9. Ibid.
10. Ibid.
11. Ridgway, *Soldier*, 129.
12. Devers, *Devers' Diary*, November 1944.
13. Maule, *Out of the Sand*, 261.
14. Ibid.
15. Ibid.

Index